Falling Down

Falling Down

*The Conservative Party and
the Decline of Tory Britain*

Phil Burton-Cartledge

VERSO
London • New York

First published by Verso 2021
© Phil Burton-Cartledge 2021

1 3 5 7 9 10 8 6 4 2

Verso
UK: 6 Meard Street, London W1F 0EG
US: 20 Jay Street, Suite 1010, Brooklyn, NY 11201
versobooks.com

Verso is the imprint of New Left Books

ISBN-13: 978-1-83976-036-5
ISBN-13: 978-1-83976-039-6 (US EBK)
ISBN-13: 978-1-83976-038-9 (UK EBK)

British Library Cataloguing in Publication Data
A catalogue record for this book is available from the British Library

Library of Congress Cataloging-in-Publication Data
A catalog record for this book is available from the Library of Congress

Typeset in Sabon by Biblichor Ltd, Edinburgh
Printed and bound by CPI Group (UK) Ltd, Croydon, CR0 4YY

For Simon Speck

Contents

Introduction

Smiling for the cameras, Chancellor of the Exchequer Rishi Sunak served up orders for unsuspecting customers at a central London Wagamama. This was 8 July 2020. Earlier in the day, Sunak rose in the House of Commons to present his mini-budget: a package of measures designed to rescue Britain's beleaguered economy from the assault mounted on it by COVID-19. To try and accelerate the recovery, the most eye-catching of his measures was Eat Out to Help Out. Between 3 and 31 August, this scheme allowed for a 50 per cent discount to a maximum of ten pounds per diner at all participating restaurants, pubs and cafes. In its own terms, it was a success. Some £849 million was claimed by businesses from the Treasury, having served over 160 million meals.[1] Just the tonic the UK's suffering hospitality industry needed.

It also proved a boon for the community transmission of coronavirus. On the day Sunak announced his policy, the cumulative total of UK COVID-19 fatalities stood at 40,916.[2] The number of daily deaths was in steady decline alongside reported positive tests and hospitalisations. The hellish scenes witnessed in wards in March and April seemed long behind the country, and so things could start returning to normal. The government's furlough scheme, which paid up to 80 per cent of employees' wages while workplaces were closed, could be wound down. People could be told to go back to work. Schools could open for the new autumn term on time and government insistence on (limited) in-person teaching in colleges, sixth forms and universities was deemed possible. This was despite predictions of a second deadly wave of coronavirus infections with even higher casualty figures than the first. In a report published in mid-July, the Academy of Medical Sciences was arguing for the maintenance of 'active containment measures' to depress any incoming wave.[3] And in August, the government's Scientific Advisory Group for Emergencies forecast up to 85,000 extra COVID deaths over the winter and argued for the return of some quarantine measures enacted earlier in the year.[4] The government ignored this advice.

During autumn and winter cases built up to the point where the government had to introduce two new national lockdowns, neither of which was as stringent as the first. It also turned out that Rishi Sunak had helped lay the groundwork for the second wave by boosting infections when community transmission was very low.[5] As such, thanks to utter complacency, not only has the number of deaths more than doubled since Eat Out to Help Out's announcement to over 126,000 at the time of writing and the NHS been overwhelmed like never before, but also the UK had to stay in lockdown until millions of (mainly older) Britons had received their first vaccine injection.

This book is not about coronavirus. It is about the party that has overseen this disaster, a party whose history is littered with a few harmful mutations of its own. It is a book about the Conservative Party and tells the story of how the world's most successful liberal-democratic party and the acknowledged preferred party of British business has come to a place where, it would seem, its policy prescriptions, strategic objectives and day-to-day decision making not only are harmful, but seemingly work against the interests of British capitalism and, at times, appear at odds with its own political interests. Many of these features were visible when the party returned to government (with the Liberal Democrats) in 2010, and yet it has gone on to win three further elections in the meantime. A case of adroit politicking, voter masochism or something else?

As a veritable (for some, a venerable) institution occupying an enviable status as the natural party of government in the United Kingdom, it has been also a trailblazer that has pioneered privatisation and deregulation in an advanced economy. It has survived, evolved and thrived for the better part of two centuries. The Conservatives therefore not only are a model case study in the longevity of parties in competitive party systems, but also are fundamental to our understanding of Britain's politics, its class structure and the character of its state. These alone are reasons enough for a serious attempt to understand the state of the Conservative Party in the twenty-first century.

Studying and analysing the Tories can, but should not, be an academic exercise. Labour needs to understand its electoral nemesis, which it has the tendency to underestimate – despite its opponents' winning ways. Trade unions must grasp why the Tories hold them down. Workers need to know why the Tories happily enforce low pay, short-term contracts and dead-end jobs that leave their time and talents squandered and why the Tories are content to lock millions out of the acquisition of property. Campaigners against deportations, against racism, against the scapegoating of whole communities have an interest in how and why they are used as a political football by the Conservatives. On issues from equality for women, trans acceptance, racism, the environment and the climate crisis, to anything and everything that might make life better or more tolerable – all these concerns and causes can reliably find the Tories standing in their way.

The role the Conservatives play as self-appointed defenders of privilege, of the establishment, as the custodians of British capitalism and their preparedness to use state power to enforce these ends mean that any and all projects of a liberal, nationalist, Labourist or socialist hue have to know their enemy. Or they can, and will, get beaten. Arguably, a factor contributing to the repeated victories of the Conservatives is the lack of attention paid to this task by the party's many opponents.

Apart from day-to-day politics, what role does the Conservative Party play as an institution of British capitalism? How and why is it so important to the custodians of capital, and how is it consistently successful in presenting the minority interest of the monied and well-heeled as the general interest? Where does the Tory Party sit in the Westminster system, in the web of class relations and in the UK's political economy, and to what extent are the Tories both symptom and cause of British exceptionalism, most recently expressed in the vote to leave the European Union and the disastrous management of the coronavirus crisis?

This brings into sharp relief contemporary writing about the party. Most political commentary appearing in the British press reads embarrassingly like fandom, full of praise for the visionary qualities and overdone patriotism of the party's leading lights. Instead of seeking to explain what's happening in the party and providing snippets of information to help their readers piece together the whys and wherefores of policy, strategic decision making and blunders in office, the voluminous press coverage the party attracts instead obscures its workings, rendering the Tory party a mysterious and charmed entity that just happens to win elections a lot. Structural relationships are only hinted at, with the occasional exposure of a tie between X politician and Y business. Good or bad policy is a mark of personal qualities or the right/ wrong ideas. To suggest that considerations of interest and class have some bearing is 'determinist'.

This book makes no apologies for breaking with this stunted and inadequate tradition, as any work of materialist analysis must. It is inconceivable to consider the Tories as anything other than the institutionalisation of moneyed interests, a network and permanent mobilisation of elites fed by commercial relationships and buttressed by privileged access to and patterns of control and influence over state power. If, however, that was all the Tories were, this would be an excavation of the bones of an extinct political animal, not the means of understanding the anatomy of a thriving apex predator that has devoured any and all challenges (and not a few challengers). It is therefore not enough to say that the Tories are a ruling-class party, the political articulation of capital or simply a reflection of the political preferences of a privileged section of the electorate. Its accomplishments, its trajectories and, strange as it might sound at the time of writing, its long-term decline demand analysis and consideration.

4

Up until 2019, it looked like the Conservatives' demise was uncomfortably close for their adherents. Since the end of the 1980s the party has been the last word in fractiousness; the argument could be made that the party had merely endured the turbulence buffeting it. Indeed, from the general election of 2017, which saw Theresa May's Conservative Party lose its majority, to mid-October 2019 no peacetime party of government had ever experienced such a prolonged and unprecedented period of intense crisis. As the May government stumbled against electoral and then Commons opposition without, it was consumed by insurrection from within. Likewise, the initial period of Boris Johnson's government prior to the 2019 general election, if anything, marked an intensification of the European drama that has gripped the party for over thirty years. Yet despite expelling critics and threatening to trample over the rule of law, Johnson was able not only to unite behind him a powerful coalition of voters that routed their opponents in England and Wales, but also to see the Tories strike deep into the Labourist heartland.

To suggest, then, that the Conservative Party is suffering from long-term decline might, at best, be received as a provocation and, at worst, the delusional fever dream brought on by the worst electoral disaster to befall Labour since the 1930s. Facts, however, are no respecters of soaring dreams and darkest pessimism. The sociology of the Tory Party, the character and trajectory of its support, the shifting nature of class in Britain and four decades of market-first policymaking are locking millions of people out of property and asset acquisition (above all, housing) and feeding a brewing crisis – a crisis of Conservative political reproduction.

The Conservatives and their supporters will be toasting 2019 as a famous victory for many years to come, and subsequent newspaper articles, think tank reports, magazine features, academic conferences and edited collections have disproportionately focused on the possibilities and viability of the Labour Party after Jeremy Corbyn. Yet few, if any, are talking about the problems accumulating for the Tories. Their electoral hegemony is facing perhaps its most significant challenge since conceding the vote to working men. While the party has received many an obituary since the 1832 Reform Act and has faced down crisis after serious crisis, the twenty-first-century mole burrowing away at the party's foundations cannot be easily deflected from its single-minded task.

The party's chief problem is younger voters, who are keen to vote for almost anyone but the Conservatives. At first glance, this might not seem like a problem at all. As former Tory leader and foreign secretary William Hague observed at a conference in early 2020, 'There is a never-ending supply of older voters.'[6] Young people eventually become old, turn Tory and vote regularly.

This is complacent. The numbers since 1992 suggest a greater likelihood of supporting the party among older cohorts of voters over time, and the pattern has moved from a relatively shallow correlation to stark polarisation between young and old in the 2010s.[7] However, it does not necessarily follow that voting conservative is simply an outcome of growing older.

To understand the juncture of this crisis we must consider the Tories in the context of the development of the political system that they are embedded in and, more than any party, have shaped for nearly two centuries, and particularly so over the last forty years. It is the Tories who have steered the course of British politics, and so the crisis they face is a destination arrived at on their own terms, because of their own decisions and against the backdrop of a political economy and class structure they actively fought to bring into being. Less a case of the bourgeoisie creating their own gravediggers and more one of the Tories doing the spadework themselves.

What follows is an account of how we came to this impasse where, despite repeated electoral triumphs, the Tories have sowed the seeds for, but have so far put off, a destructive reckoning. This is a narrative of splits in the ruling class occasioned by periods of open class warfare and the modelling of what we might call the Tory state. It is also a tale of how the party had a near-death experience which it overcame, but only by postponing an inevitable demise. This is a story of a forty-year political cycle following the pattern of ascendency, slump and ascendency again. As in economics, the boom determines the character of the bust, except in this case the first period of rising fortunes also enabled the second period of success, while conditioning its decline and fall.

As such this book comes with some necessary caveats. As a work of limited size, this has concentrated on political matters and on sketching the broad trajectory of the party from the Thatcher years to the present. Some aspects of the Conservative Party have had to be neglected. For example, the deregulation of the City in Thatcher's 'Big Bang' and the subsequent financialisation of the state, the long Tory dominance of the countryside, the relationship between the party and different sections of business, and whole swathes of policy are skipped over or dealt with tangentially. This is not to say that they are not important, but the focus is on the politics of the party, on how it remade the British state in its image and has continued to cultivate its mass appeal.

To understand where the Conservative Party is, where it is going and what it has accomplished, it is necessary to get to grips with what the party is. Understanding its sociology, its relationship with class and the UK's political economy, and that between party and state is crucial if we are to grasp not just how the party repeatedly wins general elections, but how it has been able to move with the times and capitalise on shifting social trends in ways that have alluded its Labour opposition. This is where we begin.

1

Dimensions of Decline

For anyone interested in the sociology of elite power in the UK, the Conservative Party is the indispensable machine for arranging and repeating patterns of dominance and subservience across British society. And this is reinforced by its historic propensity to win elections and form governments. As such, the British political system, or at least that part of it concerned with Westminster, is best characterised as a one-party system given how politics pivots around the Conservative pole.

Thanks to their centrality to British political life, the Tories attract a great deal of commentary on a day-to-day basis, and this is reflected in the books published on the party. The politics shelves in bookshops are weighed down by tomes in which politics is soap opera. The grist to this mill are the rise and fall of careers, rivalries petty and great and the he-said-she-said dramas of committee room, backbench and Commons tearoom manoeuvring. This finds its pinnacle in biographies and autobiographies, and the tradition of former prime ministers responsibly penning a memoir about their time in office is well-established. The reader is treated to glimpses of who's married to/related to/went to school or Oxbridge with whom, who are best friends and regular dining partners and so on. This is a world in which big names are thrown about with abandon and are always amenable to phone calls, chats over coffee, dinner. No academic study of elite behaviour would ever be allowed access to these groups of people to study them, and so pen portraits by a client journalist must do. The picture this draws is one of a roughly cohesive and interchangeable group sitting atop politics, business, the media and the state consciously pursuing a rather narrow range of interests. As a microphysics of the shifting alliances and movements of the Tory elite, it is invaluable.[1]

This is the inescapable and hegemonic form of political coverage for popular audiences and characterises establishment politics of all shades. There is a second tradition which is academic and tends more towards the historical and political-scientific than sociological. Here, the Tories are (strangely) not as well served as Labour. There are plenty of histories of the Tory Party, and one notable but sadly dated study of the party membership. Unfortunately, for the period following the Thatcher years there is comparatively little in way of analytical literature. The party is better served in the specialist journals in terms of policy analysis, commentary on rule changes and aspects of party history, but again it is dwarfed by commentary on Labour. Then there is the third tradition: the analysis of the Tories from the left but like its mainstream academic counterpart it is surprisingly thin. Compared to the library of work on the Labour Party and the voluminous quantities written about Labour and its place in leftist strategy, the Tories have seldom merited book-length treatment. This is not to say that there is no commentary, but comparable studies situating the Tory Party and its role in articulating and organising ruling interests are relatively few. And what there is tends to be old. Understandably, the triumph of the Tories in the 1980s attracted a great deal of coverage, but work since has been patchy and piecemeal. The contributions of Stuart Hall, whose work on Thatcherism will feature later, have cast a long shadow over leftist and mainstream political-science work on Conservative Party politics and, arguably, one can see echoes of Thatcher's authoritarian populism in Conservative Party electoral strategy still.

Yet, arguably, this was the point when much original thinking about the Tories effectively ceased. With a few exceptions, critical or radical treatments of the Major years,[2] in which much of the policy groundwork for the New Labour project was bedded down, are few and far between. As for the dog days of the Tories themselves between 1997 and 2005, and their rejuvenation under the

Blair-modelled leadership of David Cameron, there is, again, little leftist comment of note. A welcome exception is Richard Seymour's *The Meaning of David Cameron*,[3] which analysed the Conservative Party's rebranding exercise as a superficial gloss on a party uncomfortable with the modern world, but argued that the party remained a ruling-class enterprise determined to use the 2007–8 economic crisis to push a remaking of Britain under the guise of 'austerity populism'.[4]

Who Are the Conservative Party?

The 2019 general election saw the Conservative Party return 365 Members of Parliament, up forty-eight seats on their 2017 outing and winning 13,966,451 votes (43.6 per cent) – the Tories' best raw-numbers performance since 1992. The 2019 intake of 107 MPs is substantially larger than those elected under Theresa May (twenty-seven), and David Cameron in 2015 (seventy-four). According to reports produced by Conservative Home,[5] for 'Boris' Boys and Girls', thirty-six new MPs were women (34 per cent); five were from black and minority ethnic backgrounds; fourteen per cent were privately educated and 29 per cent hailed from state schools. Given the political sensitivities around schooling, the authors note that these numbers depended on candour, suggesting that the figures are not entirely reliable.

Eleven had prior careers in the law, twenty-two had some experience of the public sector, six had some third-sector/charitable-association employment and fifty-three had a business, managerial or banking/finance background. The professions account for twenty-one parliamentarians and, given the rhetorical emphasis on Brexit and working-class revolt, only six were employed in working-class occupations prior to election.[6] Interestingly, forty-five (42 per cent) members had previously been Conservative councillors, whereas fifty-one (48 per cent) had previously stood as parliamentary candidates for the party, all save one who contested a seat for UKIP. Lastly, thirteen MPs had previously held a role working for an MP, the party or another Tory elected official.

Away from Westminster and in the devolved administrations in Scotland, Wales and London, as of June 2021 the Conservatives respectively possess thirty-one Members of the Scottish Parliament (MSPs), sixteen Welsh Assembly Members (AMs) and nine members of the London Assembly. Furthermore, in the last European Parliament elections in May 2019 they returned just four MEPs with 1,512,809 votes.

Following their advances in the May 2021 local authority elections, the Conservatives hold 7,680 council seats (compared with 5,964 for Labour and 2,535 for the Liberal Democrats). They govern all save three of twenty-four county councils as majority administrations. The three (Cambridgeshire, Cumbria, and Oxfordshire) not run by the Tories are ruled by coalitions. Of district councils, 103 out of 201 authorities have Tory majorities, and a further seven are governed by either coalition with a Conservative component or as minorities. Lastly, fifty-eight unitary local authority areas have returned twenty with majorities and five more in coalition or governing as a minority.

All councillors are required to be members of the Conservative Councillors' Association (CCA) for an annual fee of thirty-five pounds. Council candidates can become candidate members at a reduced rate of twelve pounds, and there is a two-tier associate membership structure open to candidates and 'those who have a keen interest in local government'.[7] Members receive a quarterly magazine, email bulletins carrying news updates, pages of online resources, the opportunity to bid for campaigning grants and access to CCA staff who can assist with policy enquiries.

On the demography of the Conservative councillor base, the Local Government Association does not subdivide demographic data by party affiliation, making available data patchy.[8] A report undertaken by the Fawcett Society looking at the 3,560 council seats won by Tory candidates in the 2019 local authority elections found 1,075 (30 per cent) were women. This is versus 35 per cent of all councillors, and 45 per cent returned by Labour in the same electoral round.[9] Interestingly, of the ten authorities named and shamed by the same report for having the worst representation (i.e., fewer than one in five councillors are women), eight are run by Conservative-majority administrations. In a 2018 audit of the ethnic composition of London borough metropolitan districts[10] and unitary authorities, some 10.9 per cent (112) of ethnic minority councillors were Tories – versus 84.2 per cent (864) who were sitting for Labour. With 1,026 councillors in total identifying as minority ethnicity in this sample, it is reasonable to assume that if it was expanded to cover district authorities too, the number is still likely to be very low.

Of the party's membership, figures have proven hazy and elusive over the years. This is not helped by the equally fuzzy criterion of what counts as a member. One can be a member of the local Conservative Association bar or club, which still exist in some places, and be counted. There are also historic difficulties in Conservative Campaign Headquarters (CCHQ, formerly known as Conservative Central Office) obtaining a comprehensive list, this being a competency devolved down to – and often jealously guarded by – the associations themselves. Therefore, an early 2018 report on party membership pegged it at 149,800 based on a December 2013 estimate provided by CCHQ.[11]

Thankfully, the 2019 Tory leadership contest provides a more robust figure. While the number of ballots issued was reported at 'over 160,000', it transpired that a number had been issued twice.[12] Some 139,318 votes were returned (92,153 for Boris Johnson, 46,656 for Jeremy Hunt and 509 spoiled) with 87.4 per cent turning out. Computing these numbers suggests an overall membership in July 2019 of 159,403 – slightly below the figure briefed to the media. A modest increase compared to 2013, but feeble in comparison to the dramatic growth enjoyed by Labour, the Liberal Democrats, the Greens and the Scottish National Party over the same period.

Compared with the last time the party balloted its membership, this is a marked decline on the 2005 leadership contest. No turnout figures are available, but ballots cast then amounted to 198,844. Claiming that the party has experienced growth since Johnson's election, in October 2019 on the fringes of party conference James Cleverly, the then Conservative Party chair, announced a membership of 191,000.[13]

Conservative membership has three tiers as of January 2021: a five-pound rate for under-twenty-sixes, a standard rate of twenty-five pounds per annum and a fifteen-pound discounted rate for serving and former members of the armed forces. The 'benefits' advertised include financing campaigns(!), choosing candidates, voting in leadership elections, participating in local Conservative Associations and special campaign groups (such as the Conservative Women's Organisation, which, as an affiliate, does not receive funds from the party proper),[14] 'privileged' party information and an opportunity to contribute to policy discussions. In line with the vague character of membership, prior to William Hague's 1998 constitution it was possible to join the Conservatives without paying a subscription provided the member agreed with its aims and values. Hague mandated a compulsory financial contribution, and these subscriptions are split between the (professional) party and the association as determined by the Party Board.

The role of members in the party has been the subject of controversy since the modern party was founded by Robert Peel in the 1830s. Broadly, there are three aspects to the Tory machinery, which was confirmed in 1981 by a Court of Appeal ruling. It found that 'the separate bodies which make up the party cooperate with each other for political purposes but maintain separate existences for organisational purposes'.[15] At the summit sits the Parliamentary Conservative Party, which provides the ministers and leadership, and the operation is run via the Whip's Office. This enforces discipline, manages welfare issues arising from honourable members and reports to the party leader. Policy formation is also the parliamentary party's prerogative, though, in practice, it emerges from negotiations and struggles between leading figures – typically ministers. For example, Britain's entry into the Exchange Rate Mechanism in October 1990 came about after protracted struggle between Margaret Thatcher and Nigel Lawson, with input from Cabinet members and Treasury and Bank of England officials.[16] Interestingly, the privileges afforded MPs in the party's hierarchy are not extended to MSPs and AMs in the devolved regions, nor was this the case with MEPs or Conservative Groups on local authorities. They tend to reproduce on a smaller scale the preeminence of the elected representatives of the bodies they sit in, but under the shadow of possible overrule from Westminster and CCHQ.

The second is the professional party: CCHQ and the apparat, including full-time activist staff based in the nations and the regions. The third strand is the voluntary party. The basic unit is the Conservative Association, which (usually) corresponds to parliamentary constituencies and organises the ward branches in each district. Every association is a member of the National Conservative Convention (NCC, before 1998 the National Union of Conservative and Unionist Associations), which coordinates campaigning and exists in tension with the apparat and the parliamentary party. The NCC and its associations also enjoy a certain autonomy; every association determines an affiliation fee and is responsible for recruitment and discipline. Before 1998 there were no bodies above the association executive to which excluded or sanctioned members could appeal, which presented the centre with some difficulties in the event of local controversy.

Associations have historically enjoyed independence from the national party, which they tend to guard jealously when centralising leaders are in office. For example, if CCHQ wants to make use of association assets or favours candidates it wishes to impose on safe seats, this can invite localised rebellions, though never on the same scale as the internal warfare Labour experienced in the 1980s and after 2015. Since 1998, each association is expected to accept the Mandatory Rules set out in the Conservative Party Constitution, but has the freedom to adopt its own rules via an annual general meeting provided they are constitutionally consistent and subject to approval by the Party Board. There are also provisions for the federation of two or more associations if, for example, a constituency organisation in a particular locale is no longer viable.

The NCC formally meets twice a year in what is described as 'effectively the parliament of the Voluntary Party'.[17] This comprises association chairs and executive officers, who are elected by the rank-and-file membership, along with representatives from the Young Conservatives and the Conservative Women's Organisation. The

NCC receives reports and elects four members to the Board of the Conservative Party. Unlike other parties, these meetings – which coincide with the annual spring forum and party conference in late summer or early autumn – are not forums for policy making, though there is a constitutional stipulation that they 'provide a focus for views of Party Members and act as a link between the Party Leader and Party Members'.[18]

Sitting alongside the NCC are area councils and area management executives (AMEs). An area council brings together associations in each geographical area, and in turn elects an area management executive to act as a regional coordinator of resource distribution and campaigns. AMEs have the power to run organisational initiatives such as recruitment drives, training constituency officers and resolving disputes within and between associations, up to and including rule breaking. AMEs elect three regional coordinators in their area for a maximum of three consecutive years, one of whom is designated chair. These provide organisational leadership in each area and are responsible for the implementation of strategies handed down by the Party Board.

The Party Board itself comprises the party chair (appointed by and accountable to the leader), who serves alongside two deputy chairs: one appointed by the leader and another elected by the NCC. The rest of the board has four positions additional to the chair reserved for the NCC, the chair of the parliamentary 1922 Committee, the chair of the Association of Conservative Peers, the deputy chairs of the Scottish and Welsh Conservatives, the chair of the Conservative Councillors Association, the party treasurer (also appointed by the leader), a further member who might be nominated to the board with its approval, a senior staff member from the professional party appointed by the board's chair, a further member who might be co-opted by the board with the leader's approval and lastly three MPs elected by the parliamentary party.

Constitutionally, the board's writ is supreme. It 'shall have power to do anything which in its opinion relates to the management and administration of the Party'.[19] Among its stipulated responsibilities are the review and approval of the party's accounts, the maintenance of the national membership and the list of approved candidates, the organisation of party conferences, compliance with legislation governing political parties, managing the NCC, dispute resolution and membership discipline.

Despite the tensions between the voluntary and the professional party, members' subordination is enshrined by party statute. Rank-and-file influence over the direction of the party is diluted by the number of elite or leader placements filled on the board, and their input on matters of policy diverted down the route of consultancy via the Policy Forum. Nevertheless, despite the meagre awards and rights available to ordinary Tory members as determined by the constitution, like any party with pretensions to winning elections and forming governments, membership is a necessity.

First is the standard political science argument that party membership fulfils a linkage function, bridging the gap between elites/leaders and the constituency that the organisation typically fishes among. Because members are more numerous and are more likely to be 'normal people', they transmit up the hierarchy and to party representatives the everyday pressures and attitudinal changes they experience. As party memberships whither, the linkage function becomes attenuated, representatives and elites grow more remote, their legitimacy declines, the party is imperilled and, if taking place simultaneously across several parties, the quality of liberal democracy declines.[20]

Second, all parties need a volunteer base to undertake election-eering activity. In the age of social media and money spent on the so-called air war, someone must deliver the leaflets and, occasion-ally, knock on the doors. These are tasks that cannot be outsourced when the spending limits of the election period come into force. Related to this is finance. While the big donors to the Conservatives are often shrouded in secrecy and hide behind fundraising affairs like the annual Black and White Ball or dining clubs that act as clearing houses for anonymous donations, the rest of the voluntary party is always a crowdfunding opportunity and, thanks to membership subscriptions, the source of a stable base income.

Third, members are a necessity because they provide a ready cadre of potential candidates. The Party Board delegates candidate responsibilities to the Committee on Candidates, which operated two lists for UK and (until 2019) European Union parliamentary elections. This body is responsible for the selection and periodic review of those included on the lists, and they comprise the pool from which associations must draw when selecting their candidates.

As subordinate and constitutionally shackled party members are, like any other party – despite recent experiments in the UK political system – the Tories need a voluntary body as much as they require votes.[21] It is therefore interesting that party membership is currently bumping along at historic lows. Taking James Cleverly's autumn 2019 barroom figure of 191,000 in good faith, since the early 1950s the party has slumped from over 2.5 million members to about 5 per cent of its previous size.

Who, then, are the members the party have managed to hold on to? According to survey work carried out with YouGov, Tim Bale and colleagues suggest that women make up 29 per cent of Tory members (versus 39 per cent of political party membership taken as a whole), with an average age of fifty-seven (down two years on an earlier study), and 38 per cent of members were sixty-six or older in 2017.[22] Four in ten enjoy an income of over £30,000 a year, while one in twenty reported £100,000. This might appear surprising given the popular perception of the party as wealthy and for the wealthy, but it is consistent with 42 per cent of members holding degrees, the disproportionate numbers of retirees in the party membership and how the self-employed make up 26 per cent of members.

Bale et al. also found that 44.5 per cent of members had joined since the 2016 EU referendum, and 33 per cent resided in London or the South East of England. On attitudinal matters, 56 per cent styled themselves as being on the right of the party, 34 per cent supported cutting taxes further and one in five think too much emphasis is placed on climate change. On Brexit, two-thirds supported a no-deal outcome.

These mark significant changes compared to the party of a generation ago. According to their survey undertaken in the early 1990s, Paul Whiteley and colleagues noted, 'The typical Conservative Party member is retired, comes from a middle-class occupational background, is an owner-occupier, and possesses few educational qualifications. Men and women belong to the party in roughly equal numbers.'[23] They found that 51 per cent of members were women. The average age then was sixty-two, but with half the membership aged sixty-six and over. Two-thirds self-reported as middle class compared to 19 per cent working class, but 40 per cent said they were from blue-collar backgrounds. On longevity, 35 per cent had been members for at least twenty-five years, whereas only 19 per cent had joined within the previous five years.

Considering the fieldwork was done not long after Margaret Thatcher's resignation and the pall she cast over British politics, the attitudinal evidence suggests that the grassroots were somewhat resistant to the values and policies she favoured. On socially conservative measures, 70 per cent believed repatriation of migrants should be encouraged and 69 per cent would like to have seen the death penalty restored. Yet on economics, while 68 per cent thought market forces improved the National Health Service, 74 per cent believed unemployment benefits should be enough to maintain a reasonable standard of living, 81 per cent believed the government should intervene and spend money to alleviate poverty and 64 per cent thought workers should have more of a say over their workplace.

Has the character of party activism changed? According to Whiteley et al., 28 per cent of members had given money on a frequent basis, and 18 per cent had put a poster in their window. This compares to 63 per cent of members who had never delivered leaflets and 77 per cent who had never canvassed. Forward to the present, asked by Bale et al. 'Which of these have you done for your party in recent years?', only 11.3 per cent of members had donated money on top of their subscription and 12.2 per cent had attended a meeting. On campaigns activity, 21.6 per cent had displayed a poster, 30.5 per cent had delivered leaflets and 21.3 per cent had canvassed during the 2017 general election (in 2015, the figures were 29.6 per cent, 43.5 per cent and 36.5 per cent respectively).

This suggests an increase in activity between the 1990s and 2010s, while the sudden drops between elections might be politics fatigue (both coming so close together, and a year after the EU membership referendum) and the fact that the 2017 contest was unscheduled while, under the provisions of the Fixed-term Parliaments Act, the date for 2015 was set many years in advance, allowing members and activists plenty of notice. But it might also be the case that increased activity is symptomatic of the Tories losing a hinterland's worth of inactive members, making the activist base more proportional.

This diagram of the Conservative Party, as we will see, is not without consequence. Understanding the party's basic organisational principles draws attention to how successive Tory prime ministers conceived of the relationship between government and state. Surely it is more than coincidence that the pre-eminence of the executive within the party parallels the authoritarian approach to statecraft taken by Thatcher and her successors, in which the state is haphazardly centralised with the diminution of points of institutional authority outside the Cabinet. It is almost as if experience of a party where the leader's authority has little to no constitutional checks, and running such a party, confers a certain habit of governing once a Tory leader enters Number 10.

In short, we have a picture of a successful party of government which, while smaller than its Labour opponent, is no less active in terms of its membership and possesses a more enviable electoral record. Given recent successes, which include growing support while in office, in what meaningful sense can the Conservatives be said to be in decline?

The Argument for Decline

Despite the relative paucity of literature about the Conservative Party, it has nevertheless yielded three theses of decline. Curiously, two of these are from within the tradition of Tory commentary and, though separated by forty years, two were published at the height of Conservative power. The accounts from the right are

Geoffrey Wheatcroft's *The Strange Death of Tory England* (published just before David Cameron put the party back on the path to government) and Ed West's *Small Men on the Wrong Side of History* (appearing months following Boris Johnson's election triumph).[24] From the left, *Thatcher and Friends: The Anatomy of the Tory Party* was published in the immediate aftermath of Margaret Thatcher's crushing victory in 1983.[25]

Taking the most contemporary first, West's book argues that the 2019 election victory papers over several structural issues, which he understands as 'a result of demography, cultural trends and its [the Conservative Party's] disappearance from many national institutions and sectors'.[26] Assuming a semi-autobiographical tone throughout, this former *Telegraph* blogger and contributor to the Catholic press found, much to his chagrin, that as he grew older there was not much evidence that his contemporaries were becoming more conservative. Indeed, the failure of this middle range of Generation X voters half-way through their working lives to turn conservative (and vote Conservative) ensured that Theresa May's election was derailed.

This was indicative of a wider process of cultural change which West likens to the Reformation. Social liberalism is on the march, morality is governed by an intolerant laissez-faire (i.e., prominent figures find themselves hate figures if they nod against prevailing political correctness, or what the right now like to call 'woke' politics) and, from the conservative point of view, people tend to be growing more progressive and radical as they age. The victories of Trump and right-wing strongmen elsewhere, Brexit and Johnson's 14 million votes are therefore blips along the road to a distinctly non-conservative future.

As a polemic against the cultural domination of social liberalism in the United States and the UK, West provides few clues to explain the decline of conservatism. He gestures towards the argument, popularised in political science by Ronald Inglehart's post-materialism thesis,[27] that rising affluence has meant growing economic security and employment. As a consequence, materialist issues around pay and jobs lose efficacy. This development spells the end of class politics and the dominance of identity politics as the new fulcrum of radicalism. As West puts it, 'progressives are naturally better suited to good times, and since things have been getting better over the past seventy years, so the world has become more liberal . . . modern liberalism [therefore] is more like Type-2 diabetes, the side-effect of a society with too much good stuff'.[28] West also locates the spread of liberalism, and therefore conservatism's eclipse, against the post-war growth of universities and the preponderance of liberal-minded academic staff, collapsing church attendance and a relationship observed in the US between high house prices in a given district and the propensity to vote Democrat. All these mean that younger people more generally are not growing conservative as they age.

There is some merit to West's case, even if he is short on explan-atory detail. The growth of social liberalism and women's increasing freedom from traditional gender roles, enabled by the feminist movement and the availability of contraceptive techno-logies, has seen greater rates of participation in the labour market and increasing economic independence. Combined with rising house prices, women and men are marrying older, if at all, and leaving children until later. This, for West, is significant because marriage and childbirth have significant conservatising effects around gender roles and one's ontological sense or place in the world. It follows that women's receptivity to conservative values is pushed to later in the life course. This is a problem for conservative parties (at least where they remain mainstream parties of the centre-right), because traditionally they have disproportionately appealed to and commanded the votes of women. For example, Sarah Childs and Paul Webb note that the first time Labour out-polled the Tories among women was in 2005, before reverting to the historical mean in 2010. This gendered disproportion was much larger in the past, with gaps of up to 14 per cent recorded in the 1950s.[29] A move away from conservatism among women, rein-forced in the last three elections, will pose the Tories a great deal of difficulty considering their past dependence.

Focused more on the changes to the Parliamentary Conservative Party, Geoffrey Wheatcroft's account of Conservative decline locates it in the recomposition of the party's elected cadre from the 1960s onwards. Characterised as a class battle, Wheatcroft's fundamental thesis offers little in the way of conceptual clarity but is indicative of a real process. Introducing his work, he locates the sea change in Tory fortunes to the early 1960s and the battle over Harold Macmillan's succession. He writes,

> A kind of class war within Conservative ranks would be brought into the open, and the party would be forced to reinvent itself, something it had often done before, but in this case for the last time. Two factions would engage, one of them upholding the old regime ideals of privilege through service and lineage and the virtues of an hereditary governing class, the other, of the contrary cause *carriére overte aux talentes* and of worth proved by ability rather than rank or connection. One faction would win, and go on to transform the country: thanks in part to that victory, the Tories would reach the end of the century in terminal decline.[30]

Iain Macleod, Churchill's health minister and the former minister of labour and colonial secretary, was the trigger for an overhaul of the Tory way of doing things. In early 1964, Macleod wrote up his recollection of the 1963 leadership contest, in as far it could be described as such. He argued that Macmillan's replacement by Sir Alec Douglas-Home was an Old Etonian stitch-up, of preferment and position selecting for its own. Macleod himself hailed from a middle-class background and attended grammar school, and so this dispute – in which he dubbed the *cognoscenti* the Magic Circle – had a clear class dimension. As Wheatcroft notes, among the nine grandees party to Home's enthronement, eight were Eton old boys.

An affront to democratic politics certainly, but for Wheatcroft what came next drove the nail into the coffin of the old Conservative Party. Upon Douglas-Home's own resignation in 1965 the Vaticanesque method of election was replaced by a ballot of the parliamentary party. However, rather than adopting a simple method the process required a victor to have an absolute majority of votes and a 15 per cent surplus over and above the tally of the next-placed opponent.

In the first historic exercise of Tory internal democracy, Edward Heath polled 150 votes, Reginald Maudling 133 and Enoch Powell fifteen. To satisfy the new rules a second ballot was held to confirm Heath in position, even though his opponents withdrew. Ten years later, in the dog days of Heath's premiership, a committee under Douglas-Home revisited these mechanics and recommended an annual ballot, provided that a challenger to the incumbent could find a proposer and a seconder, and the 15 per cent surplus was expanded to cover all MPs (i.e., the entirety of the electorate), not just those who voted. As such, when Margaret Thatcher challenged Heath the results were 150 votes to Thatcher versus 119 for Heath, with an also-ran campaign from Hugh Fraser mustering the support of just sixteen MPs. Come the second ballot, Thatcher retained her lead with 146 votes (52.9 per cent) versus seventy-nine for William Whitelaw, Geoffrey Howe's nineteen, Jim Prior's nineteen and four for John Peyton.

This established the passage from the aged, patrician governing class to the career politician who won leadership elections irrespective of merit and depended on popularity (or, in the case of Thatcher's elevation, was the least unpopular). Arguably this remained the case until Theresa May succeeded David Cameron in the brief summer 2016 contest.

For Wheatcroft this triumph of the career politician called time on what Alexander Gallas calls the 'gentlemanly capitalism' of the post-war period, and its healthy (some might say conservative) respect for established institutions, the cultural memory of the depression and acceptance of the compromises and limited industrial power sharing.[31] The career politician had no such ties – nor, for that matter, direct experience of responding to these concerns.

This process accelerated under Thatcher (her intakes 'were new professional politicians from a new class who were in politics as a trade and for the money'),[32] and allowed for an arrogant, brash and authoritarian approach to government that, over the course of Thatcher's reign, alienated natural Tory supporters among professional strata and the public services.

Summarising these two accounts of Conservative decline, the displacement of social conservatism by social liberalism and the dissipation of the grandees and the dominance of the parliamentary party by the petit bourgeois (self-made or otherwise) and by the politics-as-vocation cohorts, while conceptually fuzzy, offer two narratives that provide insight into how the party has changed over the decades, and are suggestive of explanations more social scientific in nature that go beyond the personalities and blunders of successive Tory leaders. As accounts go, they are a beginning. As they stand, they are limited and require firmer footing.

John Ross's *Thatcher and Friends* offers a materialist framework for understanding what was happening to the Tories in the early 1980s. Appearing shortly after Thatcher's 1983 triumph, it – like the present work – makes the counterintuitive case for Conservative decline. Ross, however, roots his analysis in two empirical observations. The first are long-term voting patterns. Between 1846 and 1931, the overall trend in Tory votes was upward while the old Liberal Party entered into steep decline between 1859 and 1951, a fall from political grace that, from 1886, saw the Tories beat their old rivals in twenty-five out of twenty-six elections.

On performance between 1931 and 1983, fluctuations from election to election reveal a tendency for the proportion of Tory votes to decline. When the party won office, it was thanks to a lower vote (though not necessarily seats) than the preceding election, with the sole exception of 1955, when the Tories hit a post-war high. Likewise, periods in opposition saw them do worse than the previous parliament where they were in opposition, apart from 1945–50. The 1979–83 period of Thatcher's triumph was consistent with this decline. Indeed, in vote terms the 1983 victory was only 2.4 per cent higher than that commanded by the party in 1945 and was, at the time, the lowest recorded by a Tory prime minister.

This leads Ross to several conclusions. First, the Tories were shedding mass support in those areas gained during their ascendency prior to 1931. Second, decline is indissociable from a pattern of periodicity in the British party system itself. Rather than being a two-party system with parties taking their turns in office, Ross suggests it is a one-party system in which one dominates for a long period. There are four such periods: the 1688–1783 dominance of the Whigs, followed by Tory ascendency between 1783 and 1832. They were displaced by the Whigs/Liberals from 1832 to 1886, and again the Tories assumed their supremacy from that point on, albeit with fluctuations in support and temporary interludes out of office. It only operates like a two-party system in transitional moments from one period of dominance to the next. What, then, is driving this process and therefore Tory decline?

The rise and decline of the Conservative Party, and of the modern British party system, is a product of the rise and decline of British imperialism itself. To attempt to overcome the consequences of that, British capitalism must progressively abandon the old economic formulas and link itself to new rising forces. For Ross, this meant the powerful European capitalisms of the EEC. This entire reorganisation of the mechanisms of the British economy in turn required a complete change of the party system. The events of the last thirty years are simply the manifestations of this.[33]

How has Ross's argument fared in the years since? Returning to it in the immediate wake of the May 2010 general election, he suggests that the trends confirm his thesis.[34] Following 1983, the Tories won elections with successively lower proportions of the vote, even though on one occasion (1992) they won more absolute votes than any party at any other time. Three years later, Ross was convinced that the Tory-led coalition government was going to founder, boxing itself into its South Eastern heartlands.[35] In popular-vote terms, he calculated that the Tory vote declines by around 0.2 per cent per year, and that this yields a swing factor of 5 per cent, determining the difference between defeat and victory. Looking ahead to the 2015 general election he forecast 34.6 per cent if the Tories did well and won, and 30.3 per cent if they lost.

Unfortunately for Ross's theory, matters did not turn out as predicted. In 2015 the Tories emerged strengthened from their coalition with the Liberal Democrats with 330 seats (excluding the Speaker, John Bercow), a majority of twelve seats and a proportional increase to 36.9 per cent of the vote. In 2017 under Theresa May's leadership the Conservatives suffered a net loss of thirteen seats, but the vote share surged to 42.3 per cent – 13.6 million votes – a tally comparable to Thatcher's at the height of her success. And then in 2019 under Boris Johnson the Tories polled 43.6 per cent and almost 14 million votes – the highest in absolute numbers since John Major and the best percentage since 1979. Contrary to expectations since hitting rock bottom with 30.7 per cent in 1997, Tory fortunes have improved from election to election. We do not see failure and retreat but rather consolidation and advance.

Recent performance therefore poses theories of decline some difficulties. For West, the advance of social-liberal culture is yet to resolve itself in Conservative defeat. For Wheatcroft, the replace-ment of the grandees by careerists might have sown the seeds for the traumas inflicted by New Labour, but the generational replacement of these cadres by cohorts of Tories who are more short-termist, and even more determined to bang on about Europe, is yet to lay them low. And for Ross's argument, the dislocation of British capital from the 'sensible' trajectory of European inte-gration might not have stopped the fragmentation of the party system, but nor has the Tory Party been struck down. All of this begs the question: in what meaningful sense can the Conservative Party be in decline?

A New Theory of Decline

The growing institutional weight of the labour movement from the 1930s onwards introduced an important stabiliser into the manage-ment of class politics and economic-order politics. The specifics of the post-war settlement need not detain us here, except to mention the peculiar and somewhat singular experiment with British Keynesianism whereby trade unions were partially integrated into the system of economic management, underpinned by a shared approach to (nearly) full employment on the part of both govern-ing parties, and a generally more benign period of economic expansion ensured rising living standards and the growth of mass consumption.[36] This introduced powerful tendencies towards the privatisation of leisure, was a boon to social mobility and in turn provided an impetus to property ownership and a decline in the immediacy of traditional community institutions.

This was not felt most acutely among the trade union movement at first – trade unionists and workers covered by collective bargaining kept on growing right up until 1979. It instead primarily affected the social roots of the Conservative movement. It was Jeremy Bentham who reportedly first referred to the Church of England as the Conservative Party at prayer, and it is striking how closely declining attendance matched the post-war fall in Tory Party membership. Christmas and Easter attendance fell from 5 per cent of the population to 2 per cent between 1960 and 2015, and Sunday attendance has declined from 3.5 per cent to just over 1 per cent from 1968 to 2015.[37] As a prop for associational life outside party meetings and social clubs, it is reasonable to assume that this institutional feeder and reinforcer of conservative values has less purchase as an organ for bringing together those who might otherwise be inclined to follow these values into the party.

The second point worth noting is social mobility. A common touchstone and aspiration of Tory programmes, the social scene the party provided in the 1940s and 1950s allowed for a certain degree of social mixing, where association members could rub shoulders with upwardly mobile professionals, managers, employers, the odd aristocrat and, of course, local and national politicians. These networks were a good way for the young and ambitious to get ahead, in terms of both finding 'suitable' partners and making contacts to maximise one's employment opportunities.

However, post-war evidence from Europe about social mobility found that the upwardly mobile become less conservative with the change in social location – a story different to North America's.[38] This suggests something of a mercenary attitude to association membership, and with mobility purposes served and other priorities taking over there was little need to maintain the relationship – though this did not necessarily mean a change in voting habits.

Thatcher's authoritarian approach to government compounded the processes of atomisation further. The attacks on the trade union movement and the nationalised industries not only broke the back of organised labour, but further destroyed tens of thousands of small businesses – natural conservatives – while accelerating the move towards privatised individuality, which impacted on conservative institutions like the Church and other civic organisations such as the Scouts and Guides movement, as well as informal community ties and spiritedness. Following Wheatcroft's argument, this is a direct consequence of the relative independence afforded to the careerist (and petit bourgeois) core of Thatcher's Conservatives and with it a light-minded approach to the party's existing mass support. There was little to no perceived social or political cost to Tory MPs who enthusiastically voted through each piece of legislation, green-lighting the Thatcherite assault on the social fabric.

Paradoxically, privatised individuation under Thatcher, pursued by all governments since, has its roots in the authoritarian state. For Thatcher, as we will see, this was indispensable for her political project, which promised the restitution of authority. In implementation, this meant a reordering of the state in which more powers were centralised in the executive and alternative bases of authority and competence in the state's institutions were undermined, muted, stripped of their powers or abolished. Add this to the privatised leisure opportunities of mass-market consumerism, facilitated by the extension of personal credit, and we can see how the committed base of the party eroded. This process accelerated in the Thatcher years. Yet this supposes something of a conundrum. While Thatcher's reforms attacked the institutional solidarities that helped sustain mass Conservatism in the post-war period, one might suppose that a cultural turn to individualism and the good life defined in acquisitive terms would be fruitful for the Conservatives. Politically speaking, six outright wins and two where the Tories were the largest party out of eleven elections since 1979 would appear to bear this out. Yet, despite outright centre-right dominance, and the precious little New Labour did to challenge the market-fundamentalist authoritarian consensus, how has the triumph of the right led to the growth of social liberalism as the emerging de facto cultural outlook, and how in turn does this gnaw at the foundations of Tory viability?

The expansion of the state in the developed capitalist nations was not solely thanks to the institutionalisation of the labour movement and the move to tripartite corporatism in economic management. The lessons of the Depression demonstrated that the state needs to attend to the conditions of the production and reproduction of class relations more systematically. The expansion of the welfare state and nationalised industries, with the stress on full employment, was the key to social stability, with the consequence of drawing millions of workers into direct employment by the state.

Many, as was the case in Britain, were producing commodities under state direction and ownership, but others were employed to produce relationships. These jobs were not concerned with producing surplus value, but reproducing social relations, institutions and technologies of population management that advanced capitalist societies depend on. It was service-oriented towards a (mass) client base and was, to all intents and purposes, in the business of producing people.[39]

This 'immaterial labour' underwent a double expansion in the 1970s. States, despite the best efforts of leaders like Thatcher, carried on growing in size while becoming internally more complex, with powers dispersed among semi-autonomous (and occasionally competing) institutions, under the command of the executive in the last (or, where politically expedient, first) instance. Simultaneously, some responsibilities were sold or contracted out to the private sector, while increasingly the offshoring and decline of manufacturing saw jobs replaced by an expanding for-profit service sector, such as retail, call centres, adult care and, more recently, the gig economy – all supported by growing armies of administrators. The younger the demographic, the more likely their experience of work is under the conditions of immaterial labour, of the production of intangible services, knowledges and relationships.

This is where matters become problematic for Conservatism. Immaterial work is fundamentally about relationships and draws on social competencies for the benefit of an employer. This sociability demands an aptitude to rub along with others from all kinds of backgrounds, with all kinds of characteristics. Employment is simultaneously social production and social performance, and this makes tolerance fundamental to an economics based on intangibles produced by cooperative, social activity.

Social liberalism, therefore, is not simply the result of successful struggles against discriminatory practice and oppression, but their subsequent incorporation into the logics of capital accumulation; it is the spontaneous common sense of new vectors of exploitation dependent on the social capacities of human beings, and therefore privileges tolerance, empathy, communication and care with a (low-grade) antipathy towards arbitrary authority, hierarchy and coercion. Social conservatism as practised by the right, with its emphasis on tradition, authority and the identification and vilification of undesirables and scapegoats, cuts fundamentally against the prevailing (and expanding) social-liberal common sense. Their way of the world jars with younger workers' experience of the world.

This goes some way to address the oft-noted context of the stark age polarisations seen in the 2014 Scottish independence referendum, the 2016 EU referendum and the 2017 and 2019 general elections. Older workers and the retired in the main have a different experience of working life and are the least socially liberal demographic groups, and as they pass away those experiences and values pass with them; until social conservatism reinvents itself in a manner more compatible with the spontaneous everyday lives of the majority of the working-age population it is not going to reproduce itself like-for-like, with obvious consequences for centre-right parties.

Yet why is there not only an attraction for the old particularly to the Conservative Party in the United Kingdom, but also a similar preference noted in liberal-democratic polities generally? Is it really the case of one's simply growing more conservative with age, and that the transition from liberal to conservative values that Ed West frets about in his arguments is getting pushed back to later in the life course? The answer to this question resides in the experience of class or, more precisely, the experience of being 'declassed', and the acquisition of property, of a general ontological tendency of life after work and a strong trend of the social being bound up with asset ownership conditioning consciousness.

As YouGov reported of the 2019 general election, 45 per cent in the 60–69 age bracket voted Conservative, with an additional 16 per cent supporting Nigel Farage's Brexit Party (BXP).[40] In the 70-plus demographic, Tory support climbed to 58 per cent and that for the BXP fell back slightly to 14 per cent. In other words, 61 per cent and 72 per cent of older voters, just under and just over two-thirds respectively, supported parties of the right. Comparing the figures with 2017, then we found that 58 per cent of 60–69s supported the Tories (and 20 per cent supported the UK Independence Party) and for the 70-plus group it was 69 per cent and 2 per cent for each, indicating a solid bloc of right-wing voters that grew very modestly between the two elections.[41]

Age polarisation, however, appears to be a conjunctural characteristic stemming from the UK's referendum on European Union membership in June 2016, with both elections overshadowed by the vote to Leave and its subsequent impact on politics. YouGov numbers for the referendum showed a stark age gap.[42] Those aged 18–24 voted to Remain by 71 per cent to 29 per cent, whereas the respective figures for 50–64s was 40 per cent versus 60 per cent, and in the over-65s Leave led by a large margin – 36 per cent Remain versus 64 per cent Leave. However, prior to this, age polarisation in British politics was still present. At the 2015 general election, 61 per cent of the over-60s supported the right (45 per cent Conservatives, 16 per cent UKIP).[43] In 2010, all age groups were more likely to support the Tories, apart from the 18–24s, where Labour led by a single point. Yet, again, there was a more pronounced support for the Conservatives moving up the age ranges, topping out at 44 per cent for over-65s.[44]

What might appear to be conjunctural is an exacerbation of a trend found in British politics at least since 1992, as Figure 1.1 demonstrates.

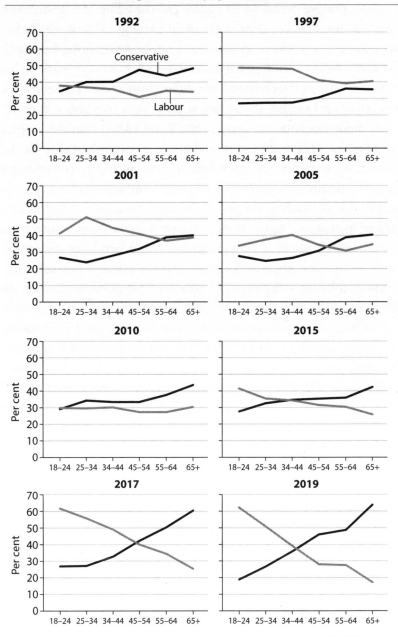

Figure 1 Vote by age over time

Source: Ipsos Mori, 'How the voters voted in the 2019 election', ipsos.com, December 2019

What is it about the experience of being old that accounts for this now-persistent feature of British politics? The first is the weak magnetic force of the experience of retirement. This is not to say retirement is a uniform experience or a luxurious life, but one's relation to social life is transformed by giving up work. This affords a certain freedom and the inclination to do as one pleases. In a society where the individual is formally sovereign, independent and therefore the arbiter of what is right and what is wrong, it can tend towards atomisation and a relative withdrawal from the social, compounding the individuating tendencies present since the ready availability of privatised leisure. Additionally, most retired people are dependent on fixed incomes from their (public and private) pensions. Hence most pensioners move from a structural location conditioned by waged labour to another, somewhat analogous to a petit bourgeois position. The obligation to the employer is replaced by the obligations of family and individual inclination, but because of the fixed income, retirement also means little opportunity to make good shortfalls, either imposed by disaster, price rises, pension fund collapse or government policy. Therefore, like the petit bourgeois dependent on their own efforts and their modest amount of capital to survive challenging market conditions, retirement is a social location in which anxiety exercises an overhanging presence.

The political behaviour of structurally anxious locations has been well known since Marx's day. Marx himself wrote about how the middle class, small businesses, the peasantry and the lumpenproletariat comprised the backbone of support for Napoleon III's authoritarian regime in France after 1851. Trotsky and many others have noted that the mass appeal of fascism and right-wing populist parties rests on similar strata, despite none of these movements and parties articulating their politics in transparently straightforward class terms.[45] The ontological embedding of uncertainty finds relief by sublimating politically into a series of common themes exemplifying change and the unfamiliar, such as (the perceived habits of) young people, the trajectory of popular culture and 'outsiders' used as scapegoats: sexual minorities, travellers and immigrants. The flip side of anxiety is the longing for certainty, and this desire can be incorporated by governments or political projects promising to short-circuit the messy complexity of the real world and reduce matters to simple, binary truisms, all the while promising to give outgroups, the fixations of these anxieties, a good hiding in the name of authority, discipline and the nation. It is therefore unsurprising that attitudes of these kinds, and the politics they inform, draw more support from the retired than from the working-age population. It helps explain not just the growth in support for socially conservative and authoritarian values among the elderly, but also why Brexit – sold as an assertion of the sovereignty and will of the British nation – was disproportionately popular among these age cohorts.

Nevertheless, the experience of retirement is a comparatively weak tendency, a predisposition that can be overridden by attachments to working-life identities, relationships with family, one's social circle and previously existing political loyalties. Yet the data and the stubborn loyalties that older voters have to right-wing parties cannot be denied any more than the propensity for the affluent to vote Conservative.

The strong magnetic force that the Tories have benefited from, however, is property, which, combined with the experience of retirement, strengthens the petit bourgeois-adjacent tendencies described. As we shall see, central to Thatcher's strategies for breaking up her opposition were her efforts to try and manufacture Tory voters. Through council house sell-offs, the advancing of subsidised, low-cost mortgages and latterly the so-called popular privatisations of gas, telecoms and electricity, expanding the scope of property acquisition and share ownership saw millions buy into the Thatcherite dream. Not everyone buying their council house turned Tory, but these experiments in a property-owning and share-holding democracy helped build a significant enough layer of voters to help the Conservatives through three subsequent elections.

This was to have long-term consequences for the Tories' electoral fortunes. Between 2001 and 2017 there was consistent transference of voters from Labour to Conservative among the over-65s. This represents the cohort of voters who were able to get on the property ladder in the Thatcher and Major years entering the age bracket, as well as shifts in party policy oriented towards them. Labour under Tony Blair was clear about its intentions to leave the Thatcherite settlement intact, but by 2005 fatigue and the fallout from the Iraq War saw increasing numbers desert Labour. By 2010, the trashing of Labour's reputation for economic competence by the stock market crash, and the soothing noises made by David Cameron to protect pensioner incomes from the consequences of austerity, meant that there was a sharp move to the right among the old thanks to increasing numbers of property owners reaching retirement age.

Far more likely to own property than younger cohorts of the employed, paradoxically, the trappings of a comfortable retirement – homeownership benefiting from rising asset prices, second or more homes put out to rental, index-linked pensions and a modest quantity of shares – exacerbate ontological unease because one has more to lose if the economy or governments turn against one. From a rational-choice point of view, it makes perfect sense to support governments that will not move to tackle private renting, build social housing to undercut it or allow for too much new housing in general to keep asset prices inflated. Any kind of policy deviation or uncertainty around its continuance must be resisted and voted against. Hence there is even more of a longing for an authoritarian government that will leave the chips to lie where they lie, with more of a predisposition towards nostalgia-tinged certainties and a firm reaction against threats to this set-up. This is where we start seeing real dangers for the future of the Conservatives.

The problem the Conservatives have is that their coalition of elderly voters is not being replaced because the conservatising effects of old age are breaking down for the layers beneath them. Increasing conservatism is not an essentialist feature of the life course, but is due to passage into the small business-adjacent location of retirement and, more importantly, the consequence of acquiring property. The overriding difficulty for the Tories is how property acquisition is eroding over time as asset-price inflation is barring young people from buying a house and driving more into the private rented sector, an issue exacerbated by a dearth of publicly subsidised housing.

This cannot simply be fixed by building more and offering subsidised mortgages, because high property prices and the proliferation of renting are very much in the interests of the Tories' coalition of older voters, among whom are a not inconsiderable number of petty landlords who rent out old family homes or other properties. Keeping this base loyal, which disproportionately turns out at election time for the Conservatives, means that the Tories have an electoral interest in pitching their programme at them, even if the price the party will pay is decreasing political viability in the medium to long term. If this was not bad enough, the Tories have visibly set themselves up as a barrier to the aspirations of younger people by reinforcing age tiers and conditionalities for the minimum wage and access to social security, the tripling of tuition fees for those moving into higher education, the stymying of opportunity, holding down real pay and therefore living standards and fanning the flames of illiberal culture-war positions.[46] Even if the Conservatives are able to square the circle of reconciling the interests of the rising electorate with those who regularly support them and the conservatising effects of age are jump-started by a new policy package, there is no reason to believe these policies could overcome the toxicity they're bedding down into younger demographics.

This is how we can meaningfully discuss the long-term decline of the Tory Party. The patterns identified by Ross explain the party's fortunes up until 1997 and the doldrums of the early 2000s, but to explain their subsequent rise and consolidation we have to pay attention to the expansion of property ownership in the 1980s and the electoral consequences of this cohort of voters as they move through the life course and age, ultimately culminating in the appearance of a generation war in which the old have accumulated property, and continue to do so, while younger working-age people are disproportionately locked out of the system.

This has meant that the accumulation of support for the Tories, their appearance of success and mass appeal are strongly rooted in a declinist dynamic. Small wonder the party is most enthusiastic about constituency boundary reviews and new forms of voter identification designed to suppress the votes of those outside its coalition, and has enthusiastically aped the populist politics of UKIP, the Continental far right and Donald Trump. Any triumph under these conditions is based on foundations of sand, and election victories become increasingly difficult the longer they persist.

The Conservative Party as a Ruling-Class Party

So much for the Tories' mass appeal, but how to account for the stable bedrock of the Conservative Party: the British bourgeoisie itself? Why does it win and continue to win over most millionaires and billionaires, remain relevant to them and keep the loyalty of those sectors of capital when they might be pursuing policies favourable to another sector and detrimental to theirs?

Ralph Miliband argued that the state acts as guarantor of capitalist relations of production thanks to inertia. He argued that economic elites and (senior) state personnel tend to be drawn from similar social backgrounds, underpinned by inequalities in education, privileged career pathways and what would be referred to today as the social capital that attendance at elite institutions offers. This cultivates a common outlook and a common concern in maintaining the fundamentals just the way they are, which means the contemporary cast of politics and, above all, the balance of the capital–labour relation: the power of employers versus employees. As he observed, 'top civil servants . . . are not simply conservative in general: they are conservative in the sense that they are, within their allotted sphere, the conscious and unconscious allies of existing economic and social elites'.[47]

As guarantor of the class character of the capitalist state, Miliband's argument drew a great deal of criticism (including a bad-tempered exchange between him and Nicos Poulantzas in the pages of *New Left Review*), but this approach does have the benefit of putting social relationships at the centre of analysis. These are key for understanding strategic decision making, and institutional inertia over time repeats, reiterates and reaccomplishes the state's character. It is not simply spontaneously and magically capitalist. This also makes specifying the social relationships that constitute political parties, and for our purposes the Conservative Party, more grounded. For instance, on conservative ideas and parties in liberal democracies, Miliband notes,

> conservatism, however pronounced, does not entail the rejection of all measures of reform, but lives on the contrary by the endorsement and promulgation of reform at the least possible cost to the existing structure of power and privilege . . . conservative parties . . . remain primarily the defence organisations, in the political field, of business and property. What they really 'aggregate' are the different interests of the dominant classes. Precisely because the latter are not solid, congealed economic and social blocs, they require political formations which reconcile, coordinate, and fuse their interests, and which express their common purposes as well as their separate interests. These purposes and interests also require ideological clothing suitable for political competition in the age of 'mass politics'; one of the special functions of conservative political parties is to provide that necessary clothing.[48]

Miliband provides a heuristic for teasing apart the structural processes and laying bare their content as material and mutually constitutive connections between people, albeit people who inhabit nodes within the economy and state – the social and political worlds that confer on them power, influence and control. The study of mainstream political parties requires that they be considered part of the complex of institutions and organisation encompassing the state system and, as we are in the business of specifying structural relations, how parties articulate, express, win over and perpetuate certain interests. By not treating the state as a 'thing', in Bob Jessop's phrase, there is the possibility of an approach that can capture the fluidity and movement of social relationships between elites.[49]

It also helps provide a basis for answering questions such as why the state pursues certain 'non-class' policies, such as the Conservative Party's historic preference for socially conservative positions of gender, race, ethnicity and LGBTQ rights. Or why certain businesspeople support a party that does not align to 'their' capital's interests, such as the machine builder and long-standing Tory funder JCB following the Tories' long, lackadaisical attitude towards manufacturing. This means moving materialist analysis away from a homology to rational-choice approaches to economics and politics – that is, the crude assumption business and bourgeois politicians *always* act to further the interests of capital and have perfect information about the circumstances of their tactics and corresponding strategies, rather than something more socially situated.

In the first place, bearing in mind Miliband's approach, this requires bourgeois preoccupations to be always already socially embedded in cultures, doxas, networks and institutional and organisational contexts, and variously framed by the pressures of this conditioning, and their opinions/ideas to be formed over the course of a lifetime's participation in these milieux. That is, decision making always takes place under conditions of what John Goldthorpe refers to as situational rationality – decisions anyone makes are meaningful to them and benefit them in some way from within their consciousness of the lifeworld they inhabit.[50] Hence those watching out for a catch-all explanation for why some manufacturers align with the Tories are going to be sat in their hide for a long time.

The second point is obvious but is largely missing from Marxist discussions of ruling-class decisions. Capital is not omnipotent. Individual capitals can be frittered away and destroyed. Not only are decisions made situationally, but the perceptions of one's interests (be it about investment opportunities or a policy initiative) can be mistaken. Businesses fail all the time, and some do so because of wrong decisions. Likewise, politicians fail, whether they prove incompetent or make the wrong call at a given juncture. Success is always bought off the back of the failures of others. Analysis must be open to the possibility that agents, whether individual, collective or institutional, make bad decisions that can run counter to an 'objective' appreciation of their interests.

The same, then, is true of political strategies. For Lenin, politics was more an art than a science due to the bewildering variables in play at any one time. The complexity of any given juncture, the weight of situational rationality and the activities of others ensure that an unfiltered continuity between interest, decision and outcome is difficult to accomplish. An analysis of politics must proceed on the ground that everyone is flawed.

Where does this leave the Conservative Party? It means understanding the party as a historical condenser of business interests, as a voluntary organisation that is nevertheless a key actor in the UK state system, a vehicle for the politically ambitious, but above all a collective working to reproduce itself as a collective; and it does that by – mostly – winning elections, disorganising its opponents, defending governmental power and authority and providing a setting (among many) to allow establishment figures to network. It is a means by which old, safe political elites are replaced by new, safe political elites.

Understanding the Tory Party as a collective accomplishment endowed with significant political advantages means paying attention to the decisions it makes that directly or indirectly impact its ability (or otherwise) to maintain itself as the primary party of government. For example, key sections of commercial and financial capital voted with their feet and warmed to the cocktail-party offensive launched by Tony Blair after 1994, with Labour's promise to leave the fundamentals of the Thatcherite settlement intact even more congenial than refreshments and access offered at posh soirées. These layers of capital abandoned Labour after the 2008 crash destroyed Gordon Brown's reputation for economic competence, despite taking the measures that saved their system, and migrated back to the Tories with promises of protecting capital from austerity.

However, the issue of Brexit badly split these interests, but without Labour providing a safe harbour and alternative, significant commercial and financial concerns variously backed the so-called Remain movement and, temporarily, the Liberal Democrats. Despite Brexit being 'settled' by the 2019 election, the political splits in capital are far from healed, even though Boris Johnson has repeatedly talked up his grand infrastructure schemes to provide the possibility for profitable (state-backed) investment opportunities now that EU markets come with barriers to them. The decline of the Conservative Party, then, is not just a matter of boxing off growing sections of the electorate, thereby imperilling its mass support; it is also a story of a party increasingly in hock to certain sections of capital whose short-term interests sit uncomfortably with the collective interest of British capital as a whole.

Therefore, given the character of the Conservative Party, just as its organisational diagram privileges the party elite sitting as Tory MPs, the bulk of our analytical focus is on parliamentary conservatism. This – or, to be more precise, the Cabinet/Shadow Cabinet – is the party's cockpit, the executive that decides the strategic direction, defines the politics and steers the state. Hence the need to emphasise the tactical and strategic choices these figures opt for, especially in the absence of day-to-day accountability to the wider party and the electorate in between elections. This structural characteristic of British conservatism has shaped forty years of Tory statecraft, and ultimately the decisions taken by successive leaders and prime ministers to keep the party viable have conditioned its fortunes: a path that led to catastrophic electoral defeat in 1997, and the long-term decline of its electorate. The party, so long the master of its destiny, now faces an increasingly more difficult future, a future it has done more than any other political force to bring about.

2

Thatcher

Introduction

Accounts of Thatcher's time in government often stress overt class struggle, the financialisation of economy and state or the project of building a popular hegemony by recasting British politics and society in the Tories' authoritarian image. There is a danger, however, in crediting Thatcher and her lieutenants with too much foresight and supposing that 'Thatcherism', with its stress on deregulated markets, privatisation, competition, choice and self-responsibility underwritten by an authoritarian, centralised state, was present from the very beginning. That the Tories came to power in 1979 armed with strategy documents and a wish list of policies and set up several private working groups on economic policy, industrial relations and social policy does not mean that a cogent political philosophy was fully formed or possessed clear-sighted objectives.

The Tories won the 1979 general election off the back of Labour failure: heightened industrial disputes, growing inflation and a promise to deal with the malaise. The roots of this crisis were multiple: the relative decline of Britain vis-à-vis its competitors; the spiral of inflation kicked off by the abandonment of Bretton Woods by the United States combined with the oil price shock; and, latterly, the UK's haphazard and poorly institutionalised linkages between state, business and the trade unions for the purposes of economic management. Restoring social peace and a sense of national pride was the overt objective, hence Thatcher's famous recitation of St Francis of Assisi outside Downing Street.[1] Yet what are often overlooked are her concluding remarks: 'I just owe almost everything to my own father. I really do. He brought me up to believe all the things that I do believe and they're just the values on which I've fought the election.' In her own terms, what was to follow was the application of this common sense.

Thatcherism achieved three core and interlinked accomplishments: the restoration of the authority of the state in law and order, economic and social policy terms; the striking of a new class peace through confrontation with the labour movement; and a bedding down of neoliberal individualism and governance. The consequences of these feats changed the Tories and their Labour opposition, and they also had profound impacts on the political composition of Tory support. Thatcher's decisions were explicitly concerned with laying the basis for continued electoral dominance, driven by the realisation that, despite a decade of electoral success, the Tories were nevertheless in decline.[2] Ironically, it was the success of these efforts to secure the party's continued electability that undermined the party in the long term, and set up a secular dynamic of decline with which Tory leaders after Thatcher, whether in government or in opposition, continue to contend.

Understanding Thatcher's record in government means dividing it into three fronts: class politics, economic-order politics and state-order politics. This covers the context, preparation and waging of class war against a labour movement that the Tories argued was overweening, and ultimately put workplace authority and the powers of the employer class into question. Away from the overt battles forced on the workers' movement, the day-to-day business of economic policy, particularly following the 1984 miners' strike, had an overall strategic aim of transforming the bulk of the population into rational-choice economic actors through the institutionalisation of competition, self-reliance and officially mandated entrepreneurialism. Selling council housing stock to tenants, making available cheap mortgages and cheap credit and encouraging a revolution in small share ownership by privatising strategic state-owned sectors of the economy comprised the popular economic offering that Thatcherism went to the electorate with. Lastly, the assertion of the state against the organised working class had its corollary in the battles Thatcher waged within the state apparatus itself, a fight that saw the professional autonomy of experts undermined and formally scrapped, as per the case with teachers and civil servants, and authority centralised in the government itself. Thus the Thatcherite offensive was a class project.[3] Reasserting capital and its interests over everything else necessitated a strong, centralised executive capable of carrying the project through. Thatcher was successful, even if her poll tax was to prove an imposition too far, but her time in office set the parameters of politics for the decades after and, though neither she nor any of her strategists could have known it, for Tory success in the 2010s and the long-term decline now menacing the party.

Class War and Class Peace

During the 1970s British capitalism was in dire straits. In GDP terms, the economy shrank in twelve of the forty quarters and reported growth under 1 per cent in another twelve quarters. Along with the rest of the developed world, the UK experienced a two-year recession between 1973 and 1975 in which GDP contracted by 3 to 4 per cent – growth beyond the starting point of the recession was not achieved until late 1976. During the same period, Edward Heath's Conservative government announced the three-day week of limited electricity consumption and rolling blackouts in preparation for a showdown with the miners. The measure was in force from 31 December 1973 to early March 1974, with Heath determining this period of emergency to be the best time for an election, one which resulted in the temporary political paralysis of a hung parliament.

Unemployment, though low by twenty-first-century standards, was above the post-war average, fluctuating between 3.5 and 4.8 per cent of the work force. Retail price index inflation rates saw strong movement as oil prices tripled, prices increased and organised workers struck to ensure wage packets kept up. With the onset of the 1973–5 recession, the rise in unemployment was accompanied by a steep inflationary gradient, topping out at over 22.6 per cent and reaching a second peak of around 15 per cent as the Tories settled back into office in 1979. For the bulk of the decade double-digit inflation was a fact of life. Furthermore, the economy suffered internationally with an acute drop in the balance of payments, registering a 4 per cent deficit in the current account, a very weak pound and, in 1976, the Labour government going cap-in-hand to the International Monetary Fund for a loan.

The Labour governments between 1974 and 1979 had a difficult time getting on top of the crisis. The country was treated to the spectacle of a Labour government cutting social security and winding down the public services that its constituency was dispro-portionately dependent on. In 1976 Chancellor Dennis Healey oversaw £3 billion worth of austerity cuts but this seemed to have little impact on the UK's economic wellbeing.

Such disruptions coincided with an era of rising labour organ-isation. Trade union membership had steadily increased from 4.4 million members in 1933 to around 13 million in 1979.[4] This meant that approximately half the workforce were organised, and nearly all workers were covered by collective-bargaining agreements. The 1970s also saw the highest numbers of strike days since 1926 and the General Strike, ranging from a low of 3.3 million days to a high of 29.5 million days in stoppages across the decade. This increase is striking when compared to the 3.3 million days lost annually on average between 1945 and 1969.

The 1970s was also the decade of significant advances for the women's liberation movement both culturally and at work, with the Equal Pay Act coming into force in 1975. Likewise, anti-racist and LGBTQ liberation movements were challenging ingrained preju-dice and were at the forefront of struggles against the growing street presence of the National Front. The post-war social order was barely thirty years old and it was beset by economic problems, a rising tide of class conflict and the opening of new fronts of mobi-lisation and struggle threatening to destabilise the social order.

There were plots and rumours of plots on the part of the establishment and a generalised sense of crisis among ruling circles.[5]

The post-war malaise was simultaneously a crisis of labour discipline, of state authority and of irreverence towards received tradition. Nevertheless, crisis moments and movements of decomposition find tendencies to recomposition running alongside them. As trade unionists mobilised to protect living standards, the inchoate sense of chaos incubated an authoritarian counter-current, of which the National Front was its most extreme expression. The other was the loose conservative movement of think tanks, pressure groups and newspaper editorial offices. The latter were responsible for the confection of moral panics about a mugging epidemic, which talked up the incidence of violent crime on British streets, scapegoated black youth as the root of the problem and cultivated demands for 'action', i.e., new laws, intensive policing, tougher sentences, heavy-handedness and moral absolutism – just the recipe for sections of the population upset by one convulsive crisis after another.[6] These panics ran alongside and nourished moral watchdogs – such as the Festival of Light and the National Viewers' and Listeners' Association, both associated with the mercurial moral guardian Mary Whitehouse – helping coalesce a body of conservative opinion epitomised by Thatcher's election and her own brand of conservatism.

Indeed, Thatcher's marketing of her economics reflected the authoritarian mood with discussions of tight money and market discipline,[7] and argued that state intervention in the economy caused industrial unrest. Clasping the invisible hand in the tight grip of regulation and trade unionism was symptomatic of weakness and of 'socialism', which Thatcher codified as antithetical to British values. Therefore for Stuart Hall the crisis of the 1970s was a crisis of consent, of establishment parties who could not rule in the old way, of government and state on whom expectations had grown as their capacity had diminished, and of a general collapse in the acceptance of state authority.

On Thatcherism, Stuart Hall's remarkable work is often the starting point for Marxist accounts of the Tories in the 1980s.

While Margaret Thatcher was still in opposition, Hall argued that there was more to Thatcherism than simply letting the Tories have another turn in government before relinquishing the reins, as per the alternate administrations between 1964 and 1979. Thatcher was more than an office-seeking politician; she had a project for remoulding British society. In the context of a crisis, her 'authoritarian populism' combined a hard law and order position with tough anti-immigration and nudge-nudge racist rhetoric. It was an us-versus-them-ism, a virtuous 'we' against a non-white, semi-communist, semi-totalitarian other. Hall was worried, and later proven right, that Thatcher's Tories might create an alliance between factions of different classes to sustain them in office for an extended period. The populist rhetoric went with the promise of a popular capitalism – a shareholder, homeowning democracy. Freedom to buy one's council house, freedom from strikes and union bullies, freedom to be successful – this was Thatcher's promise as she waged class war against the labour movement and other undesirables. Closing state-owned industries, creating vast private monopolies out of state-owned assets and using North Sea oil revenues to fund tax cuts for the rich; Thatcher sought the greater subordination of Britain to the blind whims of capital. For these reasons, the labourism of the late 1970s – statist, authoritarian, technocratic – was ill-equipped to handle the crisis in the system and see off the new kind of politics Thatcherism articulated.

In his seminal essay 'The Great Moving Right Show', Hall notes how the resolution of the crisis on capital's terms meant confronting and defeating the labour movement. This is what Heath tried to do during the Three-Day Week period, but his efforts were undermined at the outset by the government's dependence on the ad hoc tripartite scheme for managing British industry and organised labour's participation in it. Similarly, Labour faced more acute difficulties given the perceived need to balance the books on the backs of the workers and its status as the labour movement's political wing. In other words, how could the party of the workers resolve the crisis by making the workers pay for it?

Hall et al. characterised the situation as one of catastrophic equilibrium, where neither capital nor labour was able to inflict a decisive defeat on the other. Therefore, among the responses to this conjuncture, Thatcherism represented one route out. Its aim was not the defence of a dysfunctional status quo, but its recasting on more favourable terms. In this sense Thatcherism was simultaneously an elite movement, a current of opinion of leading politicians, state personnel, intellectuals and, of course, business leaders condensed and institutionalised in the leadership of the Tories under Thatcher, and a subaltern movement of popular (but reactionary) discontent with British capitalism – hence its superficial radical and anti-establishment sheen.

What Thatcher offered was a hegemonic project: the construction of a new popular consent around the restoration of state authority, a return of conservative decency versus the permissive society's moral rot. It threatened to end union 'bullying' and industrial strife and, crucially, the striking of a new settlement that meant social peace and certainty. This was the promise of a conservatism where everyone knew their place and had a place. In the absence of such a body of ideas, which largely cohered as a consistent whole after the fact, the central objective of Thatcher's – the defeat of the labour movement – might not have been possible.

Thatcher's election was only possible because of a changing of personnel within the party. As outlined by Wheatcroft, the old governing class, of which Macmillan was the epitome, were products of the Depression and the war. For them patricianism and its articulation in one-nation Conservative terms was the best way of managing labour discipline and securing continued profitability. Theirs was a universe of gentlemanly capitalism underpinned by chummy relationships and personnel circulation through the Treasury/Bank/City all the way to the top of big business and Parliament itself.

Yet by 1979 the Macmillanite layer of ruling-class politicians were increasingly pushed out of their pre-eminence in the Tory Party once the semblance of democracy was introduced. They were rapidly being replaced by the rising generation of careerist

MPs. As Peter Storey notes the established common sense, which Heath and the bulk of the older parliamentary party subscribed to (with the notable exception of Enoch Powell) was reviled and the newer cohorts of entrants were more combative and coveted confrontation over conciliation.[8]

The reasoning for this was threefold. As younger politicians they had no direct experience of the 1930s and 1940s and so their political habitus was formed under conditions of class peace and rising living standards. Second, this generation largely came from outside big business and had prior careers either in the professions (the law, mostly), small and medium-sized enterprise and other backgrounds. Norman Tebbit, for example, entered Parliament in 1970 after a career as a pilot and a trade union official. More than a few lacked the exalted origins of their peers, and barely any had experience of managing large numbers of staff. This meant negotiating with workforces subject to collective bargaining was absent from their skill set, which manifested as an aggressive attitude to industrial conflict. As a cohort they lacked a personal stake in and experience of good industrial relations.

In addition, MPs drawn from a petit bourgeois background, which Thatcher personified, were not afforded institutional privilege in the shifting tripartite structures of the post-war order, and so appeared at a remove from it. Indeed, one of the conceits of this class location is their independence vis-à-vis class conflict: that they are above it all and can look down on each of the contenders with equanimity when in fact their existence is threatened by the movement of one or the other. Therefore, while Thatcher and the radical Tory right hated unions, they also were scathing of the conciliators among their social betters whose power and position were handed to them instead of earned by the sweat of their meritocratic brow. As the then Tory MP Julian Critchley observed, 'businessmen with flat provincial accents . . . small town surveyors and estate agents, the politically active middle class which began taking over the constituency parties, have now taken over Parliament itself'.[9]

When Thatcher was elected, she was some way off making her revolution permanent in the Tory Party, never mind the country. Still, from the outset the objective of dealing with the labour movement was the priority. In his examination of Thatcher's strategy, Alexander Gallas suggests her concern was twofold. First, she wanted to hold her cross-class alliance of voters together, which he characterises as a power bloc.[10] This was followed by the standard practice of bourgeois politics, which alternates between, on the one hand, class politics and direct confrontation with and management/regulation of organised labour to secure the reproduction of wage labour and disrupt its nascent collective strength, and, on the other, economic-order politics, the everyday business of policy, budgets, industrial strategy and so on.

On becoming party leader in February 1975, Thatcher set up four secret Tory working groups. One of these, the Authority of Government Group, led by Peter Carrington, a hereditary peer who had held Cabinet positions under successive administrations from Douglas-Home onwards and was later appointed NATO general secretary, pre-emptively addressed emergencies that posed a threat to government authority, such as another miners' strike. While conciliators of the old school and class-war hardliners sat on the group, in the event of confrontation with the miners they recommended continuously updated contingency plans, the building up of coal stockpiles, public relations strategies to counter support for any strike, and redesigning access to power stations to make them difficult to picket. It nonetheless cautioned against all-out confrontation and recommended picking and choosing battles.

More revealing was the Nationalised Industries Policy Group set up under another peer, Nicholas Ridley. His remit was the management and privatisation of these businesses and he linked their successful sell-off to confronting and breaking union power. Like the Carrington group it advocated flexible tactics involving conciliation and retreat when the situation demanded and aggression when possible, while retaining fidelity to the plan. Also crucial were recommendations made about language use. Rather than setting out objectives in class terms, finding new ways of fostering divisions among workers on a 'non-class' basis was an explicit tactical objective. One suggestion was defining the public as consumers who were being hit in the pocket by irresponsible, militant 'producers'.[11] This document was leaked to and published by the *Economist* in May 1978.

The Ridley document was noteworthy because it addressed hegemonic concerns. In addition to the specifics of how to wage class warfare, it articulated a two-nation conservatism. Instead of building generalised consent for the Thatcher project, Gallas notes, this was a 'just-enough' strategy. Constituting a power bloc and an election-winning coalition was premised upon opposing a nation of law-abiding decent people to a minority of malcontents and troublemakers. Employers in private industry were encouraged to award workers handsome pay rises, thereby using rising living standards to undercut solidarity with public sector and nationalised industry workers. Policies were to be developed to give them assets like shares and property so their fortunes might increasingly be tied to market performance over and above what workplace collective action could secure for them. Not only might this divide workers; also it would provide a material incentive for (some) workers to vote Tory.

Sir Keith Joseph's group, whose *The Right Approach to the Economy* document was published at the 1977 party conference, made the case for 'economic liberalism' but was clear it required a repressive approach to industrial relations. Freedom for capital was only possible if labour was shackled in chains. The *Stepping Stones* report written by businessmen John Hoskyns and Norman Strauss, but commissioned by Thatcher and Joseph, argued for a fundamental shift in Britain's political economy that favoured future Conservative election victories. This systematic approach was, again, contingent upon defeating the unions.

The preparation for confrontation was very much behind the scenes. For example, in 1981 in line with the Ridley plan that defeating the miners was key to their anti-union strategy, the government set up a Cabinet committee on coal whose remit was tracking coal's movements, existing stocks and demand. Personnel changes were made to the leadership of the Central Electricity Generating Board and the National Coal Board (NCB), the nationalised business to which coal mining belonged.

While these were proceeding, the overall approach to industrial relations in the first term was overtly characterised by a focus on economic-order politics – for instance, cutting inflation by limiting the money supply and lowering taxation levels. Direct taxation was reduced, with the top rate of income tax falling from 83 per cent to 60 per cent while Value Added Tax was almost doubled from 8 per cent to 15 per cent, and exchange controls and bank lending restrictions were lifted, precipitating the 1980s credit boom. The Employment Act of 1980, overseen by leading Tory conciliator James Prior, introduced government-financed secret ballots for putative stoppages, the outlawing of secondary picketing, restrictions on the closed shop – which needed 80 per cent workplace approval before a new one was set up – and targeted 'coercive recruitment' by unions.

This annoyed the hardliners on the Tory benches, but upon Prior's replacement by Tebbit in autumn 1981 it was clear that this was part of a longer-term strategy. Small steps were preferable for the moment so the government did not appear too far ahead of public opinion and, it was hoped, the meantime could be used to build support for future legislation. Therefore the 1982 Employment Act tinkered further with closed-shop provisions, outlawed union-only tendering (i.e., trade union recognition could no longer be listed as an essential condition for the winning of a contract), allowed for selective firing of striking workers and increased the civil penalties unions were liable for if they undertook unlawful strike action.

Another measure, justified on economic grounds, was to have an important impact on the balance of class forces. The concern with inflation, a bugbear of monetarist economics, saw the government raise interest rates. This affected the money supply by making the pound more expensive on the international markets and, by extension, British exports less competitive. The abolition of currency exchange controls saw capital flight out of the country and therefore less available for domestic investment. Additionally, the Tories introduced private sector management practices into the nationalised industries and imposed upon them tough new borrowing rules.

In this new commercialised world, many nationalised enterprises were unable to meet the wage bill and were forced to lay off hundreds of thousands of workers with the happy consequence, for the Tories, of weakening manufacturing unions and enabling mass unemployment as a not-so-subtle warning against worker militancy. Insolvency coincidentally provided the government with good excuses to privatise industries that backbenchers and press allies had characterised as lame ducks. Therefore manufacturing, which had been in long-term decline, collapsed along with the government's poll ratings.

Since taking office the government had trailed Labour, and this mushroomed into regular double-point deficits with the SDP split from Labour and its alliance with the Liberals from October 1980 onwards. There was evidence of modest recovery in early 1982 prior to Argentina's occupation of the Falkland Islands and South Georgia, after which double-digit poll leads for the Conservatives were the norm. Alongside this, elements of the two-nation strategy started to be enacted. Layers of the working class were offered the opportunity to become homeowners through council house sell-offs, which were taken up with alacrity. The disciplinary effects of meeting mortgage payments would not have been lost on the policy's architects, so not only does the assumption of asset ownership bend one's awareness to the rise and fall in its value, but also the need to make regular payments to the mortgage provider curbs the appetite for militancy. It was a measure for securing class peace (on Thatcher's terms), undermining workplace collectivism and nudging voters towards supporting the Tories and their suite of homeowner-friendly policies.

The initial opening of the two-nation strategy was overwritten by the 'wartime' patriotic fervour and gratitude Thatcher benefited from, enabling her to consolidate her base among those least likely to be negatively affected by her programme. As Dennis Kavanagh observed,[12] 70 per cent of small-business people supported the Conservatives in 1983, as well as private sector, relatively affluent and non-unionised workers identified by Ridley as a key constituency to keep sweet (variously assimilated to 'Essex man' in media parlance), who also benefited from tax cuts and falling inflation. A split opposition may have also helped,[13] but, notwithstanding the decline in absolute support, a substantial number of trade unionists also voted Tory. Only 39 per cent of them voted Labour.

Ian McGregor, appointed NCB chair, immediately set about putting the thrust of the Ridley plan into action. Initially, this meant closing over a third of the UK's pits with seventy-five out of 186 to be shuttered and the loss of an additional 45,000 jobs over two years. Come March 1984, these objectives were scaled back but nevertheless remained (purposely) provocative.

That month the NCB announced the immediate closure of twenty pits and with it the loss of 20,000 jobs. Ostensibly due to 'costs' of £1.3 billion the mining industry was adjudged to lack viability. From 8 March the National Union of Mineworkers (NUM) executive authorised rolling stoppages, and it was expected that a snowballing of local lodges would follow the militant lead. However, in some localities the strike call was voted down, most notoriously in parts of Derbyshire and in the Nottinghamshire coalfield. These were areas in which the most modern pits were located and with them the highest pay. As his history of the strike in Nottinghamshire suggests, Harry Paterson notes that the area was the site of an attempted breakaway during the previous confrontation between the government and the miners in the 1920s.[14] Furthermore, the culture of solidarity underpinning miners' communities elsewhere in the country was absent. Disproportionately, these mineworkers had moved to the area attracted by higher pay and therefore were not subject to the collectivism exerted by community cohesion and local family ties. Hence, in the absence of a national ballot, Thatcher could pose as the champion of democratic rights, which gave her the political cover necessary to use heavy-handed policing to keep these pits open, as well as fund the breakaway Union of Democratic Mineworkers.

Among other tactics Thatcher used was importing coal from overseas (notably 'socialist' Poland) and receiving shipments in smaller ports to avoid sympathy action from dockworkers. Coal transports were removed from trains for the same reason and contracts handed to non-union road haulage firms, all the while treating the dispute as if it was a private matter between the miners and the coal board in which the state got involved where matters of criminality and the law were concerned. This was a conscious attempt to depoliticise the strike, even though ministers met twice weekly and Thatcher herself was closely involved, having regular phone calls with Roy Lynk – the Nottinghamshire area NUM president and leading light among working miners.

Meanwhile, despite an impressive solidarity movement in support of the miners, official backing from the rest of the labour movement was muted. The National Union of Railwaymen and the Associated Society of Locomotive Engineers and Firemen voted to black scab coal (hence the haulage firms), but the TUC was quiescent and there was little vocal support from Labour's front bench. In short, the strategic objective of (relatively) isolating the miners through divide-and-rule tactics worked.

Where additional disputes did threaten, Thatcher settled quickly. The two most significant were a nationwide dock workers' dispute and another by pit deputies, organised in the separate National Association of Colliery Overmen, Deputies and Shotfirers union. The latter was strategically vital as pit deputies had overall responsibility for health and safety and, if they were not present, a pit could not operate. Despite an 81 per cent vote in favour of strike action, the NCB was able to offer inducements enough to stop the pit deputies from striking – in retrospect the most short-termist decision ever taken by a British trade union.

Therefore, with isolated and increasing numbers returning to work over the 1984–5 winter, the NUM executive narrowly voted by ninety-eight to ninety-one to end the dispute in March. Thatcher had won and the backbone of the labour movement was broken.

Thatcher's complete dominance of the Tories undoubtedly assisted her in her battle against the miners. With a huge majority in Parliament the more conciliatory voices in the parliamentary party were sidelined. Coming into force just prior to the miners' strike, the 1984 Trade Union Act narrowed the definition of what could be accepted as a lawful dispute. It meant they could only proceed with compulsory secret ballots. Hence, under the law, the miners' dispute was unlawful because its rolling wave of localised votes did not meet the stipulated criteria of a nationwide ballot by a simple majority – though later the High Court found that the NUM could not be forced to hold a national ballot.

With the miners defeated, the Tories could tighten the legislative screws on the labour movement further without having to proceed with the same level of caution. There were three further Acts during Thatcher's premiership that confirmed unions' subaltern status.[15] These involved introducing secret postal ballots for internal union elections, the provision of state assistance to individual members wishing to take legal action against their union for not following balloting procedures, and an expectation that unions repudiate unofficial action.

As such, when Rupert Murdoch's News International moved into dispute with the print unions after clandestinely introducing new technology that could run his presses with a tenth of the workforce, anti-union legislation was called upon to sequester funds while heavy-handed policing repeatedly clashed with pickets. The result was a second strategic defeat for the labour movement. Victory recast the balance of forces between capital and labour through methodical planning and the imposition of a settlement, and Thatcher's successors bedded down the ways in which the state dictated terms at the behest of business. It meant that the Tories' restructuring of the post-war social order could proceed with little subsequent opposition from organised labour.

State-Order Politics

In addition to economic-order and class politics, we can add a third overlapping term: state-order politics. The 1979 Tory manifesto put it thus, 'THE MOST DISTURBING THREAT [sic] to our freedom and security is the growing disrespect for the rule of law. In government as in opposition, Labour have undermined it. Yet respect for the rule of law is the basis of a free and civilised life.'[16]

This refers to the restoration of the state's authority both as the repository of official authority, its legitimation as such, and as the accepted guarantor for commodity exchange, the regulation of sterling, and overall custodian of the reproduction of the capitalist relations of production. Reaffirming its authority was the essential precursor to Thatcher's set-piece confrontation with the miners.

Thatcher's state-order politics and social conservatism were explicitly concerned with the construction of racialised others as a means of rehabilitating state authority. It was a classic move typical of her two-nation conservatism. In *Policing the Crisis*, Stuart Hall and his colleagues drew attention to the racialised characterisation of the mugger. Parallels were explicitly drawn between 'epidemic' levels of violence and lawlessness in British cities and large numbers of black youth who, after Enoch Powell's infamous 'rivers of blood' speech, were coded as especially dangerous and unpredictable. Against the backdrop of a generalised slippage in state authority, economic crisis and the rising tide of class struggle, looming anxiety around racialised dangers helped empower the National Front, and consequently provided a small but significant constituency for Thatcher's social conservatism.

In the 1979 manifesto, the Conservatives promised the introduction of a British Nationality Act, which would introduce 'firm immigration control' as the guarantor of 'good community relations'. These controls meant restricting work permits, curtailing the right to stay in the country, limiting entry to family members, quotas and taking 'firm action' against illegal immigrants – though explicitly ruling out compulsory repatriation. Interestingly, these were placed in the manifesto's section on 'law and order', alongside the promise of tougher sentencing and more police on boosted salaries.

When Thatcher's Nationality Act was introduced in 1981 it made changes around the right of abode and modifications to automatic entitlement to UK citizenship – crucially the removal of the right to citizenship by virtue of birth. Instead, an infant was entitled to citizenship if they were born in the UK and at least one parent held British citizenship. The British Nationality Act also abolished the right of abode for non-British citizens, and Commonwealth citizens had to apply for naturalisation – it was no longer a simple matter of having it granted by registration. And citizenship could no longer be acquired for women by marrying a British man.

A second opportunity to reaffirm the tight relationship between racism and authoritarianism came in 1981. Riots broke out in Brixton in April followed by a summer of disorder in London, Liverpool, Leeds, Manchester and several smaller English cities. The background was the deteriorating economic situation, but the precipitating factor was heavy-handed policing targeting black youth as part of an ostensible campaign against burglary.[17] In the face of insurgency, the government immediately moved to depoliticise the Brixton riots as a public-order matter – a line summed up famously by Norman Tebbit, then the employment secretary, with a glib 'I grew up in the '30s with an unemployed father. He didn't riot. He got on his bike and looked for work, and he kept looking till he found it.' The Scarman report commissioned in the aftermath did find a pattern of racial disadvantage and social exclusion. It precipitated the 1984 Police and Criminal Evidence Act, which issued a prescribed police code of behaviour and introduced the Police Complaints Authority to try and inculcate trust and a measure of accountability.

Also significant was the showdown with Irish Republican prisoners. In 1976 the government had withdrawn special-category status from incarcerated paramilitaries, who responded with a dirty protest and, in 1980, fifty-three days of hunger strike. On that occasion the government offered some concessions, but when they failed to materialise the second hunger strike began in March 1981. This struggle, which famously saw Bobby Sands elected in a by-election from his prison cell, nevertheless failed. For Thatcher, sticking with a line used later against her trade union opposition, said, 'we are not prepared to consider special category status for certain groups of people serving sentences for crime. Crime is crime is crime, it is not political.'[8] Upon Sands's death, Thatcher told the Commons, 'Mr. Sands was a convicted criminal. He chose to take his own life. It was a choice that his organisation did not allow to many of its victims.'[9] However, following the strike the government did grant all the prisoners' demands bar the refusal to undertake prison work activities. As a set piece it had the desired effect from Thatcher's point of view. The *Guardian* summed up the mood with its observation, 'the Government had overcome the hunger strikes by a show of resolute determination not to be bullied.' In other words, the Tories had faced down one of the British state's enemies and won.

More important for the fortunes of the Thatcherite project was the occupation of the Falklands and South Georgia by the Argentinian junta in early April 1982. Though the government had ignored warnings throughout 1981 concerning the likelihood of an invasion, and had scaled back its presence in the South Atlantic pending a defence review, Thatcher said the government was prepared to assemble a task force to retake the islands if they were occupied.

Amid patriotic scenes when the task force set sail, the government's poll ratings dramatically improved. After Britain rejected attempts at mediation by the US State Department, the short war was successful, with Argentinian forces surrendering on 14 June. By martial prowess – British forces sustained 255 deaths to Argentina's 655 – Thatcher was able to restore state legitimacy by locating the war as part of her project of national rejuvenation. Hence, during the miners' strike, her widely reported remarks at the backbench 1922 committee meeting on 19 July 1984 described General Galtieri as the enemy without and likened the miners to the 'enemy within'.[20] The restoration of state authority through standoffs cultivated a sense of a government that would not compromise in seeing its will done, which was essential for the use of force in the industrial battles to come.

Economic and Political Authoritarianism

Authority, however, was not confined to the rehabilitation of the state's repressive role. Considering that Thatcher located the Tory programme as undoing the legitimacy of the state on matters of economic management, she did reinforce government and particularly the Cabinet as the cockpit of decision making – chiefly, in the running battle against inflation and, relatedly, defending sterling from speculation on the international money markets. The second was a simultaneous attack on the leftover corporatist institutions and practices, and so-called vested interests – professional organisations (and their autonomy) and 'expertise' more generally.

In the 1979 manifesto, the control of inflation is positioned at the heart of Tory economic strategy. It observes, 'The pound today is worth less than half its 1974 value. On present form it would be halved in value yet again within eight years. Inflation on this scale has come near to destroying our political and social stability.' The solution offered was reducing the money supply and cutting public spending, euphemistically described as the 'gradual reduction in the size of the Government's borrowing requirement'. It explicitly rules out price controls as ineffective against inflationary pressures.

Yet despite these pledges Thatcher's first government did not match up to its tough talk. Between 1976 and 1978 Labour had reduced inflation from 24 per cent to 8 per cent. In the first year of Tory government, it jumped from 11.4 per cent to 21.9 per cent. Some of this was out of the government's hands, such as the sudden cut to oil production and subsequent price shock thanks to the Iranian revolution in 1979, but not all. The abandonment of Labour's incomes policy meant industry and collective bargaining found their own level above the old targets, and the Tories stoked inflation by doubling the standard rate of VAT from 8 per cent to

15 per cent in Geoffrey Howe's first Budget. The counterproductive strategy continued into 1980 with the scrapping of foreign-exchange controls and the deregulation of the domestic credit market. Hence the Medium-Term Financial Strategy of that March set targets for cash in circulation and monies held in bank deposits, which were missed – both had grown as prices increased.

Just under a year later, the government faced a different problem. Increasing production of North Sea oil led to an appreciation in the value of the pound, and interest rates remained above 12 per cent between November 1978 and July 1982, gradually exerting deflationary pressures on the economy. Taken together with Thatcher's policies on the nationalised industries, the results were that UK exports became more expensive and less competitive while imports were cheaper, leading to a collapse in manufacturing output and rapid growth in unemployment to 3 million by the close of 1982. But it achieved the objective of forcing down inflation from January 1981's 13 per cent to December 1982's 5.5 per cent.

In Philip Stephens's account, the government responded to deflation by measures aimed at a gradual devaluation of sterling.[21] This meant abandoning a money-supply strategy with more public spending cuts, cuts to interest rates and tax increases to the tune of £4 billion. This caused a rapid depreciation of the pound that stabilised around the time of the 1983 election and brought permanently low inflation of below 5 per cent thereafter (notwithstanding a brief peak above at decade's end) – albeit at the price of decimating manufacturing.

Throughout this period, Thatcher made a virtue of facing down her critics by ignoring them or, when they were from her own party, dismissing them. When 364 economists wrote an open letter to *The Times* that month criticising the economic strategy from the standpoint of Keynesian commonplaces, they were brushed aside.[22] When Cabinet colleagues challenged Thatcher and opposed her in meetings, by September all were either sacked or demoted. Similarly, she appointed Robin Leigh-Pemberton, then the chair of NatWest Bank, to the governorship of the Bank of England on grounds of fidelity to her own thinking and numerous party connections – his predecessor, Gordan Richardson, had opposed the government's money-supply controls. Thereafter while the government eschewed direct intervention, it retained a hands-on approach to managing the see-sawing fortunes of the pound in the money markets that later led to Thatcher signing up to the Exchange Rate Mechanism.

This was evident in the relations with the professions too. In 1977 Callaghan's government commissioned a report into the efficacy and failings of the National Health Service since the war. Known as the Black report, it was famously buried by Thatcher's government because its conclusions – general health had improved but inequalities persisted, and the NHS required extra funds if it was to tackle them adequately – were not to its liking. It was released on August Bank Holiday 1980 with a limited print run, and Social Services Secretary Patrick Jenkin wrote in its foreword that the recommendations were 'not realistic' in straitened economic circumstances and this was 'quite apart from any judgement that may be formed of the effectiveness of such expenditure in dealing with the problems identified. I cannot, therefore, endorse the Group's recommendations. I am making the report available for discussion, but without any commitment by the Government to its proposals.'[23]

This dismissive attitude to arms of the government not in Thatcher's favour extended to the civil service. Having already identified the state as a drag on economic activity and informed by monetarist dogma of the 'disastrous' consequences of state intervention, it is unsurprising Thatcher viewed the state's employees with some suspicion. According to Eric Evans,[24] she despised the civil service's ethic of neutral 'non-political' professionalism and its culture of persuading ministers of the merits of an alternative course should a policy prove unworkable. Because senior civil servants were not political in the sense of a commitment to an overall strategy (beyond the preservation of their status and expertise), they comprised a strategic blockage. As a cadre of administrators, they had kept British 'socialism' chugging along since the war.

Nothing summed up the government's hostile attitude better than a blacklist of militant civil servants Thatcher instructed MI5 to draw up in 1985.[25]

Thatcher's struggle with the civil service was part of her authoritarian programme. Within days of entering office, Thatcher invited Derek Rayner from Marks and Spencer's into Downing Street as an adviser on Whitehall waste. His Efficiency Unit was set up in tandem with Parliament's Public Expenditure Select Committee, which had its own remit to look at spending reductions. However, rather than looking for quick savings, Rayner moved in the direction of comprehensive remodelling after an initial round of 'scrutinies' had taken place.[26]

In line with the campaign against 'waste', in the winter of 1980–1 the government moved into dispute with the civil service unions. In its characteristic disdain for expertise, the government set aside the usual method for calculating the basis for pay negotiations by ignoring the groundwork done by the Pay Research Unit (PRU). The unit undertook the task of comparing civil service grades with commensurable occupations elsewhere as a means of uprating pay. Interestingly, in advance of the 1979 general election Thatcher argued for the PRU's retention.[27] This also meant ignoring the National Pay Agreement by attempting to impose a pay settlement of 6 per cent – uprated to 7 per cent after pressure.

This sparked a twenty-one-week strike among civil servants which, ultimately, was unsuccessful, and Thatcher scrapped the PRU. The government also scrapped the Civil Service Department, which was concerned with staffing and pay, and these key functions were taken over by the Treasury. Recruitment and promotions were merged with the Efficiency Unit and brought under the purview of a new body, the Management and Personnel Office, and located in the Cabinet Office. The defeat of the unions meant the government could then proceed to implement the recommendations following the post-strike investigation into civil service pay. The Megaw report targeted national collective bargaining, recommended breaking up the system into sectoral bargaining and suggested more managerial determination of pay in line with performance.[28] The year 1982 saw the launch of the Financial Management Initiative (FMI), which worked to embed business-informed management practices across the civil service and introduced computerised budgeting. However, the FMI did not lead to satisfactory results quickly enough. From 1983, with the appointment of Robin Ibbs, a serving director of chemicals giant ICI as the Efficiency Unit's chair, the 'efficiencies' found meant significant job losses. Overall, between 1979 and 1986 civil service staff shrank by a fifth.[29]

The government was by no means finished with the civil service, however. The Mueller report in 1987 underlined the (perceived) necessity for sectoral bargaining,[30] while the Efficiency Unit-commissioned Next Steps review in 1988 saw the civil service broken up into semi-autonomous departments. Reflecting on this time, the incumbent permanent secretary of the Department for Business, Energy and Industrial Strategy said that it generated real excitement across the civil service 'through a new set of focused and lean public agencies, with their own staff, strategy and leadership structures'.[31] This meant leaving behind a core Whitehall bureaucracy subject to changed ways of working, while the 'autonomy' for the arms-length agencies – which would grow to encompass 75 per cent of civil servants – could have closer relationships with business and be free to develop their own managerial styles and accountabilities. This dispersed approach would, it was believed, allow for more marketisation of public services and expand the scope for privatisation.

Similar approaches were applied to health and education. Having dismissed the Black report in 1980, in 1983 Thatcher appointed Sir Roy Griffiths, a director (and deputy chair) of supermarket chain Sainsbury's, to review the management of the NHS. His recommendations involved an arm's-length management board and the appointment of general managers in health authorities and hospitals, with budgetary and performance responsibilities. The NHS should also be governed by a Health Services Supervisory Board chaired by the secretary of state and responsible for strategic direction and budgets.

The Griffiths report was meant to produce a clear leadership structure. In practice, the move to 'general management' meant the importation of managers from the private sector schooled in customer as opposed to client/patient delivery, but this was done to 'secure the best possible services for the patient'.[32] The best possible services were, in line with the Thatcherite ethos, interpreted in instrumentalist value-for-money terms. This was also when ancillary NHS services, like catering and cleaning, were contracted out to private providers on a cost–benefit basis.

This was followed towards the end of Thatcher's premiership by the 1989 White Paper *Working for Patients*. This explicitly positioned patients as service-/treatment-seeking consumers, and the NHS's role was to facilitate choice by providing information and making them aware of their rights vis-à-vis the health service. Repositioning the patient required an NHS fit for health consumers, and the diagram of a responsive, more marketised and customer-friendly health service was introduced in the 1990 National Health Service and Community Care Act. Prefiguring fully fledged marketisation, unwieldy but relatively straightforward relationships of bureaucratic authority were henceforth mediated by an internal market. Health authorities were responsible for assessing healthcare needs in their locality and required services were purchased from NHS providers. These consisted of existing healthcare providers which were converted into NHS trusts, and competed with one another for 'business'. This resulted in localised variations for what was and was not available (what the British press much later christened the postcode lottery, or health lottery), and criteria were increasingly formulated for denying treatments on financial as opposed to clinical grounds.[33]

Education was also ripe for repurposing according to similar principles, though this did not take place until after the 1987 general election. Thatcher's key ally and ideological soulmate Keith Joseph was appointed education secretary in 1981. Sceptical about comprehensive education because it was a state-provided public good, he believed in market provision and argued that the Tories should 'foster excellence and elites rather than equality of condition'.[34] However, the attack on comprehensive provision did not begin with Joseph.

The 1979 Education Act allowed local education authorities the right to allow schools to introduce selection at secondary-level entry – it did nothing to address streaming of pupils within schools.[35] The 1980 Education Act introduced the Assisted Places Scheme, which provided scholarships for state pupils in private schools – the funding for which would not come from new money but from the existing schools budget. Until its abolition in 1997 the scheme funded 75,000 pupils with an accumulated cost of £800 million.[36]

These, however, were side issues. The appointment of Joseph in 1981 meant that education had assumed some importance for Thatcher's project. In the first term the autonomy of schools would be weakened by the introduction of 'parent power' via vouchers that could 'purchase' education services from outside the state system, followed by the growth of central government's influence over the national curriculum. After 1983, teachers (and their troublesome unions) were brought to book by imposing greater government oversight over teacher training and curbing professional influence on curriculum development, reducing the leeway afforded to local education authorities.[37]

Joseph was to drop the voucher scheme in 1984 owing to its complexity but pressed ahead with overtly political changes to the curriculum. Derek Gillard notes that this included praising entrepreneurial activity and pushing the government's retention of its nuclear arsenal as questions of war and peace. The Tories also returned to parental control with their 1984 Green Paper *Parental Influence in Schools*. This proposed a board of governors for each school formed from parents, who had input into formulating admissions policy, issuing annual reports to parents and responsibility for an annual meeting of parents with the right to pass resolutions that must then be considered by the governors' board.

The target of these reforms was the local education authority (LEA). Their numbers on governing boards were kept steady with the number of parental governors, but representatives of staff and business could sit, thereby diluting their influence. Additionally, appointment and dismissal competencies remained with the LEAs but they had to consult with governors. 'Political indoctrination' was explicitly disallowed, and while the head teacher was responsible for disciplinary issues these were derived from principles determined by the governing board. The Act also abolished the Central Advisory Council for Education in England and Wales, a body that provided research and reports about the education system and offered expert knowledge and significant specialised advisory capacity.

Most notably, the Act made sex education compulsory but its content was prescribed by a circular issued in September 1987: 'Pupils should be helped to appreciate the benefits of stable married and family life and the responsibilities of parenthood.' More explicit was the authoritarian tone taken towards homosexuality, in Clause 22.

> There is no place in any school in any circumstances for teaching which advocates homosexual behaviour, which presents it as the 'norm', or which encourages homosexual experimentation by pupils. Indeed, encouraging or procuring homosexual acts by pupils who are under the age of consent is a criminal offence. It must also be recognised that for many people, including members of various religious faiths, homosexual practice is not morally acceptable, and deep offence may be caused to them if the subject is not handled with sensitivity by teachers if discussed in the classroom.[38]

In 1988 the government introduced the standardised general certificate in secondary education for final-year pupils. It provided cover for, and confirmed, the internal selection processes existing within schools by allowing schools the power to enter candidates according to previous mock results, thereby offering a gamed picture of a school's pass rate. It also represented a power grab affirming government control over curriculum content. Each subject area and standards were governed by national criteria covering all exams, whose determination and approval sat with the secretary of state.

This centralising mood was reflected in the erosion of teachers' autonomy. Forced into a response, the teachers entered into dispute with the government in 1985. In February teachers organised by the National Union of Teachers began a programme of rolling strikes for an uplift of £1,200 per year to compensate for a decade of meagre salary settlements. Some 2,000 schools were closed and a further 20,000 were impacted. It also involved considerable action short of a strike, such as stopping meetings with parents out of school hours and participation in playground supervision at lunchtime. However, as with other industrial disputes the government was able to tough it out and the action, which lasted into 1987, was called off. Kenneth Baker, education secretary since May 1986, oversaw the abolition of pay negotiations with the unions and replaced it with an advisory committee which made recommendations to the secretary of state without any union input. However, this applied in England and Wales only; Scottish teachers kept their negotiating rights.

The combination of centralisation and humbling of the teachers paved the way for the Tories' 1988 Education Reform Act. In the 1987 manifesto, the party set out four key objectives in line with the priorities recognised in its first term. These were a standardised core curriculum, the devolution of budgetary control to all secondary schools and a wave of primary schools, parental choice – giving them the right to send their children to schools of their choice while schools would be forced to take pupils up to their physical capacity – and the option of schools to leave LEA control for direct government funding. These principles fed into the legislation, which allowed for city technology colleges (autonomous schools part-funded by the department), but also required partial private funding, a proviso encouraging close relationships between schools and business. The proposals provoked public debate and opposition but, having been returned with a comfortable majority, the government pressed on without offering concessions.

Given the centralising tendencies and general authoritarianism, the last key area of consideration was the recasting of local government. The first major piece of legislation was the Local Government, Planning and Land Act 1980. An example of economic-order politics, it paved the way for development corporations to regenerate urban areas left empty of industry, and most notably led to the redevelopment of the London Docklands into the Canary Wharf complex. It also conferred upon the secretary of state the power to direct local authorities to put contracts for roads, construction and maintenance out to tender. It also abrogated many planning functions to the development corporations so that economic redevelopment could be driven from above without the participation of or consultation with local authorities.

Most significantly, local government finance was changed. This gave government the power to vary the monies going to councils and introduced a penalties system. If an authority overspent, its subsequent grant would be less, and the loss would grow in line with the overspend. This was codified in 1982's Local Government Act and provoked a movement against rate capping among councils. While some Conservative administrations were opposed to this big-stick approach, it was Labour councils in the forefront of the struggle.

The precipitating factor was the 1984 Rates Act in England and Wales. In response to the government tightening the purse strings, councils made up the shortfall by increasing local rates, which comprised domestic rates falling on homeowners and business rates – the two constituencies identified by the Tories as 'their people'. The new Act placed limits on what local authorities could raise locally, with the government capping rate increases from authority to authority. This led to several notable confrontations.

At the height of the miners' strike, Labour-run Liverpool City Council, led by members and supporters of the Militant tendency, forced a confrontation with national government by setting an illegal budget and campaigning for extra funds. In a rare (if temporary) victory for the left in the Thatcher years, the council was successful in repatriating £20 million for the housing budget in exchange for a legal budget.[39] This helped bring rebellious council leaders together, and while Labour's official line was to disown illegality, at the party conference that autumn motions supporting illegal budgeting were carried.

The settled position of the councils was to not set a rate and keep on postponing the budget meetings. Therefore, with no concessions from government, the councils had, under the law, until 10 March 1985 – twenty-one days prior to the beginning of the new financial year – to pass a legal budget. Failure to do so meant individual councillors becoming liable for substantial fines, or a surcharge, if the district auditor, responsible for checks on council spending and other activities, determined, following an extraordinary audit, that the failure was down to wilful misconduct. These were not fixed penalties but determined by the money lost to the local authority. Councillors could also be removed from office.

In the event, only Lambeth and Liverpool went the distance in delaying a legal budget and eighty-one councillors in total were surcharged, expected to find £126,947 in Lambeth and £106,103 in Liverpool between them. They were also disqualified from public office and, in the case of the latter, the surcharge climbed to £333,000 by the end of a lengthy court battle.

The Local Government Acts of 1985 abolished the Greater London Council, a perceived hotbed of left-wing opposition to the Tories, along with six metropolitan county councils. This was followed by the 1986 Act, which explicitly stated that all councils had to have a budget set by 1 April each year. The 1988 Act was the summation of the preceding decade of Thatcher's dominance. It enshrined the principle for competitive tendering, regulated housing benefit and specified the role of auditing and rules governing local authority publicity. This did not herald a qualitative change and was more a tidying-up exercise from previous legislative activism. However, its notoriety was secured with the inclusion of Section 28, which said, 'A local authority shall not – a) intentionally promote homosexuality or publish material with the intention of promoting homosexuality; b) promote the teaching in any maintained school of the acceptability of homosexuality as a pretended family relationship.'⁴⁰

1988 also saw the passing of a fateful piece of legislation: the Local Government Finance Act. The roots of the Community Charge, or the poll tax, as it became popularly known, were in the rate-capping rebellion. As the 1987 manifesto observed,

> The extremists have gained power in these areas partly because too few ratepayers have an interest in voting for responsible councillors pursuing sensible policies. Many people benefit from local services yet make little or no contribution towards them: this throws too heavy a burden on too few shoulders.⁴¹

As a replacement for the rates, the poll tax was ostensibly designed to renovate local government. The new tax was to be variable across local authorities, with taxation levels directly related to how much a council spent. The thinking was that taxpayers would want to see low bills landing on their doormats, therefore creating a political urgency among all parties to ensure that council monies were spent efficiently and to provide only those services the local electorate thought were necessary. Unsurprisingly, given the low-tax agenda, Thatcher assumed that the Tories would benefit most of all. As a famous party-political broadcast suggested at the time,⁴² it was convinced that 'extravagances' like local authority-backed 'gay seminars' would be electoral bromides under the new system.

Unfortunately for Thatcher, the poll tax backfired spectacularly. Instead of being levied by household under the rates system, it operated under the user-pays principle. As all adults are beneficiaries of local authority-provided services, they are all 'users' and therefore were liable. In practice, for many households this meant an overnight doubling of the rates bill. It fell heaviest on those least able to pay because the lowest-paid tended to cluster in local authority areas with the highest levels of need, and therefore correspondingly greater spending on public services. Its implementation in Scotland led to the development of anti-poll tax unions, which pioneered a strategy of mass mobilisation and non-payment.

This was followed a year later in England and saw some 17 million people refuse to pay. Ugly demonstrations besieged city halls and culminated in a violent confrontation at the national anti-poll tax protest on 31 March 1990. Over the course of the year local government found it incredibly difficult to collect the tax, and the court system became clogged up with non-payers. It was very clear to all but Thatcher herself that the policy was a non-starter – the authoritarian had reached the limits of her authority, and she was duly removed.

Reflecting on the government's programme for remodelling the state it is striking that the complete dominance of the executive mirrors the structure of the Conservative Party itself. Consider, for example, how – until the leadership of William Hague – the membership did not have a say in who led the party, had no bearing on policy formulation beyond the regular round of *consultative* fora and their influence on the direction of the party was refracted through local association grumbling and representations to their honourable members, if they had one. This did not mean that Thatcher abandoned statecraft and no longer had to manage opposition within the state system itself, but rather consciously eroded the institutional basis for it. This left a legacy of authoritarian custom and practice adopted by subsequent governments of a differing political hue.

The Return of *Homo economicus*

While Thatcher's distinctive state-order politics prepared the ground for the government's confrontation with the labour movement, the strategy did not end when the last miners gathered behind their NUM banners and marched into work. It persisted and became inseparable from her distinctive politics of individualism. In retrospect, a great deal has been made of an interview Thatcher gave to the *Sunday Times* in May 1981. After a wide-ranging discussion of comparisons of the UK's place in the world, she concluded the piece noting,

What's irritated me about the whole direction of politics in the last 30 years is that it's always been towards the collectivist society. People have forgotten about the personal society. And they say: do I count, do I matter? To which the short answer is, yes. And therefore, it isn't that I set out on economic policies; it's that I set out really to change the approach, and changing the economics is the means of changing that approach. If you change the approach you really are after the heart and soul of the nation. Economics are the method; the object is to change the heart and soul.[43]

We have seen that Thatcher entered office with a determination to, as she saw it, reverse Britain's decline by curbing the power of the labour movement and undoing the fundamentals of the post-war economic order, but this was also guided by pragmatic considerations. Some of what became 'Thatcherism' was born of the exigencies of political opportunity and events, particularly when it came to state-order politics, but other parts were driven by the constant preoccupation of any government: re-election. Her embrace of individualism was as much about manufacturing new Tory voters as it was breaking up the supports for collectivism among working-class people and the strength the professions had built up as 'monopoly' providers of public services. It should be noted that this individualism was far from the libertarian ideal of the neoliberal imaginary. The heavy-handed policing of black and minority ethnicities and the legislative rollback of LGBTQ rights were demonstrative of a two-nation Toryism in which the state conceded respect to some but not all, for self-interested political reasons.

Thatcher did not invent individualism, nor the fundaments of neoliberal individualism with which she is identified. Traditionally, Thatcher's Britain has offered itself as a paradigm case of what a neoliberal society looks like.[44] To apply broad brush strokes, neoliberal policies involve withdrawing the state from economic management and service provision and leaving the market to take up the slack. Based on the ideological notion that market relationships produce the most efficient outcomes, evacuating the state

74

from the economy by privatising state-owned industries, deregulating finance and curbing union power generates the greatest good for the greatest number.

Politically speaking, the overriding objective moves on from the maintenance of full employment to key indicators of economic health: quarterly GDP growth, low inflation, low public spending and low tax rates. However, this is not all neoliberalism is; it is also a mode of governance. The individual is constituted and related to as if a mini-capitalist looking to maximise acquisitive desires through the judicious deployment of skills and time in competition with like-minded (like-constituted) others. One is constantly invited to make choices by institutions designed with this express subjectivity in mind.

Indeed, being a neoliberal subject isn't an imposition in the sense of domination. It is a subjection of enforced choice. As a mode of subjection, neoliberalism is successful because it supports a socio-economic system founded on the private expropriation of socially generated wealth while depoliticising these relations and making capitalism appear the spontaneously natural way of doing things. That is, everything is the outcome of choices being made by rationally self-interested actors. The fact capitalism is a class system in a permanent state of crisis is effaced and rendered invisible from the standpoint of neoliberal subjectivity. The politics appropriate to this situation where, effectively, there is no such thing as society, only individuals and their families, is technocratic, managerial politics.

Nevertheless, key aspects of neoliberal individualism predated the emergence of neoliberal governance under Thatcher. In his genealogy of the individual, Ralph Fevre argues that contemporary individualism is rooted in the late eighteenth century and subsequently evolved into two distinctive forms.[45] The first stems from Tom Paine's revolutionary politics, which privileged the dignity of the human being, and could only be realised by storming the bastions of tyrants and monarchs and throwing out everything incompatible with it. His was an individualism in which character was tied to the moralities of one's choices, and not the behaviours expected of one's fixed station in life. In Paine's hands there was a moral responsibility to disseminate this creed.

Yet, simultaneously, Paine's understanding of the individual was couched in property rights. Fundamentally, individuation is an effect of the market and property differentials. Navigating life called upon the exercising of one's critical faculties in the full realisation that people/citizens were not equally endowed by virtue of their station. Individuality could therefore only be attained by tackling inequality – hence Paine advocated universal education, a proto-welfare state and a basic income. Therefore his work epitomises the two great strands of nineteenth-century individualism. The first Fevre refers to as the 'sentimental' kind, emphasising self-actualisation and discovery, moral choice and purpose, and mutual respect and recognition of others. This could not be prised away from the second strand: 'cognitive individualism', that of the self-interested individual looking out for their interests in the marketplace. These two dimensions of individualism soon assumed national characteristics. The British tended towards sentimentalism, of a philosophical 'respect for human dignity, autonomy, privacy and self-development'. This includes Adam Smith, who has undergone the subsequent fate of having had his analysis of markets and invocation of the 'invisible hand' disarticulated from his moral philosophy and the condemnation of exploitation. Meanwhile the American iteration emphasised 'the right to property and to make a living as one chooses, free-thinking, self-help, minimal government and taxation, and free trade'.[46] In America's case, this cognitive individualism grew increasingly hard-nosed, especially in the absence of a consistently strong labour movement exerting a collectivist pressure on the polity, and America's Cold War-era othering of its totalitarian Soviet opponent.

Cognitive individualism further inculcated a cultural repurposing of the primary production units of the economy – the big corporate entities. In managerial literature, the firm and even more so big business were and are custodians and facilitators of individualism. This was because the managerial caste that came to dominate them marketed their expertise as the specialists in human relationships – they 'knew' how to engineer the workplace to get the most out of employees. Key to this was individuating the worker, which undermined collectivist impulses from employees, but also meant having to treat them as individuals. This was aided during the 1970s as equality legislation meant that the sorting of workers moved away from classifications based on prejudice and discrimination to performance metrics and attitudes. There was an elision between work-positive mindsets and the moral acquittal of one's individualism. With an emphasis on individual achievement, cognitive individualism was deepened in the workplace.

This bedding down of cognitive individualism spread from middle-class corporate culture into the working class. Aspirations measured in terms of material goods and funded by disposable income, and later by credit, was a lifestyle bought into by enough of the electorate to provide a potential mass base for Thatcher's overt neoliberalism. In other words, the Thatcherite programme was as much a response to significant cultural shifts within Western individualism as the clamour for authoritarianism. Indeed, as individuating processes eroded the bonds of class during the 1960s and 1970s, those who felt it most keenly were, perversely, more likely to find the authoritarian promise attractive. Therefore it appeared that voters were demanding more opportunities for individualism, and like any halfway competent politician Thatcher and her programme was responding to the demand, and indeed looking towards growing this section of the electorate.

We've already seen how education and health reforms were conceived in terms of parental and patient choice. But among the first targets for Thatcherite individuation was housing. In the 1979 manifesto, the Tories set out three policy goals: the extension of homeownership through a combination of tax cuts and shared ownership schemes (it also explicitly linked the government's cuts programme to keeping interest rates low, thereby helping mortgage payers), the selling off of council- and housing association-owned properties to tenants at a discount and the liberalisation of the private rented sector.

While ideologically congruent with Thatcher's petit bourgeois instincts, Tory housing policy had the happy consequence of appealing electorally to the culture of acquisitive individualism – and therefore being popular – as well as deepening individuation further and inducing important conservatising effects. This is well understood and is often commented upon, and has subsequently been proven to condition voting behaviour; in 1983, the Tories had a twenty-two-point lead among working-class owner-occupiers.[47] However, as Pattie and Johnson noted in their overview of the electoral consequences of homeownership, council tenants who took advantage of the policy were likely to be pro-Conservative anyway, and those who were not subsequently became less inclined to support Labour without necessarily transferring their votes to the Tories.[48]

In this sense, mortgages were disciplinary technologies; the need to make monthly payments under pain of repossession should curb militancy and produce an individuating debt pressure, but simultaneously endow the mortgage holder with an appreciating asset that, again, should direct their interests towards maximising its value. This is something the Tories understood and saw as a means for manufacturing voters for their party while undermining Labour and therefore dispersing the opposition. Additionally, a further consequence was the transformation of housing into profitable investment opportunities for big business. Appearing under Thatcher's name as early as 1974, a piece for *The Daily Telegraph* argued that the Tories should be seen as the owner-occupiers' party, while noting that 'rent control has driven private and institutional capital the pension and insurance funds [sic] – out of housing for rent, or indeed out of housing generally. We have yet to find a way to bring it back, but we must, if we are to succeed in the long run.'[49]

The Tories enacted their manifesto promise in 1980, and by 1983 trumpeted the existence of a million extra homeowners. They framed Labour as a barrier to ownership, noting that it had,

> met these proposals with vicious and prolonged resistance and is
> still fighting a rear-guard action against wider home ownership. A

78

Labour government would take away the tenant's right to buy his council house, would prevent councils selling even voluntarily at a discount, and would force any former tenant who wanted to sell his house to sell it back to the council.[50]

The Tory manifesto that year pledged to extend the right to buy by offering greater discounts, making access to mortgages available to buyers in the private sector and providing support for build-to-rent. It also promised greater rights for council (note, not private) tenants to undertake repairs to their homes themselves and force the local authority to reimburse them. Come the 1987 manifesto the Tories promised very little that was concrete, apart from an aspiration to extend ownership – though it did not stop them from trumpeting how two out of three homes were now owner-occupied. Using the familiar language of choice, more attention was devoted to renting.

Apparently, the small private rented sector was preventing labour mobility because there was not a ready supply of rented accommodation. Their two-pronged proposal involved extending a system of assured tenancies in which the period of a tenancy was 'freely agreed' between renter and landlord and introducing a system of shortholds to bring empty properties back into use. The manifesto also laid out proposals for council stock transfers which allowed for setting up tenants' cooperatives with control over their rented housing, and the provision to transfer ownership from the council to an outside organisation if the tenant wished.

When these proposals were enacted by the 1988 Housing Act, landlords could charge whatever rents they pleased – but this was, theoretically, curbed by the rental market itself and the government caps on the amount of housing benefit that could be paid to private landlords. Second, renters had the option of referring them to a rent assessment panel if they believed the sums they were paying were above market rates. However, the landlord's power to seek a Section 21 notice to evict a tenant ensured that this remained a right on paper only. The shorthold tenancies, mostly favoured by landlords, meant that members of a renting household had no succession rights if the contracted tenant died. The landlord could take possession of their property with the full weight of the law behind them after the expiration of a fixed rental period.

Therefore, by way of summary, Thatcher's housing policies worked to individuate social and council housing tenants, while the restructuring of private rental empowered the landlord and effectively rendered the renter powerless under the law – only the fickle character of the market was any guard against rising rents. Indeed, Tory attempts at renewing private renting were about providing inducements to homeowners to become landlords them-selves, further expanding the base of their natural constituency.

If property was the basis of Thatcherite individuation, then it was not surprising that other avenues for pursuing the inculcation of *Homo economicus* were pursued. The 1979 and 1983 manifestos unveiled a rolling programme of privatisations, ostensibly to keep government borrowing and interest rates low, and in the latter doc-ument conceding that only the full force of market competition can hope to make nationalised firms competitive and customer-focused. It pledged to privatise British airports, aerospace manufacturer Rolls-Royce, car maker British Leyland and, crucially, two of the biggest nationalised monopolies: British Telecom and the British Gas Corporation.

In 1984 the government sold 50.2 per cent of its shares in what became BT, but preceded this move by setting up a market in tele-communications in niche services – a consortium of institutional investors coming together to found Mercury Communications to offer some competition. To create buy-in for the move, the govern-ment was able to undercut trade union opposition to privatisation by offering British Telecom employees a tranche of free shares, which 90 per cent of the workforce took up. However, to secure the sale the government had to backtrack on market liberalisation so the corporation's management would go along with the privatis-ation. Prior to the share issue the government undertook a marketing campaign to try and attract small and first-time inves-tors, and from its point of view it was a success. As the Institute for Government notes,

. Although the share offer was significantly oversubscribed, the flotation was regarded as a great success. More than three million ordinary shares were offered for sale and by the 28 November, when the offer closed, the shares had been 3.2 times over-subscribed. Dealing in the shares began on 3 December at a purchase price of 130p (50p on application and the rest to be paid in instalments). The total amount raised was £3,916 million and nearly 96 per cent of eligible BT employees became shareholders in the company.[51]

This set the tone for the privatisation of British Gas two years later. While Telecom's denationalisation was the largest to have taken place anywhere at that time, the sell-off of British Gas was to exceed it. Abolishing the corporation in the Gas Act 1986, flotation was preceded by a memorable press and television marketing campaign which exhorted the public to 'tell Sid' about the share issue.[52] This series of adverts culminated in finding the eponymous Sid on a mist-shrouded hilltop, when he promptly disappeared, no doubt to get his application in before the hapless climber finished telling him about it. Shares were offered at 135p apiece for a minimum purchase of 100 shares, which gave the company a value of £9 billion. Some 1.5 million shareholders were successful in purchasing them.

While trumpeted as examples of popular capitalism and the creation of a nation of small shareholders, privatisation was never as popular with the public as is often imagined – though not unpopular enough to prevent the Tories from winning the 1987 general election.[53] However, concerns about privatisation warded the Tories off from pursuing the privatisation of water and electricity before that election, though once back in office they proceeded rapidly with the move. This, as before, was justified in terms of efficiencies only the private sector could provide.

Upon Thatcher's assumption of office in 1979, as part of her governance package for the nationalised sector, the then regional water authorities were prevented from borrowing for infrastructure projects, which later allowed Thatcher to castigate them for failing to invest, thereby strengthening the case for privatisation.[54] The regional electricity boards were privatised just as Thatcher was leaving office, coalescing into the 'Big Six' that have dominated the market for energy ever since.

The number of individual shareholders between 1979 and 1991 grew from 7 per cent of the population to 25 per cent, or approximately 12.5 million people.[55] This was popular capitalism, but one that benefited the Tories' side of the two-nation divide they had actively fostered since coming to office.

The last key plank of Thatcherite individuation was for those who fell through the cracks of the market and were, conceivably, outside the tent. The 1979 manifesto did not signal an assault on the welfare state. Social security was criticised for being too complex and unwieldy while perpetuating absurdities, such as taxing benefits. They proposed raising the tax threshold to remove the poorest from tax liabilities while aspiring to a short-on-detail tax credits system. Concrete promises were thin, with lay language on simplifying the system and 'increasing work incentives', while also cracking down on fraudulent claims and promising that 'rules about the unemployed accepting available jobs will be reinforced.' Despite this, there was an assumption in the Tory leadership – one Thatcher and Keith Joseph shared – that comprehensive social security systems undermined the work ethic. If benefit payments were too high, they acted as an artificial pressure on the market to raise wages above their natural level to attract workers, with consequences for economic efficiency and inflation. If the market, for whatever reason, did not move, then workers were incentivised to stay at home and subsist on state handouts instead of getting a job. Thatcher was concerned not with welfare's abolition, but with its residualisation. During her first term the growth of unemployment thanks to the shuttering of nationalised industries and their supply chain ensured that spending on social security soared.

The Tories were forced to confront unemployment in the 1983 manifesto. They announced training schemes, an Enterprise Allowance Scheme to encourage the jobless to set up their own businesses, measures for building a flexible labour market such as the removal of 'restrictions' on job creation and the dividing up of full-time into part-time roles if employers deemed it necessary, and more training opportunities such as the Youth Training Scheme to manage the transition from school to work. Ostensibly this was to confer qualifications on trainees but in practice was used by employers to provide cheap labour well below the rates of normal workers – cheapening the wage bill and undercutting established staff. Meanwhile, the Tories promised nothing concrete on social security beyond protecting pensioners – indeed, since 1982 pensions were uprated in line with prices.[56]

Nevertheless, the 1986 Social Security Act made significant changes to pension provision. In conjunction with the Financial Services Act of the same year, it made it easier to opt out of occupational pensions and workers were encouraged to look to providing for their retirement via private pension plans. The 1986 Act also made significant changes to means-tested benefits, with limits placed on welfare's scope. The effects were the reduction of social security sources of income for the poorest families as claimants became eligible for finding 20 per cent of their rates, and there was a removal of benefits from students and sixteen- to eighteen-year-olds. Between 1987 and 1991, the Joseph Rowntree Foundation found that the poorest tenth of the population, the very people residual welfare is supposed to help and whose experience of social security was used to justify reform, were those worst hit by the changes.[57]

In summary, the changes Thatcher's government made responded to and deepened a kind of individualism, one referred to today as neoliberal individualism. This marked a decisive shift to its emergence as a form of governance proceeding on two levels. The changes to state institutions and the introduction of markets made many public sector organisations behave as if they were economic actors in competition for business. This meant a change to managerial cultures and the discipline exerted on employees. The second was on the individual itself. Because institutions were engineered so they could only relate to service users as customers, this placed a set of behavioural expectations and responsibilities on those wishing to access them. This emphasis on choice and self-reliance was firmly consolidated under John Major and later enthusiastically deepened by New Labour and the Conservative–Liberal Democrat coalition.

The End of Thatcher

The full details of Margaret Thatcher's political demise do not require much consideration given the wealth of analysis, reporting and memoir available – not least her own *Downing Street Years*. A common attribute noted by commentators of all political persuasions was how her downfall stemmed from her overly authoritarian style. Her enthusiasm for the poll tax, a neoliberal-governance step too far, completely overwhelmed her pragmatic instincts and when confronted with a mass movement of non-payment and violent street action her default refusal to conciliate left her position in the party rigid – and brittle.

Meanwhile, throughout 1989 and 1990 Thatcher became increasingly preoccupied with and vexed by European matters as the party's position in the country deteriorated. The 1989 European elections saw the Tories plunge to just under 34 per cent of the vote, their poorest performance in any election since 1974. And in October 1990 the Eastbourne by-election overturned a Conservative majority of 17,000, with the Liberal Democrats taking the seat. Considering the incumbent, Ian Gow, had been killed by an IRA car bomb earlier in the summer the expectation of a sympathy vote made the result more shocking.

With polling showing a possible route to salvation via a Michael Heseltine leadership, Thatcher was cut off from what was happening in the parliamentary party. According to Tim Bale's history, she preferred listening to *News of the World* columnist Woodrow Wyatt, her press officer Bernard Ingham and her private secretary Charles Powell.[58] She did not seem overly concerned when Heseltine's challenge did materialise. In the run-up to the ballot Thatcher was in Paris for a conference concerned with the Eastern European collapse, while her team in the Commons were lacklustre to say the least. Her parliamentary private secretary, Peter Morrison, was alternately found inebriated or asleep by a frustrated Alan Clark.[59] It was as if Thatcher believed that loyalty and three general election victories would carry her through.

They did not. Thatcher won 204 votes to Heseltine's 152 – which under the leadership contest rules put her four votes short of outright victory. Thatcher greeted the news bullishly, but after interviewing her Cabinet members individually came to the conclusion that she would lose a second round of voting. She announced her resignation and on 28 November 1990 left Downing Street as prime minister for the final time. It was the end of Thatcher, but in many ways still the beginning of Thatcherism.

When Thatcher entered office, she did so with the declared intention of halting Britain's decline and restoring its standing in the world. Arguably the Falklands War and her determination to stick fast to the Anglo-American alliance elevated the country's standing in terms of realpolitik, but economically speaking those fortunes remained stuck on a downward slope. Annualised growth rates between 1979 and 1997, going through busts and booms, were at 2.09 per cent of GDP per capita, stubbornly below the 2.31 per cent recorded by a crisis-ridden Labour predecessor, and the 2.59 per cent enjoyed by the Heath government. Monetarism, selling off state assets, repressing workers' rights and attacking their unions did not pay off in GDP terms.

Yet what it did succeed in accomplishing was a redistribution of wealth from the poorer to the richer. In her eleven years the poorest 10 per cent of the population saw their income decline by 0.29 per cent. For the second-bottom it was a negligible increase of 0.61 per cent and for the third 0.71 per cent. As you move up the income scale the increase gets greater, with the top tenth better off by 5.27 per cent.[60] What prevented a wholesale collapse in living standards was the ready availability of cheap credit. Private household debt stood at 73 per cent of GDP when Thatcher left office versus 37 per cent when she entered it.

On jobs, unemployment was 6.1 per cent as opposed to the 4.2 per cent she inherited from Labour. It was her singular achievement to reintroduce permanent mass unemployment, first as a by-product of her plan to destroy manufacturing and then as a disciplinary tool. The combination of policy and recession saw unemployment peak in April 1984 at 9.5 per cent, just as the miners' strike was getting under way. There were also significant revisions to what counted as unemployment; rates only included those who were specifically accessing dole payments. For example, the numbers claiming invalidity benefits almost doubled in eleven years from 770,000 to 1.6 million claimants. Likewise changes to social security that excluded students and sixteen- to eighteen-year-olds from welfare also successfully moved them off the unemployment figures.

Tory failure on jobs was disguised and denied thanks to statistical sophistry. However, it was 'mission accomplished' where trade unions were concerned. Membership slumped from 13.2 million to 9.8 million, a decline that has barely been interrupted since except for modest increases in recent years.

On housing, unsurprisingly, allowing tenants to buy their council houses at a discount meant that local authority building completely collapsed, a matter not helped by the fact their proceeds went directly to the Treasury. Considering Thatcher identified public housing as an obstacle to the creation of a buoyant property market, its diminution thanks to sell-offs – council stock declined by 900,000 homes between 1981 and 1991 – did not stimulate the building of housing overall. There was an increase in private construction but not enough to meet demand. By 1990 home completions had declined by 13 per cent compared to 1979–80, and this gap would only widen under successive governments.[61]

The party also suffered under Thatcher. The Tories captured a lower proportion of the electorate at each successive election between 1979 and 1992, but the distribution of seats afforded by the Westminster system awarded Thatcher landslide majorities in 1983 and 1987, something that eluded John Major in 1992, despite polling the most votes at any election ever.

Despite this, the party itself withered badly. Noted political scientists Richard Katz and Peter Mair have suggested that the

Tories lost 64,000 members each year since 1960.[62] This decline was not reversed under Thatcher, with the rolls standing at around half a million fewer in 1990 than 1979. In their study of Conservative Party membership, Paul Whiteley and colleagues discovered a bigger problem in the declining activity of members, as activists were increasingly replaced by weakly attached members.[63] In the first place, the selective incentives that participation offers had to compete with entertainment and individuated leisure opportunities.

Consumption practices can be used to explain membership decline across all parties in the post-war period, but it is reasonable to assume that the greater variety of choice that came with the expansion of consumer culture and cheap credit in the 1980s compounded these issues. Additionally, even then the Tories were an old person's party. In 1994, the average age was sixty-two, with half of the membership over sixty-six. Only 5 per cent were under thirty-five. Considering that the eighteen to twenty-five age bracket were the most active campaigners, at 17 per cent, Conservative politics' decreasing relevance to young people meant fewer joining, and necessary party work not getting done. The same study also found that those who felt influential in politics would more likely be active and remain so. The problem was that the conventional avenue for building a profile and having an impact on one's community as a Conservative was local government, which Thatcher had effectively stymied with her authoritarian hand.

As a party traditionally dependent on women, more women entering the labour market in the 1980s took its toll along with increased participation costs of activists, particularly when it came to time. Other changes around increasing geographic mobility and labour flexibility impacted on civic culture; the stable communities on which the post-war labour movement was built found their corollary in disruptions to the associational life of rural communities and the suburban middle class, characterised by charitable giving, and the party as a network for the self-identified upwardly mobile. This helps explain why Whiteley and his colleagues found, somewhat surprisingly, that avowed Thatcherites were a distinct minority within the party.

Not only did Thatcher dig up and pave over the party's sources of political nourishment, but also her totemic strong leadership, her not having a reverse gear and deliberately adopting a confrontational and tin-eared approach to real and imagined enemies merely multiplied opposition. Her myopic remaking of the state order even exasperated some admirers. Geoffrey Wheatcroft noted,

> Forgetting that policy must be adaptable, and exalted by her self-belief, Mrs Thatcher had cut legislative swathes through one institution after another, in the end alienating very many quite different sections of society on whom a Conservative government might be thought to depend: doctors, lawyers, academics and in fact just about every group except the police.[64]

Likewise, another admirer, the Cambridge historian John Charmley, said it might be imagined that Thatcher had 'sawn off the branch upon which the Conservative Party had always sat: the Church, the Civil Service, the universities, manufacturing industry, the media',[65] but he went on that this was to miss the point of Thatcherism; it was a crusade against those who held Britain back, and elevated the can-do above the can't-do.

Be that as it may, no supportive flourish can disguise the facts. Thatcherism did not arrest Britain's decline. It recast class relations by liquidating the industrial backbone of the most conscious and militant sections of the labour movement. The restructuring of the state system introduced neoliberal governance and provided business with more opportunities underwritten by state money. The economy moved away from making things and increasingly into service provision, and through her restriction of the housing supply set in train the next round of dynamics that would produce Conservative victories twenty years after her leaving office, but saddle them with long-term political problems from which there is no easy escape.

Thatcherism was successful in the sense that British politics was remade around the dominance of capital, an authoritarian state and citizenship defined in acquisitive terms. And the price her party paid was not just the rout of 1997, but the long-term decline now starting to manifest itself openly.

3

The Major Interregnum

The second ballot of the Conservative Party's 1990 leadership contests saw John Major emerge as the clear winner. He polled 185 votes to Michael Heseltine's 131 and Douglas Hurd's fifty-six. As he was two votes short of winning outright as per the contest rules, it was only the concession of his opponents that ensured it did not proceed to a third round. Nevertheless, Major's victory was a curious case.

Major entered Parliament in 1979, and it was often commented that his rise was a quiet one.[1] Indeed, the impression of Major's ascent within the parliamentary party was not one of someone scheming for high office, let alone capturing Number 10. Reading his Westminster curriculum vitae, one is struck by a rapid succession of offices, the longest as chief secretary to the Treasury between June 1987 and July 1989. From there he was made foreign secretary for all of three months before Thatcher appointed him chancellor in October.

One might be tempted to cast Major as the ultimate yes-man, a dependable set of hands who knew nothing of the Commons except through the prism of the Thatcher years. However, there are some biographical similarities between him and his patron. They shared a record of activism at local association level and were not overly advantaged by background. Both had petit bourgeois origins – Thatcher's relatively prosperous, Major's marked by periodic bouts of poverty – and both subscribed to broadly similar outlooks. It is telling that the index for Major's autobiography contains neither 'philosophy', 'ideas', 'values' nor 'conservatism'.

However, his observations about his first visit to the benefits office in his constituency reveal the core of his world view.

> For all of that time there were never fewer than a hundred unhappy people queuing to see the handful of stressed clerks dealing with their enquiries, and there were only thirty seats in the room. The office, I learned, had a staff turnover of more than 100 per cent a year. It was a grim place . . . I saw no reason why people should suffer such a scandalously poor service.[2]

Recounting his background, Major slides into and encapsulates a consumer consciousness. Life is a series of good and bad choices, of opportunities taken and missed. And nothing should get in the way of exercising one's choices, whether it is shoddy service, the interests vested in them (trade unions) or disruption to the smooth running of the everyday. In this sense, there was true congruity between him and Thatcher. His rapid series of promotions had as much to do with his being one of 'her people' as it did her propensity to burn through ministers. Yet this did not mean that he was a simple reiteration of his predecessor, though policy-wise there was more than enough continuity.

During the leadership election the media made much of his humble background, which enabled Major to present himself as a consensus politician attuned to listening. The perception of moving away from confrontation and authoritarianism helped transform the Tories' polling fortunes. When Geoffrey Howe resigned and made his famous speech from the backbenches attacking Thatcher, Gallup polling put Labour on 46 per cent to the Tories' 34 per cent. A month later, December 1990's figures found the Tories restored on 45 per cent and their opponents on 39 per cent. However, to maintain this lead Major had to act fast as the government was besieged by a series of problems: the global recession exacerbated by the boom-and-bust policies pursued by Nigel Lawson during his time in Number 11, the UK's commitment to the US-led response to Iraq's invasion of Kuwait and the movement against the poll tax. The in-tray was full.

The Major governments of 1990–7 lends itself to being analysed prior to and after 16 September 1992 (otherwise known as Black Wednesday), the date the UK crashed out of the Exchange Rate Mechanism (ERM) after sterling came under sustained speculative attack. It is tempting to regard this as a period of governmental crisis, where the contradictions of Thatcherism increasingly manifested themselves, requiring a firefighting approach on the government's part. This would be a mistake.

Black Wednesday coincided with the first of many sex scandals to consume Tory ministers, consolidating a reputation for sleaze. This was also a government which, following the 1992 general election, had to cope with a slim majority and the long-running sore of serious dissent over Europe. Yet it was able to consolidate Thatcher's revolution in local government and the public services, to escape the recession and – crucially for the Tories – to reverse the downward trend in house prices and close the negative-equity trap. For everything written about the Major period, his governments preserved the authoritarian settlement between the executive and the other arms of the state system. There is no more fitting tribute to Major's efforts at consolidation than the transformation of the Labour Party, under Tony Blair, into an entity broadly accepting of Thatcherite nostrums.

The Economics of Class Peace

Thatcher had cleared the decks for a Major premiership. Whereas she had faced a relatively combative and large labour movement, the combined effects of winning two strategic disputes and heaping legislative chains upon the trade unions stymied their efficacy and membership was in decline. As successful as the upsurge in activism around the poll tax was, this represented a clumsy assault on living standards and was, for the millions it drew into activity, a defensive struggle. As such the potential for it to reignite issues around the workplace and lead to a resurgence of militant trade unionism was, in retrospect, unlikely. As Major took power, however, the poll tax was still unresolved, but provided he acted quickly the solution need not necessarily erode the basic principles of the Thatcherite consensus. Another unwelcome problem was the economy. As he entered office on 28 November 1990, the UK economy had gone into recession in the previous quarter and would not resume sustained growth until early 1993.

Bound up with the economic woes was the connection between inflation and the relationship with Europe. Werner Bonefeld and his colleagues examining the Tory record note a jump in inflation from early 1988 to April 1990.[3] Major, at the time Thatcher's chancellor, was concerned with the pressure it was putting on pay demands. Ambulance drivers, Ford workers and local government workers had all submitted above-inflation claims. This itself was a consequence of strategic decisions made about economics to effectively free successive governments from 'the politics' – in other words, getting the blame for economic downturns. In the vexed relationship post-war governments had had with the value of sterling and its tendency to attract speculative attacks on the international money markets,[4] the Exchange Rate Mechanism was designed to shield participating currencies from assaults of this type by pegging the pound's exchange rate to the Deutschmark within a permitted range. If a currency became a speculative target a mixture of concerted purchasing and interest rate changes across major West European economies would maintain its standing. As the objective of monetary policy became fixated on maintaining exchange rates, economic policy was effectively depoliticised and subordinate to abstract, technocratic objectives.

Maintaining sterling's status had the result of stoking inflation. Unfortunately for the Conservatives, their 'depoliticisation' immediately struck at the aspirational Tory base as interest rates went up to mitigate inflation, thereby increasing mortgage payments and accelerating repossessions. The second consequence was the same as in the early 1980s recession; higher interest rates supporting an over-valued pound crippled manufacturing. This resulted in another round of job losses, which had its own negative multiplier effects on the growing service industry and further affected the ability to maintain mortgages. With the collapse of incomes, the demand for housing fell, which saw prices plummet 40 per cent after 1989. Many mortgage holders, particularly those at the cheaper end of the market, typically young and working class, suffered negative equity – trapped into making payments for a mortgage of greater value than the house it had been used to purchase.[5]

Given the circumstances Major had presided over during his time at Number 11 and the continued commitment to the ERM, this was a challenging economic order to manage when he finally made it to Number 10. He was fortunate in that the headlines were initially dominated by the war in the Gulf. However, despite the rapid and successful conclusion of operations there was little in the way of a poll bump for the Tories. Between December 1990 and May 1991, poll leads of a few points alternated between the two main parties with a handful of substantial Tory leads reported by outliers. Come May, however, their position began deteriorating, before recovering to an even keel in the run-up to the 1992 election.[6]

How did Major avoid severe political damage? Partly, it was thanks to the consequences of the two-nation Toryism he inherited; first, large numbers of those who lost out under the Thatcher years continued to lose in the Major years. Second, negative equity was only an immediate stress to those looking at turning over their property. If homeowners had taken out their mortgage earlier, they saw the value of their home rise and then fall, but provided they did not intend to sell they could ride it out until prices recovered and reassumed their upward trend. Events also assisted. During the leadership contest Major resolved to abolish the poll tax, which was announced in March 1991 – its replacement, the Council Tax, was implemented two years later. In the meantime, the government announced a £140 reduction in these bills, ostensibly paid for by increasing VAT to 17.5 per cent. Major was able to draw the sting out of the poll tax issue.

Then there was grandstanding over Europe, a favourite tactic of Margaret Thatcher's and a touchstone of Tory prime ministers since. In the negotiations around the Maastricht Treaty that formed the European Union, Major's stance awarded him favourable coverage from the increasingly Eurosceptic right-wing press. He won plaudits for removing overtly federalist ambitions from the document and securing opt-outs from moves towards a single currency and exemptions from the social chapter. Framed in terms of protecting jobs and enhancing the competitive edge of the UK economy, this was about protecting the sovereignty of the government over labour relations policy. European rules governing equal opportunities, minimum wages and health and safety did not apply to the UK. This condemned Britain to a low-waged, low-skilled economy. However, the preoccupation Tories had with Europe, which was largely ignored by the public, underlined their fundamental comfort. There was a general election in the offing but affording a secondary issue such prominence underlined the stabilisation of the Thatcherite settlement.

Given Major's woeful record prior to the 1992 election, how did his failing political economy carry the day? The key battleground was taxing and spending. Despite a memorable campaign of Labour dubbing then chancellor Norman Lamont 'VATman' on roadside hoardings, it was the Tories who made the biggest splash with their claim that Labour planned a 'double whammy' of more taxes and higher prices. This framing was amplified by the right-wing press and assisted by Labour's promise to increase income tax on the highest earners and spend more on public services. Despite these being found to be popular policies in attitude surveys, the prospect of more spending on the wrong side of the two-nation divide plus paying extra taxes saw the Tories mobilise the largest popular vote in UK election history. Though as a percentage they declined again, they returned to the Commons with a thin but unexpected majority of twenty-one – a fall of forty seats.

Major's honeymoon was short, however. Black Wednesday saw the UK forcibly ejected from the ERM. As Britain's membership was conceived in technocratic terms as a means of depoliticising economic decision making, the government's powerlessness in the face of speculative attacks on sterling ensured that the politicisation of the economy came surging back. On 16 September, the government increased interest rates from 10 per cent to 12 per cent and then 15 per cent, before cutting them back to 12 per cent the following day. That plus billions spent purchasing sterling on the money markets was not enough to save the pound from an enforced devaluation versus the Deutschmark, and the government had to announce the UK's immediate departure from the ERM.

The political consequences for the Tories were devastating. Posting modest polling leads since the general election, prior to Black Wednesday Major enjoyed a 2.5-point lead over Labour. In October, Gallup was posting a twenty-two-point deficit.[7] From then until the 1997 election, Labour enjoyed double-digit poll leads that only increased over time. Compounding the collapse of the government's position was the announcement on 13 October of the plan to close thirty-one of the UK's remaining fifty coal mines with the loss of 31,000 jobs. Commenting on a 'mistake that was to inflame public opinion more spontaneously than any other event in my years in Downing Street', John Major conceded that following Black Wednesday the timing was appalling.[8] He lamented, 'There are occasions when purely economic decisions have to be overridden, even if to do so has a financial cost in the short term, and this was one of them.'[9]

Despite the public outcry, marches, the (rhetorical) backing of the miners by the right-wing press and in one case a pit occupation, the government got its way.[10] It was forced to increase the total redundancy package to £1.1 billion and scale back the closures but, reflecting on it seven years after the event, Major noted with some satisfaction,

After the events of 1992, the privatisation of British collieries proceeded as smoothly as could be hoped. British Coal had succeeded in bringing coal prices down significantly, making the remaining pits an attractive prospect for investors; even the National Union of Mineworkers joined in one of the many bidding consortia.[11]

This dovetailed with the overriding concern of the Major years: making the Thatcherite counterrevolution permanent. The section given over to trade unions in the 1992 manifesto was small but reflected this logic. It promised further penalties against unlawful industrial action; further conditions attached to balloting, including making all pre-strike ballots postal ballots; and protecting existing 'achievements'. The 1992 Trade Union and Labour Relations (Consolidation) Act summarised the changes made to labour relations during the Thatcher years, while the 1993 Trade Union Reform and Employment Rights Act went further than the manifesto.

This Act addressed itself to matters of union governance and required the production of annual financial statements, calling into being a new layer of officialdom to make and track payments. Unions were also forced to hand over ballot distribution and vote counting to third parties, and, most crucially, it gave employers the right to discriminate against trade union membership. The 1996 Employment Rights Act merely specified further an already existing situation, while the 1997 manifesto showed that Major's appetite for further restrictions on the labour movement was whetted. Arguing that strikes in essential public services were an 'abuse of power', the Tories proposed to remove legal immunities from unions if their impact was judged 'excessive'. Employers would be entitled to apply for injunctions against industrial action, even if all the new rules applying to ballots were successfully navigated. Indeed, the 1997 manifesto demonstrates the distance travelled since 1979 that only one paragraph in the entire document was given over to trade unions and strike action, with the new pledges almost a vindictive afterthought.

Class peace on Tory terms meant they could continue with their privatisation programme. In 1991 and 1993 the remaining parts of BT in government ownership were sold off. These included a mix of curios, such as the British Technology Group, which was founded in 1948 with the aim of commercialising the fruits of publicly funded research, and the National Engineering Laboratory, which was purchased by the German TÜV group of companies. Also included in the fire sale was Her Majesty's Stationery Office, which published and distributed parliamentary papers and journals of record, and the back-office functions of the National Savings Bank.

Major also oversaw infrastructure privatisations, with most airports and ports being divested. The big privatisation, however, was of British Rail. Ostensibly at the behest of a 1991 EEC directive mandating the separation of infrastructure and service operation to enable 'competition', the 1993 Railways Act paved the way for privatisation by specifying the roles of the rail regulator and the rail service franchises, and how they were to be sold off to private interests. While British Rail itself was often criticised for inefficiency and substandard trains, by 2001 the privatised infrastructure operator, Railtrack, was taken back into public ownership and rebranded Network Rail. The system has also tended towards fragmentation, with routes divided up among operators, accusations of not supplying enough rolling stock and in the late 1990s concerns that privatisation had resulted in slack maintenance of track and stock, contributing to several serious crashes and disasters.

In early 1993 economic growth returned, assisted by a dramatic fall in inflation from 8.5 per cent in late 1991 to just above 2 per cent in early 1993. It remained below 3 per cent until the global crash in 2008. Interest rates saw a similar tumble from 15 per cent in 1990–1 to 6 per cent by the start of 1993. Unemployment, which peaked at over 10 per cent in the early 1990s, began to fall, reaching about 7 per cent in May 1997. House prices resumed their upward trajectory in 1995. At least on paper Major managed to overcome the legacy he bequeathed himself from his year in Number 11.

Yet there was still unfinished business when it came to state order, and his government implemented legislation that underlined the authoritarianism of the Tory settlement. Major also consolidated the hegemony of neoliberal governance across the state system.

State Authority

The politics of dancing were an unlikely target for the next round of Tory authoritarianism. The emergence of the acid house and rave scenes in 1988 not only generated a fresh wave of tabloid fury about young people and drugs, but also raised secondary issues around property rights, which were sure to earn the ire of back-bench Tories.

The Criminal Justice bill, particularly Clause 63, targeted the rave movement by outlawing outdoor gatherings of over twenty people there to dance to music with 'sounds wholly or predominantly characterised by the emission of a succession of repetitive beats'. Following the impromptu Castlemorton rave between 22 and 29 May 1992, local Conservative MP Sir Michael Spicer raised the matter in the Commons. He said,

> the numbers, speed and efficiency with which they arrived – amounting at one time to as many as 30,000 people – combined to terrorise the local community to the extent that some residents had to undergo psychiatric treatment in the days that followed . . . It is time the Government acted with a greater sense of urgency and focus against the abuse of property rights and the threat to law posed by illegal encampments on a small and a large scale.[12]

An opposition movement sprang up to defend the free-party scene, but ultimately the passage of the legislation ensured rave moved into the clubs and the rounds of officially sanctioned festivals. They have since grown into commercial behemoths.[13]

Young people dancing in fields were only one target of this wide-ranging bill. In the summer of 1991, urban unrest broke out across northern England, and extended campaigns around dangerous dogs, joyriding and, related to rave, the emergence of ecstasy as a popular recreational drug filled the Tory press. Against a background of economic malaise and accelerating unemployment, a generalised government campaign might focus attention away from persistent problems and the Tory record, and channel discontent against well-used scapegoats (young people, black people, travellers, social security recipients). In turn, this reasserted the primacy of law and order, enabling Major to steal a march on a traditional Tory issue versus their opponents. As the 1992 manifesto put it, 'the challenge for the 1990s is to step up the fight against lawlessness and violence, so that our citizens can live free from fear'. It promised steep penalties for joyriders of up to five years in jail, a new offence criminalising squatting and action against illegal encampments. When these pledges passed into law, they represented a comprehensive retrenchment of social authoritarianism.

The eventual Criminal Justice and Public Order Act (1994) attacked a suspect's right to silence. The refusal to answer questions could be later considered an indication of guilt at trial. Police stop-and-search powers were also increased, and not just raves but protests were criminalised under rules governing collective trespass. Whether these were necessary within the terms of public order policing is debatable – at a warehouse rave in Gildersome in 1990, 836 partygoers were arrested.

The effect of coarsening the discourse, of 'condemn a little more and understand a little less',[14] as John Major might have said of his efforts, appeased the tabloids and ensured that concerns about civil liberties were a fringe issue. In a retrospective of the time, the journalist Ally Fogg noted that Tony Blair, Labour's then shadow home secretary, elected to abstain on the bill when it came before the house – presumably to avoid looking weak on an issue where he did not want to challenge the Tory/tabloid consensus.[15] Indeed, his subsequent record saw New Labour pursue restrictions on liberties entirely consistent with the authoritarian Tory line.

Accompanying law and order was the consolidation of the Thatcherite approaches to the NHS, education, social security and the civil service. The National Health Service and Community Care Act, with its creation of an internal NHS market, came into force, appropriately enough, on 1 April 1991, and was followed by the Patient's Charter on 1 October. Having been a cornerstone of the NHS since, despite revisions, the 1992 manifesto promised the introduction of targets for waiting times, a simplified system of complaints and comparative health information concerning standards achieved by *competing* authorities to facilitate public choice.

Despite opening the NHS up to patients so they could scrutinise its performance, the government was less interested in professional assessment of its reforms, as Ray Robinson, the head of the

Institute of Health Policy Studies at Southampton University, then complained.[16] In a review of research undertaken on the restructuring of the health service, he found a tendency for the internal market to increase costs around the drafting, taking on and monitoring of contracts between health providers where previously an administrative relationship existed. The rights to information about the NHS were enshrined in 1995's Code of Practice on Openness in the NHS, and in 1996 the government abolished a slew of regional health authorities, replacing them with regional offices of the NHS Executive, which was tasked with NHS management and advising the Department of Health about policy.

The NHS was also the site for one of John Major's long-standing legacies for public services: the introduction of the private finance initiative (PFI). PFIs were set up to attract private capital into public service infrastructure on very favourable terms. Introduced in 1992, they tied public bodies into long-term contracts for the delivery of new buildings and the provision of maintenance. Typically, under the terms of these schemes a business, usually a construction company, would build a hospital for a contracting party, like a hospital trust, and effectively charged them a mortgage over a twenty- to thirty-year period. In most cases the companies concerned operated the facility and had responsibility for maintenance over the course of the contract before the asset transferred to the public sector. This was useful for governments affecting a fiscally prudent stance because the capital outlay for projects did not appear in the public-spending figures. Instead, costs over time could be buried in the balance sheets of NHS bodies, lost amid general health spending.

The suggestion that PFI was considered an accounting trick in Whitehall apparently 'horrified' Major's chancellor, Ken Clarke, who enthusiastically pursued the project.[17] The second justification was classically neoliberal. Resting on the dogmatic view that public sector organisations were congenitally inefficient because they responded to bureaucratic diktat rather than living and dying by the signals from the market, the default assumption was that PFIs would do a better job of delivering value for money.

Nearly thirty years after the fact, the criticisms ventured of PFIs at the time have been borne out. Far from offering efficiencies, contracts proved more expensive to maintain in the long run – much more expensive than if the government had simply borrowed money and built new hospitals outright. The decades since have seen the failure of firms who profited from PFIs, most spectacularly the construction firm Carillion. In this case it took on as many contracts as it could handle to inflate its balance sheet and thereby its share price. Unfortunately for Carillion, its debts caught up with the company and it collapsed in 2018 with dozens of projects unfinished, most notably a hospital each in Birmingham and Liverpool and the disruption of 400 other service contracts. Not the extra efficiencies Major and Clarke had in mind.

Although it was a Tory scheme for funnelling public money into the private pockets of construction interests, New Labour embraced the policy and made it their own. Tony Blair and Gordon Brown expanded it to all areas of the public sector, ostensibly to avoid reviving historic tax-and-spend associations, even to the point of borrowing Tory arguments concerning its viability. Asked to justify PFI given the costs, all Brown could do was to 'declare repeatedly that the public sector is bad at management, and that only the private sector is efficient and can manage services well'.[18] If any kind of public authority needed new infrastructure, PFI was the only vehicle available to get things built.

The case in education was broadly similar. The principles laid down for reorganising schooling and the curriculum in 1988 were built upon by Major. Having established a new regime of testing in schools, the 1992 Education (Schools) Act introduced a new inspectorate. Locating inspection as an important component of his flagship Citizen's Charter, the Office of Standards in Education was a means to improve standards and 'build up a base of knowledge, measured standards and information for parents on which we could truly build a renaissance of state education'.[19] An appreciation of the multiplication of paperwork for scrutiny and what this meant for teachers' workloads and time in the classroom did not trouble the Tories.

The 1992 Act required inspectors to report on quality, standards, efficiency of financial management and the 'the spiritual, moral, social and cultural development of pupils at the school'. The legislation also specified how at least one person among the inspection team should have no experience of managing or providing education in a school setting. The inspection reports were made available to the governors, the education minister and the public. If a school fell short and was deemed to be 'at risk', then an action plan was required and its implementation monitored for the duration.

The 1993 Education Act was the thickest set of prescriptions in education's history, weighing in at 308 sections and over 290 pages. There were new laws specifying the responsibility of providers, the scope of grant-maintained schools, attendance, children with special educational needs, failing schools and a range of miscellaneous matters – in all respects a rather messy tidying up of the previous decade's worth of changes.

In 1994 the Tories came for the teachers again in a straightforward power grab. The Council for the Accreditation of Teacher Education, set up in 1984 to advise the government on the approval of teacher training courses, was abolished and replaced by the Teacher Training Agency. This provided funding for training and was wholly appointed by the secretary of state. True to form, the minister had the discretion to make appointments from any professional background to the agency. In all, the mix of 'freedom' and authoritarianism saw more schools opt out of local education authority control, with new Education Secretary John Patten expressing the ambition of forcibly moving all schools to grant-maintained status, in what Gillard regarded as the reintroduction of selection through the language of specialisation.[20]

However, Patten's tenure was cut short – with some relief to teaching unions and education experts – by his sacking amid murky circumstances. Despite following the established line of march, Major is discreet apart from noting that 'his health suffered . . . I decided he needed a sabbatical to recover'.[21] The move of Gillian Sheppard to education was a conciliatory one and, unlike her predecessor, she had a thoughtful reputation and was prepared to listen to education professionals. Less abrasive did not mean a reversal was in the works. Sheppard wished to see a period of 'consolidation' in the school system so recent changes could bed down and operate. However, if the Tories were somehow returned in 1997 there was going to be a push for selection among 'specialised' schools, with an initial target of 10–15 per cent operating selective entry.

Another continuation of Thatcherite authoritarianism was in social security. Despite the best efforts of both Tory prime ministers and their commitment to residual welfare provision, the benefits bill as a proportion of GDP refused to go down. Real-term spending doubled between 1979 and 1997, an increase of around 9.5 per cent to 12 per cent of GDP. During the Major years there were two key innovations. First was the founding of the Child Support Agency (CSA) as an organisation of the Department for Work and Pensions with the purpose of locating and forcing 'non-resident parents' to contribute towards the cost of raising their children.

In the context of a generalised and media-driven antipathy to welfare, the new agency – set up in April 1993 – promised to save money and make feckless fathers more responsible. However, its initial performance was simultaneously farcical and vindictive. Rather than tracking absent parents down the CSA tended to intervene in cases where financial support between an absent and a present parent already existed and recalculated the liability, often increasing it to unsustainable levels and compounding the bad press the Major government received.

The government remained under pressure from its tabloid allies, who gleefully reported benefit fraud stories and worked to undermine social security through successive scapegoating of the unemployed, single mothers and travellers. In January 1996 the National Audit Office issued a report stating that 10 per cent of all welfare recipients had at one time or another submitted a fraudulent claim, receiving up to £1.4 billion they were not eligible for. Major's approach to these issues was to introduce Project

Work – a scheme aimed at the long-term unemployed to help them secure a job, which included a three-month period of 'community work'. As Major put it at October's party conference, 'Those who don't want to work are exposed, but those who do want to work are helped.'[22]

The second initiative was the introduction of the Jobseekers' Allowance (JSA), which made significant changes to unemployment benefit. Rebranded in authoritarian newspeak and reflecting principles of neoliberal governance, 'jobseeker' denoted how a claimant was to be addressed by the system and made (administrative and ontological) assumptions about the motivations of the jobless. Matching these normative expectations, backed by disciplinary measures should one fall short, is the allowance part of the coupling. Not only does it connote a temporary situation; refusing to call it a payment or a benefit also suggests a begrudging attitude on the part of the state.

Having passed unhindered through the Commons in the previous year, two forms of JSA were established – contributions-based JSA, which paid out for six months by virtue of previous National Insurance payments (it was one year under the previous system) and was means-tested thereafter, and income-based JSA, which was means-tested as part of the application. Eighteen- to twenty-four-year-olds only qualified for a lower rate, and applicants had to sign up to a 'jobseeker's agreement' as a condition for payment. The 1995 Jobseekers Act specified this as being available to work and actively seeking employment. It also stipulated a range of contraventions that could provide grounds for sanctioning payments, such as failing to attend Job Centre interviews, getting penalised for voluntarily quitting a job, turning down job offers, failing to apply for jobs and being uncooperative.

This blend of authority and individuation had previously characterised Thatcher's poll tax, and given the anger and disorder it provoked it was a pressing concern for Major when he took over, not least because councils' annual funding settlement from central government had to be confirmed by late January 1991, as well as the small matter of a general election little over a year away. Doing nothing was not an option as the first round of bills in England and Wales would average at £400 per person.

In his memoirs, Major says he had to rule out a generous package of a funding increase for councils coupled with big cuts to poll tax bills because the £8 billion tag for doing so was 'unaffordable' and then Chancellor Norman Lamont 'issued dire warnings about the economic consequences of such an increase in expenditure'.[23] What these consequences might have been in the context of a recession where money in the pocket could have provided a useful stimulus is left unexplored. The stopgap Major arrived at was a £1.1 billion relief package targeted at the hardest-hit. For their part, the public returned their feelings in the shattering Ribble Valley by-election defeat in which the Liberal Democrats overturned a 19,500 Tory majority.

This focused Major's mind. Prior to the Budget he insisted on a more generous scheme until the poll tax could be replaced. Lamont uprated VAT by 2.5 per cent to 17.5 per cent. Meanwhile, Michael Heseltine had been working on the Council Tax as the Community Charge's replacement. This removed the flat charge and per-person levy and was determined by property valuation, with housing organised into tiers of discrete bands topping out at £320,000. The typical bill was significantly less than the poll tax while tending to be more expensive than the rating system.

It was introduced in 1992's Local Government Finance Act and remains one of Major's lasting legacies. It also represents some deft politicking. As he remarks, the vexed issue of council funding faded when, months previously, it cost the Tories their iconic leader and menaced the party with the prospect of electoral annihilation. It also secured the key objectives of Thatcher's proposals – the enshrinement of the user-pays principle, albeit hidden behind property values, and the successful attempt to interpellate Council Tax bill payers as customers looking for value for money from their local authorities.

However, it stored up problems for the future. First, only a quarter of council revenues in 2021 are raised this way, making local government overly dependent on Whitehall for funds. Second, the banding has not been reviewed and upgraded since the initial exercise under Heseltine in 1991. As property prices have risen, this has effectively meant that the top rate of tax has stayed frozen while those on lower bandings are paying disproportionately more for services. As aiding property acquisition has been a policy objective for successive Tory and Labour governments since Major, both parties have feared the electoral consequences of revisiting the issue, which would see large increases as new upper bands are introduced – particularly so for the Conservatives, for whom these taxpayers constitute a not insignificant section of their electoral coalition.

Individualism and Neoliberal Governance

Apart from the Council Tax, the second legacy of the Major years was the introduction of the Citizen's Charter. Described as an initiative to 'increase the efficiency of public services and to make them answerable to the consumer by providing information on the cost and running of services, and by setting targets for the delivery of services', it was considered by Major his flagship policy and had a section of its own in the 1992 party manifesto.[24] It deployed the familiar language of choice, of putting 'the customer' first, and embedding competition between public sector organisations. The old rhetorical trick of praising and then condemning gets a fresh outing too, with warm words for the 'vast majority of civil servants' while attacking 'outdated working methods and attitudes', albeit fault is located in 'the system' as opposed to the workers themselves.

The manifesto also promised the introduction of league tables, inspection regimes, published standards of service, an extension of competitive tendering for local and national government, performance-related pay and even the micromanagement touch of insisting that civil servants give their name when dealing with members of the public. This consolidated Thatcher's Next Steps programme, but significantly went beyond it.

Having announced it to the public in July 1991,[25] after the election Major set up the Office for Public Service Standards to oversee the charter across the public sector. Standards in the soon-to-be-privatised British Rail, as well as in the privatised utilities, also came under its purview. Major also set up a Citizen's Charter Unit inside the Cabinet Office to push the policy through government departments, advise on implementation and work as a repository of ideas. Furthermore, a consultative body was also founded, encompassing James Blyth, then the chief executive of Boots, and Madsen Pirie of the hard-right think tank the Adam Smith Institute.[26] This saw the rapid publishing of over thirty charter statements by 1993 and forty-two by 1997. One of the first innovations pushed out by the unit was the Charter Mark award, patronisingly described as 'the Oscar for public services', for organisations who meet their targets and deliver a high degree of customer satisfaction.[27] Reflecting on it, Major said that the award

> soon became immensely popular, with many thousands of nomin-
> ations each year, and widely recognised by service users. We kept
> the standards demanding: but within five years of the Charter
> White Paper almost 650 Charter Marks had been awarded, and a
> further 350 bodies highly commended. Raising the standing of
> public servants, as well as raising the standard of service, had
> always been my objective.[28]

What the awards, the publishing of information, the targets and the competition constituted was a quite deliberate hands-off mode of governing public services. As Major earlier noted, enforcing service discipline via 'an information revolution would be just as effective a way of doing this as the left-wing device of regulation by state, quango or local education authority'.[29]

From Thatcher, Major inherited a situation where the civil service was already effectively federalised. The Charter ensured that self-determination for these departments was pushed away from Whitehall and deposited under the purview of service area management. Theoretically, decision making was closer to the coalface, making front-line civil servants more responsive to client pressure and, therefore, more likely to inculcate a responsive, customer-facing relationship between agency and service user. This dispersal of power was backed by competition between departments over metrics, and 'independent' inspectorates were set up to hold managers to account for missed targets. The flip side of this regime was a conscious effort to individuate the civil service by department and sub-department. Management itself was concerned with ensuring that employees met performance targets by a system of incentives, bonuses and advancement opportunities if they met or exceeded Charter 'wins'. This did not destroy the collectivist culture of civil service trade unionism entirely, with the two main unions merging in 1998 to form the Public and Commercial Services union (PCS). However, its corollary was a depoliticisation of public services. Issues about limited resources receded into the background as choice and service efficiency came to the fore, and claimants were individuated and expected to jump through bureaucratic hoops to demonstrate their worthiness. On this measure, Major's reforms have proven successful and there has been no rollback of the neoliberalisation of the service. The changes remain largely untouched despite waves of superficial rebrands since.

At the time, however, the significance of the Citizen's Charter was underplayed. Writing in 2005, Iain Hollingshead likened it to a 'political dodo' and quoted an (unnamed) Tory MP as saying, 'it doesn't give people any legal powers, just higher expectations and the power to whinge'.[30] NHS complaints rose by 56.7 per cent and British Gas 172 per cent, and it was associated in the public imaginary with the cones hotline, described by the BBC as 'probably the most ridiculed policy ever introduced by a British government'.[31]

While the right to complain about inconveniently positioned cones on UK motorways summed up the malaise afflicting Major's government after Black Wednesday, the mockery ensured that his contribution to the neoliberal settlement was overlooked. The principles of the Citizen's Charter reinforced marketisation and outsourcing in the guise of value for money, replaced client relationships with transactional relationships underpinned by target quotas and governed by bureaucratically prescribed responsibilities and have been imposed right across the public sector – spurring further marketisation. Tony Blair said the greatest regret he had about his time in office was not undertaking public service reform. Because Major remodelled the civil service and set its governance functions on impeccably neoliberal foundations, Blair never had to.

As a good Thatcherite, Major could not resist the temptation to ally the individuation fostered by the Citizen's Charter with another authoritarian turn. In the context of a tabloid-driven campaign against single mothers, Major repositioned a flailing Tory Party by shifting back towards conservative values. At 1993's party conference, he said,

> The old values – neighbourliness, decency, courtesy – they're still alive, they're still the best of Britain . . . It is time to return to those old core values, time to get back to basics, to self-discipline and respect for the law, to consideration for others, to accepting a responsibility for yourself and your family and not shuffling off on other people and the state.[32]

While subsequently Major was to claim this was not about pushing social conservatism (in his autobiography he insists it was a crusade against ideas 'divorced from public sentiment and from reality', characterised by a certain permissiveness and a tendency to blame society for social ills), it was certainly designed to telegraph a well-calibrated stance to the Tory editorial offices.[33] Unfortunately for Major, the campaign, quickly dubbed 'Back to Basics', backfired. Taken as a prescriptive statement about personal morality, the tabloid press homed in on the misdeeds of Tory politicians.

Between the 1992 and 1997 general elections, there were sixteen sex scandals, nearly all of which involved extra-marital affairs, and multiple ministerial resignations – including one death by auto-erotic asphyxiation and the subsequent humbling at a by-election in which another 17,000 majority evaporated. One can only imagine the press frenzy had Major's own affair in the 1980s been uncovered at the time. This did not distract the press from their campaign against social security scapegoats, but the farce ensured that the Tories were unable to reap political capital from it.

Undermining the Base

If Black Wednesday fatally undermined the government's authority, every step Major subsequently took compounded the Tories' woes. The pit closures made them appear vindictive and cruel, and the fallout from Back to Basics a laughingstock. It did not end there. Following the failure of Black Wednesday and falling tax revenues thanks to the recession, the government's budgetary position deteriorated. The autumn statement of 1992 committed the government to a modest £4-billion stimulus aimed at housing and capital investment, but, to meet previous commitments on curbing spending, cuts were announced to defence and transport, and the capping of public sector pay rises at 1.5 per cent. This tough rhetoric emboldened bosses. Against the backdrop of unemployment running at over 10 per cent, several employers risked upsetting the industrial peace and stoked industrial action, such as the Timex factory dispute and indefinite strike action at the Yarrow shipyard.

Having already increased VAT to 17.5 per cent so poll tax bills could be slashed, in the 1993 Budget Lamont levied an 8-per-cent excess on domestic fuel, slashed mortgage relief and increased National Insurance. In his memoirs, Major writes how he hoped taxing energy would be an environmentally friendly measure as the government had committed itself to cutting carbon emissions at the Rio Earth Summit the year previously. Again, like so many other initiatives, the blowback was explosive and cost Lamont his job. Reflecting in his memoirs, Major said this was the final straw following an accumulation of previous embarrassments. These included stating how unemployment was a price worth paying for controlling inflation, and inadvertently renting out a basement flat to a self-described sex therapist – a woman who, predictably enough, was dubbed Miss Whiplash by the press. He was a liability among a government of liabilities, and was therefore dispatched to the backbenches.

Lamont's replacement by Ken Clarke ensured that some pet initiatives saw the light of day, such as PFI. The application of VAT to fuel bills was especially damaging to elderly people whose fixed incomes and greater reliance on heating in the winter months left them exposed. It was also seen as unfair. Pensioner poverty in the 1990s was significant, with rates at 22 per cent of pensioner couples and 31 per cent of single male and 42 per cent of single female pensioners in poverty in 1996–7, the last full year of Major's government.[34]

The matter erupted following the 1994 Budget. Clarke announced an increase of VAT on fuel to the full 17.5 per cent, which was presented in a bill that also increased UK contributions to the EU's budget. It was a confluence of opposition as a semi-regular outburst against Europe on the backbenches met with a popular desire to see the VAT increase dropped. Labour brought forward an Opposition motion against the increase, and the government was defeated 319 to 311 votes – seven Tories voted with the Opposition with more abstaining.[35] The defeat forced Clarke to make a mini-budget a few days later, announcing tax increases on alcohol, cigarettes and fuel.

What kept Tory incompetence at the forefront of the national debate were the divisions over Europe. Having negated it as an issue in the initial round of Maastricht negotiations prior to the 1992 election, that a matter related to Europe – ejection from the ERM – should collapse the polling position was grist to the mill of the Eurosceptics. Something of a niche interest up until the 2016 referendum on EU membership, it was not among Tory backbenchers for two reasons. The first was the ERM collapse itself. While seen as a manifestation of Tory incompetence, by the same token it could be interpreted as popular rejection of a scheme aiming towards a single currency and a European super-state. Therefore Euroscepticism was popular. Second, everything about the EU cut against Thatcherite instincts. With a press full of scare stories about pettifogging rules – fanned by a future prime minis-ter[36] – it provoked the traditional instincts against bureaucracy and flagrantly challenged the primacy of the 'sovereignty' of the authoritarian state. As Thatcher herself put it in her famous Bruges speech, 'we have not successfully rolled back the frontiers of the state only to see them reimposed at the European level'.[37]

Following Black Wednesday, an Early Day Motion was signed by a hard core of sixty-five Eurosceptic Tory MPs calling for a 'fresh start' on Europe. This rebellion-minded cadre was emboldened by the narrow margin by which France, regarded as one of the most Europhile of countries, ratified the Maastricht Treaty by referendum. This rump also attracted the support of the Thatcherite pantheon, among whom were Kenneth Baker, Cecil Parkinson, Norman Tebbit and Thatcher herself. Having rebelled against the whip when Maastricht had its second reading in the Commons in the form of the European Communities Amendment bill, when it returned for its third in May 1993 Major's majority had been whittled down to eighteen seats.

As the vote approached, the rebellion intensified. For the actual vote on 20 May, Labour abstained, but on 22 July the opposition submitted an amendment that would have delayed the treaty's implementation until the social chapter was accepted. This fell on a tied vote of 317 versus 317, with the Speaker, as per tradition, casting her vote in favour of the status quo. However, the following vote that would have brought it into law was lost as abstentionist rebels voted with the Opposition. The government was defeated 324–316. The following day, the government played its final card: a confidence motion tied to implementing Maastricht without the social chapter. It passed 339–299, not least because an election would have led to annihilation.

As the party approached conference season, Major made emollient noises. Writing in the *Economist*, he said the EU should remain an association of sovereign states and resist full union, and at conference positioned the Tories as the only party against a centralised Europe. However, in March 1994 Major committed the government to accept qualified majority voting, the process by which the EU's Council of Ministers arrived at decisions.[38] He saw it as a necessary protection of democratic functioning, the Eurosceptics as another step towards federalism. While the rebels kept their powder dry ahead of the European elections in June, the cumulative damage of the previous two years of incompetence, cruelty and disunity ensured that the Tories plunged to their worst election result in the twentieth century. They emerged with eighteen MEPs, thirteen fewer than 1989, and 26.8 per cent of the vote. Meanwhile Labour, whose leader John Smith had unexpectedly died four weeks previously, took sixty-two seats on 46.2 per cent of the vote.

More agonies presented themselves in November when the European Communities (Finance) bill went before the Commons. Though entailing a small net increase in UK contributions by £75 million per year, it became a hill for the rebels to die on. Having learned the lesson from Maastricht, Major immediately presented it as a confidence issue. Labour introduced an amendment making the new contribution dependent on tackling fraud in the EU, in Major's view to cause mischief. However, despite the amendment falling by twenty-seven votes amid bad tempered scenes, the main bill passed easily. Eight Tories abstained on Labour's motion as opposed to voting against it, and had the whip removed. A further MP resigned the whip in solidarity.

The immediate consequence was the government losing the vote on VAT on domestic fuel. The whip-less rebels presented further difficulties later when they voted against the government on reform to the European Common Fisheries policy, and only half of the cohort voted with the government to maintain its right to majorities on parliamentary select committees. Nevertheless, it temporarily secured Major against any leadership challenges. Thirty-four signatures were required to force a contest, so the removal of nine malcontents made that a little more difficult. However, with the 1995 local elections looming and the need to affect a united front, the rebels were readmitted into the party without conditions or penalty that April. They repaid Major's overtures by holding 'a cocky, unapologetic press conference before decamping to College Green for triumphal television interviews. They made no conciliatory noises and refused to give any guarantees of party loyalty.' Reflecting, Major wrote, 'I thought their behaviour was contemptible.'[39]

The woes continued. The 1995 local elections came and the results were appalling. Though depressed by the number of city unitary authorities that were up for election and traditionally lean towards Labour, this observation does not apply to the borough and district councils who held elections. The Tories plunged to 25 per cent of the vote compared to Labour's 47 per cent and shed 2,018 councillors while Labour picked up 1,807 and the Liberal Democrats 487. Of the fifty-seven councils the Tories controlled prior to the election, they retained four.

Conscious of the drain that infighting was exerting, in June Major took the unprecedented step of calling his critics out publicly and addressing the Westminster whisperings about his leadership. A poll published by the *Telegraph* on 19 June showed that seventy Tory MPs wanted a leadership contest, well above the thirty-four names needed to trigger one. Major, having mulled over the idea for a couple of weeks previously, spoke to the executive of the 1922 Committee on the evening of 22 June, outlining his decision to resign as leader of the Conservative Party and stand as the incumbent candidate in a contest – an unprecedented step but one that certainly beguiled his internal critics.

It was a high-risk move. In his memoirs, Major confessed to hoping for more than 230 votes but had reconciled himself to resigning if he came in with fewer than 215 votes.[40] In the event, none of the so-called big beasts of the Cabinet put themselves forward, such as Michael Portillo, who was then the toast of the right. It fell to John Redwood, the Welsh secretary and former chief of the Number 10 Policy Unit under Thatcher. He appealed to Thatcherites and Eurosceptics and won the imprimatur of Norman – by now Lord – Tebbit, but it did not matter. The party apparatus was behind Major from the start, and there wasn't a clamour in the country for a more right-wing prime minister. Despite Redwood running under the slogan 'no change, no chance', polling showed that his putative leadership would cost the Tories up to sixty more seats than the beleaguered incumbent. The poll also found that the mood for disunity in the voluntary party was overstated, with some 90 per cent of association chairs backing Major.

Major did not get his heart's desire, but came in with 218 votes, while Redwood could only muster eighty-nine. Therefore Major got his outright majority plus 15 per cent surplus. Having comprehensively defeated his critics there was a temporary abatement of internal dissent. However, by January 1996, leadership speculation was again in full swing, not helped by an anti-EU speech by Thatcher.[41]

Triumph to Tragedy

John Major's unproblematic leadership re-election did nothing to change the fortunes of the Tories. The air of crisis, the miasma of diminished authority, the persistence of scandal and sleaze, and a fresh-looking Opposition committed to the standing settlement meant that the traditional Tory advantage in mobilising a vote via the press was diminished after the *Sun*, Britain's best-selling tabloid, switched allegiance to Tony Blair's Labour. *The Times*, the so-called paper of record and traditional Tory supporter, declared itself neutral, though it urged its readers to vote across the parties for Eurosceptic candidates.

As such, the 1997 Tory manifesto is more an exhausted than exhaustive document. It went heavy on what the party regarded as its achievements since 1979, but the proposals it offered for a further term amounted to more of the same. There was to be an extension of workfare for the unemployed, a pledge to push global tariff-free trade, ruling out the minimum wage and the social chapter, keeping taxes low and red tape to a minimum and other nuts-and-bolts policies designed to further bed down and tweak the settlements Major had consolidated.

Without anything eye-catching and huge polling deficits to make up, the Tories entered the 1997 campaign with their negative slogan 'New Labour, New Danger', with a pair of demon eyes glowering out of the darkness.[42] However, even under electoral pressure the Tories had difficulty affecting a united front. They were simultaneously menaced from the right by James Goldsmith's Referendum Party – a well-funded ginger group who recruited one Tory MP prior to Parliament's dissolution. If a Tory candidate were to declare themselves for a referendum on the UK's relation to the EU, Goldsmith's party would not stand against them and they would attract extra campaign funds from the pro-Thatcher property developer Paul Sykes. More disunity over a second-order issue did not reap the Tories any electoral dividends.

'A new dawn has broken, has it not?' noted Tony Blair in his victory speech on the morning of Friday 2 May. The Tories lost half their parliamentary party, shedding 171 seats and plunging to 165 on under 31 per cent of the popular vote. Labour returned 418 MPs on 43 per cent of votes cast (550,000 fewer than Major in 1992), awarding a majority of 179. The Tories returned no Scottish or Welsh seats for the first time in the party's history, were extinct as an urban party and held the distinction of plunging to the worst defeat of any governing party since 1832. The Tories had been utterly routed. Summing up the coming collapse, Ludlam and Smith remarked,

> by the mid-1990s, the Conservative Party had succeeded in drawing its main opponents on to its policy terrain, but was becoming less able to exploit its advantages. The bases of its electoral triumphs were visibly weakening, its membership and funding were falling alarmingly, and its reputation for unity in defence of the British state lay in tatters as it divided from top to bottom over Europe and national sovereignty.[43]

Likewise, Major noted,

> We should have been very popular. Economic buoyancy is the traditional recipe for political recovery. But it did not come in a climate in which there was no tolerance for our shortcomings [sic]. We had been in office, the public thought, for too long, and the accumulation of political debris over many years was a burden not even a strong economy could erase.[44]

Could the Tories have avoided what befell them in 1997? It is doubtful. Counterfactuals abound concerning the fate of Labour under John Smith had he lived, and yes, the double-digit poll leads were a fact of political life before Blair became leader. Blair himself proved an aggressive and wily opponent of the Tories in the Commons, while Major's party had inflicted mortal wound after mortal wound on its chances for re-election.

Was it because of Black Wednesday? Major had deftly weathered the poll tax, the Gulf War and the initial round of Maastricht negotiations, and won the 1992 general election with a record popular vote under circumstances the Tories had been widely expected to lose. It showed it is possible to successfully reinvent a party in government by a change of leadership, as Boris Johnson was to underline in 2019. However, while affecting a more consultative, one-nation style, Major entered government on Thatcherite terms and consolidated its approach to statecraft. In other words, the authority question remains central. Building on Thatcher's foundations, Major cleared out the inconvenient residues from the post-war social order and extended market principles further in education and health. His key policy, the Citizen's Charter, was easily his most significant contribution to post-Thatcher Thatcherism, and is often overlooked. It entailed a cultural counter-revolution, a sustained attack on collectivism, expertise and authorities within the state system that were independent of government. It made for a system in which government had a much freer hand over the decisions of different service sectors, while day-to-day operations were 'spontaneously' managed by the governance provided by the elaborate system of targets, penalties and incentives, and overall conditioned by pseudo-market competition.

Authoritarianism is brittle in the long run. In Major's instance, he reaffirmed the position of government as the central actor of decision making – an inescapable fact of Thatcherite politics regardless of efforts to depoliticise economic decision by technocratic frameworks of currency exchange management, or to take the politics out of public services delivery by competitive standards targets. Under Thatcher we saw how the poll tax and her refusal to countenance an alternative in the face of widespread hardship and opposition among the party destroyed her own authority, and it took a change of leadership and significant concessions to reverse it. With Major, in a moment of acute economic crisis the ejection from the ERM did the same for the authority of the party as a custodian of the state. This was compounded further by the follow-up attack on the remaining mining industry. Thatcherism established competency in the person of the prime minister as the key criterion by which neoliberal governments should be judged, and once that was stripped away and challenged from within the outcome was inevitable – a pattern we have seen repeated since.

This Thatcherite emphasis on the authority of the executive and, with it, the Conservative Party's chief instrument of pursuing its political objectives is key to understanding the preoccupation with Europe. If the executive's dominance is supreme within the state system, it was unconscionable to pool sovereignty with and concede ground to the European Union. Major tried mitigating this issue with his refusal to sign up to the social chapter, which also meant that UK employers could hold down wages and working conditions in the context of the single market and, they believed, gave them a competitive edge where foreign direct investment into the EU economic area was concerned. Yet it was not enough. The drip, drip of tabloid stories about interfering bureaucrats and absurd directives and the compromises Major made undermined his authority among a significant section of Tory MPs as a keeper of the Thatcherite flame. Therefore Euroscepticism and Thatcherism were fused and, in time, came to dominate the party.

The authoritarian dynamic within Thatcher's and Major's governments was the source of their strength and ultimate instability. However, what did this mean for the party's long-term decline? Between 1979 and 1992, the membership halved from 1.2 million to 600,000, and between 1992 and the next general election by a further 200,000.[45] One might be tempted to attribute this to the depoliticising consequences of Thatcherism. If the old corporatist structures were obstacles to realising aspiration, defined in terms of acquiring property and worldly goods, then with their dispersal by Thatcher and Major and the marketisation of services, what is the appeal of joining when there is nothing to crusade against?

Conservative associations themselves were not immune to the consequences of the Thatcherite programme. Considering mining, for example, the rapid pit closure programme stemming from the strike and the 1992 aftershock acted as a negative multiplier. Across the supply chain, businesses dependent on supplying the mines went to the wall. The loss of tens of thousands of jobs destroyed the economies of towns and villages centred on pitheads, liquidating thousands of small businesses ranging from news-agents and grocers to window cleaners, garages and hairdressers. The price of smashing the labour movement was the liquidation of sections of manufacturing and small capital, which might other-wise have supported the Tories.

There are the broader trends too. Mass consumption continued its individuating effects, accelerated by the expanding choice of home entertainment options and leisure opportunities. Unless politics directly impinged on one's life, as was the case with the poll tax, people were prepared for it to remain background noise. Hence why, despite organising a huge movement of non-payment that clogged up the courts and took to the streets, the trace it left on the political landscape was barely visible.

The politics of consumption did become a front that was able to mobilise a cohort of young people against the Tories in their attempts to shut down the free-party movement. And while the legislation was able to pass through the Commons without much trouble it foregrounded the next wave of problems that imperil the Tories over the medium to long term in the twenty-first century: the alienation of young people and their exclusion from property acquisition.

The economic balance sheet looked encouraging when Major left office, though it is worth remembering the boom he sought to take credit for had its origins in the abandonment of the ERM. On unemployment, when he took over from Thatcher it stood at 7.5 per cent, up from a low of 6.9 per cent in the first six months of 1990. Thereafter it accelerated until topping out at 10.7 per cent at the start of 1993 and then falling gradually until reaching 7.2 per cent when the Tories were defeated. Major also inherited a GDP of £292 billion in the last quarter of 1990, declining to £290 billion in the third quarter of 1991 before resuming its upward curve, reaching £337 billion in the second quarter of 1997.

Both Tory prime ministers presided over sharp recessions, and both left office with higher unemployment than had greeted them. The question is whether GDP might have been greater had neither pursued the policy orientations they did. It is a counterfactual that cannot be answered definitively, but it is worth noting that annual GDP growth across the 1980s and 1990s was lower than in the crisis-ridden 1970s.

Margaret Thatcher faced a labour movement with 13.2 million members, and left office with it reduced to 9.8 million members. This downward trend continued under Major, with 7.9 million trade unionists at the end of 1996. Working days consumed by strike action in 1979 were 29.5 million; in 1990 they were just 1.9 million. In the last full year of Major's government, they had fallen to 1.3 million, but this was something of a peak year – between 1991 and 1995 they did not rise above 761,000 and, in 1994, they fell as low as 278,000. Thatcher met her objective of taming the labour movement, and this was consolidated under Major with further repressive anti-trade union legislation.

On housing, in 1980 prices averaged at £22,600, and at the peak of the Thatcherite housing boom they had inflated by almost three times to £61,000. Because of the recession, for most of Major's years prices contracted, falling to and stabilising around the £51,000 mark. They resumed modest rises prior to his leaving office and accelerated thereafter to £247,000 in the first quarter of 2020, before falling back thanks to the coronavirus crisis. The prospect of negative equity, of holding a mortgage worth more than the value of the property it purchased, reinforced the 1990s house price squeeze as buyers were warned off. This presented the Tories with a problem.

If Thatcher's aim for a property-owning democracy was to pay off, the value of the asset needed to appreciate. If mortgage holders lost money, homeownership would not boost Tory voting. Therefore it is reasonable to assume the erosion of prices underpinned the collapse and continued antipathy the Tories faced after Black Wednesday. Unsurprisingly, with sales slowing, houses available for private purchase plunged after 1989, recovering slowly from 1993. Meanwhile, the right to buy slowed over the same period and council house building contracted to almost nothing, with housing associations taking up the development of social housing. The consequence of this meant that supply eventually could not meet demand, which spurred the house price recovery. What it also did was set the scene for the next cycle of growing Tory support as it began its long comeback following the election.

In sum, John Major's government consolidated Thatcherism with all its contradictions. It reaffirmed the primacy of the executive in the state system through a programme of centralisation and depoliticisation, abetted by the marketisation of services. The price, however, was the destruction of the party's authority. For all the non-interventionist laissez-faire framing of Thatcher and Major, theirs were activist governments who increasingly took on a voluntarist aspect. This meant that when their authority slipped it was next to impossible to salvage their position.

We can also discern the beginning of the next cycle of Tory rise and decline. Thatcher and Major's sale of public housing was calculated to generate new layers of Tory support, as well as discipline militancy through the lash of the mortgage and to provide new opportunities to the property interests comprising the core Tory support. By banning councils from making good the housing lost, they ensured that it was in strictly limited supply, which ultimately drove the house price explosion dating from the late 1990s.

Over time, younger people would be prevented from acquiring property, which in turn goes some way towards negating the conservatising consequences of age. Furthermore, policy-disadvantaging the young was made a structural feature of the social security system with the removal of eligibilities for students, the poll tax, successive youth training schemes that enabled employers to get away with poverty pay and a crime and justice agenda that particularly demonised and criminalised the young. The background was set for the generation wars characteristic of the next cycle of electoral success and government.

John Major, then, deserves to be rescued from the obscurity recent political history has cast his government into. It was pivotal for consolidating the Thatcher years, for putting the Tories on their subsequent trajectory of development and for largely developing the policy agenda that would come to be identified with New Labour and Blairism.

4

Into the Abyss

Following 1997, the Tories went on to convincingly lose two further general elections in 2001 and 2005. Given the huge majority the electorate awarded the Labour Party, as far as mainstream politics were concerned the Tories were simply irrelevant. They were not positioned to inflict defeats on the government's legislative programme and, even worse, as the Thatcherite settlement was co-opted by New Labour there were few opportunities to capture the public imagination. Therefore the Tory wilderness years prior to David Cameron were a time where they could indulge their hobby horses and did so with alacrity. For in opposition, formally opposed to a government that had adapted a great deal of their programme, the issue of Europe was practically the only issue on which they diverged from New Labour.

When Cameron was elected Tory leader, he expressed his frustration with the party's tendency to 'keep banging on about Europe'.[1] Indeed, this obsession, which contributed to the downfall of Major's government and overdetermined Tory positioning for the eight years following 1997, is treated by some, notably Tim Bale, as if it was irrational and detached from political realities.[2] This assumption is borne out neither by the place Europe occupies in the Thatcherite imagination, nor by what happens to political formations after experiencing a collective trauma.

For example, Bale notes the preponderance of a myth among Tory backbenchers of how the party lost because loyal supporters stayed home, thereby avoiding having to reckon with the millions of former voters who transferred their votes directly to Labour.

There was, however, rationality to this apparent irrationality. The emphasis on executive authority under Thatcher and Major, which was left untouched by Blair, lends itself to sovereigntist criticisms of the European Union. If government is supreme in the state system, then decisions and rules issued by Brussels would at best sit uneasily in this set-up. Encouraged by the anti-EU commentary pouring incessantly from right-wing editorial offices, assuming that newspaper coverage reflects (rather than moulds) political opinion outside Westminster, under these circumstances pushing sovereigntist politics makes sense.

Second, 'banging on about Europe' differentiates one from one's opponents (regardless of its political efficacy), but also works to cohere ideologically a shattered party and an interested electorate. With irrelevance staring the party in the face for a period, how else could it keep itself together as a going concern? From a rational-choice point of view this is poor for vote chasing, but essential for survival. The problem, however, is that this was not the foundation of a bridge back to government.

During this period Thatcher became a caricature of what she once was, but she once understood the politics of coalition building and the necessity of using policy to cohere a voting bloc capable of gaining the Tories a majority. The party's three leaders during this period – William Hague, Iain Duncan Smith and Michael Howard – were blessed by neither the circumstances, the wit nor the strategy to move on from the politics of trauma. As a result, the interregnum period of 1997–2005 was blighted by a tendency to fetishise their own irrelevance; by weak attempts to 'modernise' the party, particularly around leadership elections; by political inconsistency; by internal warfare; and by a lack of purchase outside its ranks save for a few bright moments. At the same time, they were only able to react to Tony Blair's New Labour without making any serious opposition, as both sides were effectively pursuing the same policy objectives. In their own ways the three leaders kept the party on life support and allowed a new generation to pass through its portals and on to leadership. Therefore 1997–2005 might appear time wasted by a party content in its own delusions, but it provided the personnel and motivation for a new cohort of MPs to come to the fore and (partially) remake the party in their image.

William Hague

On the morning of 2 May 1997, Major resigned as Conservative Party leader before resigning as prime minister at Buckingham Palace. This sparked a leadership election consisting of five candidates – Michael Howard, John Redwood, Peter Lilley, Ken Clarke and William Hague. Of the contestants, Hague was the freshest face, having recently been promoted to the Cabinet as Welsh secretary to fill the vacancy left by Redwood after challenging Major in 1995. Hague had briefly tasted prominence before as a sixteen-year-old lambasting Labour from the party podium at the 1977 conference, somewhat artfully telling the assembled that half of them 'won't be here in thirty or forty years' time'.[3] Entering the Commons in 1989 at the Richmond by-election, he worked first as an assistant to Norman Lamont. Within the year he was moved to the Department of Social Security, before holding the brief for disabled people and then the Welsh Office following Redwood's implosion.

Like Thatcher and Major, Hague hailed from a petit bourgeois background. He was educated in the state system before heading to Oxford. Entering the leadership contest, Hague took a leaf out of Blair's book and styled himself the 'modernising' candidate and wanted a party fit for the twenty-first century. Commenting on the efforts of the other challengers, Bale notes how Smith and Redwood used the contest to raise their profile, Clarke did not take campaign organisation seriously and Howard was wounded both by his lack-lustre performance as home secretary and his being memorably described by his former subordinate Anne Widdecombe as having 'something of the night about him'.[4] What characterised all these pitches for Bale was a lack of diagnosis about why the Tories lost, and of a strategy for challenging New Labour. Considering the shattering defeat and collapse of party morale, this was not too surprising.

Hague won on the third round by ninety-three votes to seventy versus Ken Clarke. In his first significant speech as leader, Hague unveiled his vision for the party based around six loosely defined principles: unity, decentralisation, democracy, involvement, integrity and openness. Archie Norman, the newly elected member for Tunbridge Wells and a former colleague of Hague's, was charged with advising on party reform and, interestingly, when the proposals surfaced in the autumn they sought to bring the trappings of consumerism into party structures; voters were to be seen as 'consumers' and members/campaigners as 'sales staff'.[5]

The problems with imposing these assumptions on a voluntary party were not considered, but in sum moved the party's internal regime more towards a managed democracy. On the vexed question of leadership, the Alec Douglas-Home reforms were replaced by a trigger system in which MPs could force a no-confidence vote if 15 per cent wrote to the chair of the 1922 Committee. There would then be a confidence vote based on a simple majority. Second, a postal ballot of the membership was introduced. They would get to pick between two candidates determined by the parliamentary party after several voting rounds as per received tradition. For example, had these rules applied to the 1997 contest, Hague and Clarke would have gone before the members.

The introduction of limited democracy and Hague's fluffy language masked a power grab in which a new Party Board united the three arms of the party's organisation – the parliamentary party, the professional apparat and the voluntary party organised by the National Union. In practice this enshrined the authority of the leader's office and formalised the power of (unelected) officials over independent-minded Tory associations.

Politically it enshrined principles around parliamentary, European and Holyrood and Cardiff candidate selection. While association members each had one vote to endorse candidates in selection ballots, prospective parliamentarians had to appear on an approved list determined by the apparat, which gave officials scope to weed out undesirables. Financially, the decline in membership under Thatcher and Major and the defection of several high-net-worth donors to Labour meant that the party was broke. The party had a £4-million debt and was looking at a £6-million deficit. Therefore centralising the party meant that CCHQ could, theoretically, begin raiding the cash-rich associations.

Despite threatening the organisational independence of the activists, these reforms, now rebadged as Fresh Future, went to the membership in February 1998 and were endorsed by 96 per cent of voting members on a 33-per-cent turnout. Nevertheless, there was some unhappiness. There was upset over plans for a Conservative Women's Network, and thanks to pressure from below plans to introduce all-women shortlists for a quarter of selections were dropped.[6] The limited democracy of the party leader ballot evidently trumped other considerations, however. Sadly for the party's bank balance, a windfall from raiding the associations was not forthcoming but the appointment of Michael Ashcroft as Tory treasurer did stymie the cash crisis. This was by a combination of personal donations (he began donating £1 million/year), increasing the number of donors handing over more than £5,000 a year from thirty-three to 126 by 1999–2000, and, in that final year, had managed to put the Tories back into the black.

While the Tories were reforming, Labour was introducing its agenda piecemeal. In May 1996, Major's government had set up the Dearing review into higher-education funding, which was due to report back the following summer. Arguing that universities needed extra funds to drive the next wave of expansion, the committee made several recommendations. Labour's preference was for an upfront fee made payable by students of up to £1,000 a year (with means-tested concessions) and the replacement of the grant by a loan that would later become repayable once a salary threshold had been crossed.

Considering the thrust of Tory policy in education in the previous twenty years, in his first conference speech as Tory leader in October Hague attacked Labour for introducing 'a system of student fees which will hit the poorest families hardest'.[7] Opposition couched in such terms rang hollow. The other key political initiative of Blair's first summer was referenda on Scottish and Welsh devolution. The Tories campaigned for the status quo but lost as both were passed with majority votes, albeit in the case of Wales by the narrowest of margins.

Further efforts at getting Hague noticed by the public bombed spectacularly. These photo opportunities included an unconvincing ride on a log flume wearing a baseball cap with the legend 'Hague' splashed across it. Hague was also entirely sidelined as Tony Blair affected, successfully, to speak for the nation on Princess Diana's death.

The cumulative consequence was a resounding irrelevance, which was underlined by the spectacular defeat at the Winchester by-election in November. Originally won by the Liberal Democrats at the election with a majority of two votes, a successful legal challenge meant it had to be rerun. Hague's party spectacularly turned a minuscule margin into a 21,556 deficit, aided by a collapse in the Tory vote and a mass transfer of previous Labour voters. Not the most auspicious of beginnings for a new leader.

Hague's problems were compounded by Tory opposition to popular policies. For example, Labour's pledge to implement a windfall tax on the privatised utilities to tackle youth unemployment was opposed by Hague on the ground that it would raise energy bills.[8] In the event, gas bills remained flat until the second quarter of 2002 and electricity until the second quarter of 2003. Similarly, like his predecessor Hague railed against the minimum wage and opposed the legislation when it came before the Commons. Despite the warnings of job cuts to meet the pay floor, within a month of coming into force Hague was considering dropping party opposition to it, with some suggestion of using the issue to force the resignation of Redwood, then holding the Trade and Industry brief, from the Shadow Cabinet.[9]

Hague's leadership was also menaced by Michael Portillo, one of the heirs-presumptive in the Major years who was, however, removed from contention when Labour memorably took his Enfield Southgate seat in 1997. He was not out of the Commons for long and was returned as the member for Kensington and Chelsea following the sudden death of Alan Clark. Therefore Hague retreated from previous positions, above all the minimum wage, to ensure that Portillo could not cohere support behind a policy-based critique of Hague's leadership, and promoted him to shadow chancellor.

The return of Portillo affected another significant policy change. With Labour's commitment to Tory spending plans for the first two years of office all the party could do was argue for further tax cuts and challenge Gordon Brown on an alleged taste for indirect taxation – ironic considering the alacrity with which it used VAT in office.[10] In early 1999, under the advice of Shadow Chancellor Francis Maude, Hague announced plans to reduce taxation as a proportion of GDP every year of the next Conservative government – a position that would be unworkable if tax revenues collapsed during a recession. This 'tax guarantee' disappeared with Portillo's appointment, but was to resurface again in the 2001 manifesto.

There was one bright spot for the Tories. At their 1997 conference, Hague apologised for the mishandling of Black Wednesday, and committed the Tories to opposing a European single currency for the lifetime of that parliament. It did attract criticism from grandees like Clarke and Heseltine, but already at this point their pro-EU politics put them out of sorts with the remainder of the party. Hague's Shadow Cabinet in all its incarnations tilted to Euroscepticism, and he was not afraid to repeatedly burnish these credentials. For example, at a speech the following May at INSEAD Business School in Fontainebleau, he said,

There is a limit to European political integration. We are near that limit now. I intend to make three arguments. The first is economic. The European policies that were a natural response to the problem of post-war reconstruction are not necessarily appropriate for the future. In place of the ideas of intervention and regulation we need to create a free and flexible Europe. My second argument is strategic. The fall of the Berlin Wall has completely changed the challenge facing European states. Bringing prosperity and stability to newly freed states is now the most urgent of Europe's tasks. And the third argument is political. Push political integration too far and accountability and democracy become impossible to sustain.[11]

Unexpectedly, this positioning in the immediate term proved something of a boon to the Tories. The 1998 local elections saw the Tories enjoy a net gain of 256 councillors and one local authority, though six points behind Labour in popular-vote terms. This could be interpreted as a stabilisation of their position, if not the beginnings of the path to recovery. However, 1999 appeared to suggest that Europe might indeed be the wedge issue the Tories needed. In the local elections the Tory vote crept up two points to 34 per cent, only two behind Labour, but, more significantly, they were able to gain 1,348 councillors and forty-eight local authorities while Labour lost 1,150 councillors and the control of thirty-five (while gaining three). Commenting on the votes, Bale notes that these had more to do with 'natural' seats returning to the Tories than with any wave of popular enthusiasm or discontent with Blair.

This prefaced the year's European Union elections. Standing on an explicitly anti-euro, Brussels-bashing manifesto, the Conservatives won their first national election since 1992, winning 33.5 per cent of the popular vote versus Labour's 26.3 per cent.[12] This gave them thirty-six MEPs versus 1994's eighteen, while Labour tumbled thirty-three seats to twenty-nine MEPs. This was also the year the United Kingdom Independence Party made its electoral breakthrough, scooping up a seat each in the South West, the South East and East Anglia. Turnout, however, was just 24 per cent. A post-election press conference confirmed the popularity of the defence of the pound in the Tory imaginary and guaranteed that it became the centre of their coming general election campaign. For Labour politicians, the defeat was less a verdict on the government and more one of Labour support staying at home, a lacklustre campaign and a lack of decisiveness over the single currency.[13]

At the party conference that October, Hague had decided that New Labour had won its majority on the basis of adopting

Conservative policies, and so he committed the party to reclaiming the ground lost.[14] Styling the new strategy the 'Common Sense Revolution', emulating the rhetoric of the Continental populist right he railed against 'the patronising elite who think it's intolerant to be tough on law and order and the progressive intellectuals who think that caring is spending other people's money'.

This was backed up with a personal attack on Blair, whose efforts at being all things to all people were roundly mocked.

'Tony's favourite food is fish and chips. He gets a takeaway from his local chippie whenever he is at home in his constituency'; but when *The Islington Cookbook* asked him the same question, he said his favourite food was: 'fresh fettucini garnished with an exotic sauce of olive oil, sun-dried tomatoes and capers.'[15]

This was to evolve into a two-pronged strategy: one within the conventional boundaries of parliamentary politics and the other outside it.

At conference, Hague drew on his response to the MacPherson report that explained the failure of the Metropolitan Police to properly investigate the murder of black teenager Stephen Lawrence in 1993 thanks to institutional racism to argue that we needed 'more PCs, and less PC', and jumped on the press bandwagon in support of Tony Martin – a farmer sentenced to life for shooting a burglar, despite Martin having been repeatedly targeted for break-ins.

On social issues, only sixteen Tory MPs voted for the equalisation of the age of consent for sex between men and opposed Labour's efforts at repealing Section 28. As the repeal was introduced as a bill in the Lords, the Tories applied a three-line whip against it and delayed its rescinder until September 2003. The Tories placed a considerable stress on the traditional family and the importance of marriage and used Labour's abolition of the married couples' tax allowance to claim that this was an attack on the family and the tried-and-tested underpinnings of a stable society.

On social security matters, as Labour had largely accepted the Thatcher–Major framing of welfare and had introduced its own workfare programme under the New Deal badge, the only place left for Hague to go was further to the right. The Tories made acceptance of any job mandatory on pain of losing subsequent unemployment support and tying into the families' agenda a new set of conditionalities targeting unemployed single parents once their child reached eleven years of age. On support for older people, an opportunity was missed to criticise Labour on derisory rises in state pension payments and instead the Tories' attention was focused on Christmas bonuses, the introduction of the winter fuel allowance, and free television licences for the over-seventy-fives on the ground that they were manifestations of the nanny state. Lastly, a persistent press campaign around 'bogus asylum seekers' allowed the Tories to retreat into a comfort zone of immigration-bashing and the pushing of several authoritarian pledges, such as the incarceration of all applicants while their claim is looked at.[16]

There were extra-parliamentary opportunities too. In 1993, John Major introduced the fuel price escalator with the ostensible objective of cutting car use and meeting emissions reduction targets. By 2000, the escalator made up 81.5 per cent of the cost of petrol, at which point Labour scrapped it and allowed prices to rise in line with inflation. The problem was oil prices per barrel had almost doubled within the space of a year. Sensing an opportunity, the Tories declared a July day of action on fuel prices with petitioning and leafleting, which prefaced a non-party-political protest action the following week. Commenting, Shadow Transport Secretary Bernard Jenkin said, 'The government has seriously underestimated people's feelings about this.'[17]

On 8 September a group of protesters blockaded the Stanlow Refinery near Ellesmere Port, with pickets spreading to several others. By 11 September, six refineries and four oil depots were blocked, and petrol rationing and panic buying were common sights at garage forecourts. On 12 September some 3,000 stations were forced to close due to the lack of deliveries, and the following day panic buying spread to food items. However, on 14 September the protesters started calling off their actions but warned the government they would resume if there was no change in policy.[18]

The government indeed refused to move. Hague tried capital-ising on this by calling on the protesters to stop their action and join a Tory-led 'taxpayers' revolt' against Labour – a call some-what blunted by his refusal to promise cuts to tax on fuel.[19] But the polling effect was catastrophic for Labour. Its customary double-digit lead evaporated as one subsequent poll but both parties level on 37 per cent, and a second the Tories ahead on 38 per cent to Labour's 36 per cent.[20]

What also prevented the Tories from exploiting the issue success-fully was a behind-the-scenes tussle in the Shadow Cabinet between Portillo and his supporters and the rest. Initially the Conservatives wanted to announce a 5p cut in fuel duty, which was vetoed and then reinstated, and then there was a row over who was to make it public, with Portillo insisting he take the press conference alone.[21] Hardly the 'ready to govern' countenance they wanted to telegraph at the party's annual gathering, which also happened to be that year's conference slogan. As such, the interregnum of polling leads passed and by the end of September Labour was posting modest leads, which later accelerated towards the general election – despite the outbreak of the devastating foot-and-mouth crisis in early 2001, which at its peak saw 93,000 animals a week slaughtered.[22]

The Conservative Party manifesto reiterated the pledges made over the previous two years while showing scant sign of capitalis-ing on Labour's woes. Titled *Time for Common Sense*, there was little here that would not have featured in 1997. Tax cuts, strength-ening the family, linking standards in public service to choice, tough on crime, more money for the NHS (but removing taxes on private medical insurance), increasing the state pension, opposition to more powers for Brussels ('In Europe, not run by Europe') and, of course, keeping the pound. Indeed, as election day approached Hague's rhetoric became more hysterical, arguing two weeks before polling that parliamentary democracy was threatened and Tony Blair planned to start the ball rolling on joining the euro within days of a return to office.[23]

It was to no avail. The Tory vote plunged by 1.3 million on the lowest turnout for a general election since 1918 with a net gain of one seat. A consolation was winning the newly formed Scottish seat of Dumfriesshire, Clydesdale and Tweeddale and restoring a token presence north of the border. By contrast, Labour experienced a net loss of six seats but enjoyed a nine-point margin over its rivals. Worryingly for the Tories, the Liberal Democrats continued to eat into their support and won seven seats from them, contrary to the Eurosceptic positioning designed to shore up the Tory vote. The following day Hague announced his resignation pending the election of a new leader.

The flatlining of electoral performance demonstrated the extent to which a core vote strategy could reach. Whatever the merits (or otherwise) of running a campaign that did not depart from previous messaging, the Tories could choose to believe that their peccadilloes were shared with the electorate at large. The Tory press, whose sway and opinion-forming weight was approaching its peak, were overwhelmingly authoritarian and Eurosceptic. Mistaking editorial output as reflecting existing attitudes among their readerships, a logical case could be made for banging on about the pound and appearing tough.

For example, despite switching to Labour and supporting it since 1997, The Sun's positions on a range of issues had not changed. Blair had moved his party towards it rather than there being any appreciable tack to the left on the paper's part. Hence, from a Tory point of view, appearing even tougher on Europe, tax, social security etc. might be enough to win back some of these voters. Second, the memory of the European Union elections in 1999 could be, and indeed was, read as a popular rejection of the euro and other federalist schemes – the Tories might be able to break Labour's logjam in Westminster if it moved up the political agenda. And third, the rapid collapse of the government's polling position during the fuel protests was illustrative of a certain softness in its leads.

Therefore it was mistaken but reasonable to assume that a restatement of traditional Tory pledges on tax might tap into widespread disquiet. Unfortunately for the party, however rational these positionings presented themselves in the Tory imaginary, they were illusory. Rather than seeing the EU elections and the protests as a blip, which the strong polling the government enjoyed after both these events suggested, party strategists chose to discount political realities and assume they would cut through somehow. This was underlined by the Tory response to the foot-and-mouth outbreak. While utterly devastating to British farming, given the size of the section given over to the crisis in the manifesto they clearly expected it to be more of an issue than it proved to be.

The Tories, then, were lost. Buffeted by political realities and unable to divine an election-winning strategy, a catastrophic second election reaffirmed their status as the B team of British politics and, as the next leader was to show, they appeared content with this status.

Iain Duncan Smith

The new leadership election had Michael Portillo as the favourite from the outset. Long a favoured son of the right with impeccable Eurosceptic credentials, he looked as though he would carry all before him. Again, Ken Clarke threw his hat in the ring, as did Iain Duncan Smith, the recent chairman of the party Michael Ancram and backbencher David Davis. In the first round Portillo came out top, as commentators had forecast, but only with forty-nine votes – just shy of 30 per cent of the parliamentary party. Duncan Smith was second on thirty-nine, Clarke on thirty-six, and Ancram and Davis tied on twenty-one. To determine the elimination, both bottom-placed candidates ran again in the second ballot, this time securing seventeen and eighteen votes respectively. Ancram therefore was eliminated and Davis concluded it was prudent to withdraw.

Meanwhile, Duncan Smith and Clarke had upped their tally by three and Portillo by one. In the third ballot, Portillo was unexpectedly eliminated. He polled fifty-three votes to Duncan Smith's fifty-four and Clarke's fifty-nine. Therefore, under the new rules, these two would be put to the membership. According to Bale, the presumptive heir was a victim of tactical voting by MPs who could not countenance his social liberalism – nor his admittance of several flings with men when he was younger.[24] As the proportion of Conservative MPs with socially liberal values had shrunk by almost two-thirds since 1992, a homophobic whispering campaign would certainly have swayed votes.[25]

There were also wider considerations in play. Knowing their associations, MPs were incentivised to vote for the most Eurosceptic of candidates. This was underlined by an ICM poll of members during the contest, 86 per cent of whom said Europe was an important factor determining their vote. On Clarke versus Duncan Smith, 58 per cent thought the former would split the party and just over half believed he could lead the party to an election win. For Duncan Smith, the respective figures were 18 per cent and 75 per cent(!). Unsurprisingly, Duncan Smith was able to romp home with a 61–39 win on a 79 per cent turnout. Given the 256,797 ballots cast, this suggests that the party membership had shrunk further to around 325,000.

Who was Iain Duncan Smith? The son of a Second World War fighter ace with nineteen kills to his name, he pursued an undistinguished military career after attending Sandhurst and had tours in Northern Ireland and (then) Rhodesia before retiring in 1981. He then spent seven years at Marconi, followed by stints at a property company prior to the house price crash of the late 1980s, and was then a sales and marketing director at Jane's Information Group.[26]

Given Duncan Smith's behaviour during the Major years as a newcomer who would rebel over European issues, he might, in turn, appeal to the baser instincts of the Tory faithful. Indeed, during the leadership contest it turned out that the vice chair of his campaign, Edgar Griffin, was the father of the then leader of the British National Party, Nick Griffin. He had also assisted BNP campaigning and had views less in tune with the anti-racist image Duncan Smith wished to project.[27] It was not long before the new rules brought in by Hague were used to expel Griffin from the party. This, however, was too much of a coincidence for some and Portillo and Clarke ruled themselves out of serving in his Shadow Cabinet.

Duncan Smith's election was immediately overshadowed by world affairs. The announcement of the contest's victor was slated for 11 September, and so was put back two days as a mark of respect for those killed in the attacks on the World Trade Center and the Pentagon. The party then decided to scale back the Tory Party conference. Therefore Duncan Smith's first appearance as party leader in Blackpool saw him give the briefest of speeches before hurrying back to London for the latest statement to the Commons about the US–UK bombing campaign taking place over Afghanistan. Most MPs and the Shadow Cabinet were in London already for the emergency statement and so, crisis or no, having most of the top team away was not congenial to a successful launch.

To stamp his authority, Duncan Smith moved quickly to burnish his socially liberal credentials. This meant forcing three MPs – Andrew Hunter, Angela Watkinson and Andrew Rosindell – to resign from the ultra-right-wing Monday Club. Other well-publicised contributions to conference also saw Michael Howard, now shadow chancellor, affect a concern for public services with a pledge to put tax cuts on the backburner and prioritising extra funding. However, the schemes Duncan Smith proffered in his first leader's interview emphasised voucher schemes and insurance, hardly a break with Thatcherism.

This concern for public services rang hollow. Shadow health spokesperson Liam Fox characterised the NHS as being responsible for 'serfdom' in health matters, which was later backed up by the leader himself, who likened all public services to 'Soviet-style command-and-control organisation' and refused to rule out introducing charges for visiting a GP.[28] Largely unnoticed, Duncan Smith sought to carry on with this theme, re-embedding these schemes in a critique of top-down welfare and emphasising the importance of caring for the vulnerable – an attempt to recapture some of the patrician ground the Thatcher years had dispensed with. This was undermined by further unwelcome comments from Fox. In a clandestine recording, he was shown arguing for the replacement of the NHS by a health insurance system and outlining a four-step strategy of getting there. Not helpful if one was retreating from Thatcherism, nor if a new leader's first election test was imminent.

The May 2002 local elections did not suggest a great deal. Labour's popular vote rose 2 per cent on the previous year, despite the stirrings of Iraq-related rebellion among its ranks, while the Tories were down six points on 2001 – a year that was good for them as local politics went thanks to the number of shire counties contested. Labour lost 334 councillors and a net seven councils, while the Tories picked up an additional 238 seats and nine local authorities on a 35 per cent turnout.

As the Tories entered the summer, grumbles were afoot in the parliamentary party. With the war clouds gathering and nothing distinctive to say apart from the usual fare on Europe, the party lapsed into introversion. In July, Duncan Smith reshuffled the Shadow Cabinet, moving David Davis from the party chair and replacing him with Theresa May, ostensibly proof of how much the party was embracing diversity. Likewise, to try and get noticed he jumped to the defence of Tony Blair, making it clear he would be happy to provide Tory support for military action when Iraq came before the Commons.[29]

September also afforded him the opportunity to flirt with extra-parliamentary activism as per Hague and the fuel protests. On 22 September around 400,000 protesters marched through central London. Organised by big farmers and the landed gentry under the banner of the Countryside Alliance, the demonstration was precipitated by Labour's hesitant steps to ban fox hunting with hounds – a pastime symbolising aristocratic entitlement to land, given their propensity to roam freely in pursuit of their vulpine quarry. This prefaced a rural rebellion against an urbanite Labour Party that did not understand and was not terribly interested in countryside affairs, and in fact would rather have their way of life buried.[30] Duncan Smith made sure he was present. However, if

anything, the Countryside Alliance mobilisation was a symptom
of Tory weakness. Utterly sidelined by its minuscule parliamentary
representation and the dominance of New Labour, in effect the
concerns the Tories traditionally articulated were excluded from
mainstream politics. Especially so considering that the Tory majority in the House of Lords had been slashed following the ejection
of most of its hereditary peers in 1999.

As such, matters were not going according to plan. On polling for
best prime minister, Duncan Smith had fallen behind Charles
Kennedy of the Liberal Democrats, who was benefiting from opposition to the war drive. More damning was polling undertaken by
the *Daily Mail* that found 44 per cent of association chairs believed
their leader was not a success, and 30 per cent wanted him to resign.
A survey carried out by the *Daily Telegraph* of conference attendees
found that 86 per cent did not believe the party was ready for power,
and 70 per cent thought that the affectation of compassionate
conservatism was implausible. The sense of gloom was compounded
by May's speech as the party chair, which ruffled feathers and upset
the 1922 Committee. Reflecting on the efforts made by Duncan
Smith to move the Tories in a detoxified direction, she said,

> Yes, we've made progress, but let's not kid ourselves. There's a way
> to go before we can return to government. There's a lot we need to
> do in this party of ours. Our base is too narrow and so, occasion-
> ally, are our sympathies. You know what some people call us: the
> nasty party.[31]

May attacked unnamed politicians in the party who had 'behaved
disgracefully', and those making 'political capital out of demonis-
ing minorities', warning against 'petty feuding and sniping' and
urging the party to get behind Duncan Smith. It was all very well
sounding a note for inclusion, but another thing to put it into practice. The big policy reveal was a plan to reimburse older patients
who had used private healthcare to jump queues for operations,
which again did not sit terribly well with the social justice affectation the Tories were keen to promote.

More internal controversy and flat policy were not welcome portents, and yet Duncan Smith's speech was reasonably well received. Then BBC political correspondent Andrew Marr commented that the Tories had 'allowed themselves an eruption of self-belief', and the *Sun*'s George Pascoe-Watson (positively) noted that it was a defining moment for the Tory leader. Famous now for the line 'do not underestimate the determination of a quiet man', he reiterated his party's commitment to compassionate conservatism and attacked Labour for making the lot of the poor worse. The party, he said, had learned the lessons of 1997: 'This will be remembered as the week when the Conservatives began the slow, hard road back to power.'[32]

There was a hard road, but one paved with more division and rebellion. Less than a month after conference, the government brought the Children and Adoptions bill to the Commons. The provisions were a test for the Tories' socially liberal credentials as it proposed that same-sex and unmarried couples should gain the right to adopt children. Preceded by more speculation in the press by anonymous sources over his future, Duncan Smith attempted to restore his authority by applying a three-line whip to vote against the bill's provisions. This prompted the resignation of John Bercow, then shadow for work and pensions, and the rebellion of other key Tory moderates like Clarke and, following a well-publicised Damascene conversion to liberal conservatism, Portillo. In all, forty-three MPs defied the whip by staying away or voting with the government, including serving Shadow Cabinet members Tim Yeo and Damian Green.[33]

More was to come. Upon assuming office, Duncan Smith left Hague's internal reforms intact, apart from moving the leader's office back to the Commons from Central Office. In general, during the leadership campaign he presented himself as respectful of association autonomy. However, his crisis of authority in the parliamentary party began moving through the wider party itself. He was prevented from getting his preferred candidate, the former Westminster Tory councillor Nikki Smith, selected as Tory candidate for London mayor. He blamed the party chief executive Mark

McGregor and forced him to resign.[34] This antagonised the party board, which was infuriated further when Duncan Smith appointed former MP Barry Legg to the role. In a public row the board rescinded the appointment and Legg resigned three months later, taking £160,000 in severance.[35]

Following the fiasco, the only thing preventing the letters from going into the 1922 Committee was local election performance. Labour fell to 30 per cent of the popular vote following the invasion of Iraq – the same percentage as the Liberal Democrats. The Tories gained 566 seats and thirty-one councils on 35 per cent of the vote. For the Welsh Assembly the Tory vote was up by four points on 20 per cent and they gained two seats, while they stayed static with eighteen seats and 16.6 per cent of the vote in Holyrood. Opposition to the Iraq adventure there crystallised in the Greens and the Scottish Socialist Party, who gained six and five seats respectively.

The polling position, however, improved. In June and July the party posted modest poll leads, which were seen less as a reaction to the war and its fallout and more as a vindication of the Eurosceptic territory Duncan Smith had occupied; he pledged a referendum on the single currency and the mooted Lisbon Treaty.[36] However, the customary poll lead was resumed by Labour that August and the knives were once again out for the Tory leader.

In June, the Labour member for Brent East, Paul Daisley, died and a by-election was called for 18 September – just before party conference season. In a display reminiscent of the triumphs of the Tory years in office, the Liberal Democrats overturned a 13,000 majority to take the seat off the back of anti-Iraq War feeling. Unsurprisingly, given their support for Blair the Tories failed to make any headway and in fact fell back in the seat. This set the scene for a chaotic conference, one in which Duncan Smith warned his critics to 'get out of our way' and memorably said, 'the quiet man is here to stay and he's turning up the volume'.[37] Less than a month later he was gone.

The final straw was news that Duncan Smith employed his wife as a diary secretary, sparking an investigation by parliamentary standards amid allegations this was more a grace and favour than a working appointment (the investigation later cleared him). It became clear to Tory MPs that the bullet had to be bitten. On 28 October Michael Spicer, chair of the 1922 Committee, had received the requisite number of no-confidence letters – twenty-five – and announced a confidence vote the following day. Despite defiant language the parliamentary party decided Duncan Smith could not continue, and he lost the vote ninety against and seventy-five for. And so his leadership came to its ignominious stop.

Duncan Smith's tenure was calamitous for sure, but not catastrophic. The advances it made in the elections under his watch were modest and owed more to the depression of the Labour vote thanks to the Iraq War than to popular enthusiasm for the Tories. The problem was an incapacity to quieten dissent and the outbreaks of infighting, and indeed Duncan Smith stirred it up through his own incoherent leadership. On the one hand he wanted to go beyond Thatcherism and social conservativism by affecting a care for the poor – a theme later returned to as the work and pensions minister – and move more towards liberal tolerance on inequalities. His actual positioning, however, consistently undermined this strategy.

Vouchers, insurance and markets were his supposed non-Thatcherite solutions to matters of social security. Thinking aloud about charging patients for visiting doctors and more NHS markets would have excited few outside Britain's private medicine industry there was no clamour among the public, the membership or the parliamentary party itself.

On social liberalism, the seriousness with which it was embraced was exposed as thin by his positioning on the adoption bill. This owed more to his being a prisoner of his own party. He could have chosen to take them on but, given the declining salience of social liberalism among MPs, such a confrontation was unlikely to do his leadership much good. This, however, was to have lasting consequences. It meant that when the social liberal turn came under David Cameron it could only be superficial. It also underlined the notion that the Tories were out of step with wider culture, which was progressively solidified by Labour legislation equalising the age of consent, introducing civil partnerships for same-sex couples, and efforts at tackling institutionalised forms of discrimination. It reinforced the Tories as an out-of-touch party ill at ease with modern Britain – and one obsessed with Europe.

Nevertheless, there was a kernel of sense, a reflex of realism in Duncan Smith's aim of a post-Thatcherism with one-nation characteristics, but he proved too erratic for the consistent push required. Unable to capitalise on the Iraq War debacle, unable to effectively oppose Labour on the key issues of the day and unable to mobilise discontent, Duncan Smith gifted a party to his successor that looked as far away from government as it had done on 3 May 1997.

Michael Howard

Poor decision making and a recalcitrant party did for Duncan Smith, but what enabled his exit was the presence of a clear alternative. Michael Howard entered Parliament in 1983 and held office under Thatcher and Major, topping out as home secretary in 1993. He was partially responsible for the poll tax while he held the local government brief, organised the privatisation of the water companies and was the prime mover behind the authoritarian Criminal Justice Act. For a party wedded to social conservatism, there could hardly be a more suitable choice.

Howard, like Hague before him but unlike Duncan Smith, was a skilled and fluent performer at the despatch box and earned press and backbench plaudits facing Gordon Brown serving as shadow chancellor under Duncan Smith. Additionally, what recommended Howard was distance from previous controversies. Considered a Eurosceptic and a traditionalist, he escaped definition as a factional exponent of either trend. He also possessed a relatively compelling backstory equal to Thatcher's and Major's. His parents were Jewish refugees from Romania who settled in South Wales in the 1930s and ran a clothes shop. Howard himself went through grammar school before heading off to Oxford, a career in law and continuous involvement with the Tory Party before finally winding up an MP.

At the 2003 Conservative conference Howard raised a few eyebrows by indulging a tradition reserved for the leader. Following what was clearly a leader-in-waiting speech, it was perhaps appropriate that he should be joined on the stage by Sandra Howard, his wife. Therefore, when the contest came it was no contest at all. Previous candidates like David Davis, Tim Yeo and Ken Clarke ruled themselves out of contention, while others like Michael Portillo explicitly endorsed him. A round robin letter from eighty-nine MPs registered their support for Howard's candidacy, which made any challenge to the clear frontrunner look like a fool's errand.[38] Officially launching his leadership bid on 30 October, he re-emphasised the need for the Tories to become the party of 'all Britain and all Britons' and pledged to lead it from the centre. The moment also called for a 'new kind of politics' that did not greet Labour failure with 'gleeful pleasure'.[39]

With no other candidates coming forward, a week later the 1922 Committee declared Howard the new leader and dispensed with the need for a membership ballot. It was fitting that a traditionalist be 'elected' in the manner Douglas-Home won the leadership. The attempt to form an opposition of all the talents, however, faltered with Hague, Portillo and Clarke refusing to serve in his Shadow Cabinet. Also, in a sign that might have suggested a shift away from social liberalism, he dispensed with Theresa May's 'truth-telling' services and gave her the environment and transport brief. She was replaced by Liam Fox and Maurice Saatchi, who were interested in curbing lay member influence.

Their proposals were guided by an elite suspicion of the grass roots, with the Duncan Smith interlude helping form the view that the Tory faithful could not be trusted to exercise the requisite judgement. A set of standards and obligations were imposed on candidates selected by members, which included regular updates of their activities and attending compulsory training sessions organised by Central Office. To make the party less dependent on association whims when it came to campaigning, ad hoc squads were set up to bypass their structures to mobilise activists for campaigns. Howard made several behind-the-scenes appointments – one curio was an unofficial committee comprising his three predecessors in the job, plus Clarke. Other, more significant, appointments were the promotions of David Cameron and George Osborne as his preppers for Prime Minister's Questions. And an early sign of success was the recovery of the party's financial position – the big donors started returning after a series of assured Commons performances – 94 per cent of the quarter's donations poured in after Duncan Smith's defenestration.[40]

Come the New Year, the polling position had improved. Instead of a consistent Labour advantage, poll leads swung back and forth. For instance, one poll reported a deficit of five points and another a lead of five points. On 2 January, the Tories paid the *News of the World* £57,000 to run a fifteen-point mini-manifesto setting out Howard's beliefs, central to which was shrinking the size of the state. This included the cutredtape.org campaign and a review looking at waste in public spending. So far, so Thatcherite. Yet Howard proved flexible in his principles if there was a chance of defeating the government.

After the introduction of tuition fees for students entering higher education in 1998, the 2001 Labour manifesto ruled out introducing variable or top-up fees – the putative increase of the upfront fee from £1,000 to up to £3,000 a year. In January 2003, the government committed itself to overturning its pledge that later provoked the Tories' opposition. Duncan Smith denounced fees as a 'tax on learning' and committed the party to scrapping them. Howard reiterated Tory opposition and called the plans 'absolute nonsense'.

There was also the possibility of a government defeat. Labour backbench rebellion saw an Early Day Motion noting concerns with top-up fees circulated and signed by 185 MPs. With the vote due on 27 January the Whip's Office pulled out all the stops. Concessions were offered on reviews, reimbursements, higher loans and better grants. At one stage, it was even suggested that Tony Blair had told a group of MPs recently returned from Australia that they would be denied expenses for the trip if they failed to vote the right way.[41] In the event, the government won by just five votes.

The following month, Howard kept himself in the news with two key interventions. The first was his 'British Dream' speech delivered at the right-wing think tank Policy Exchange. This recapitulated the previously heralded themes of the small state and the war on waste. Recalling his parents' clothes shops, he linked his vision of a fulfilled life to entrepreneurialism that is too often suffocated by a stifling state. Howard also committed the Tories to a free vote on civil partnerships, while making one thing very clear: 'Civil partnership differs from marriage. Marriage is a separate and special relationship which we should continue to celebrate and sustain.'[42] There was also an emphasis on classroom discipline as the route to better educational outcomes, and more on patient choice.

Later in the month, Howard travelled to Burnley to give a speech on immigration and asylum to shore up the Conservatives' right flank – particularly as the BNP was starting to make modest inroads into local government. Singling it out as a 'bunch of thugs dressed up as a political party', he warned of the shame befalling the UK if BNP MEPs were returned in the 2004 EU elections. To counter them, he admitted that the Tory Party had its own failing where ethnic minority representation was concerned, and he went out of his way to celebrate the achievements and contributions of waves of immigrants to British life.

This prefaced a new 'get-tough' policy on immigration; the Tories would not allow just anyone to claim asylum in Britain, for immigration controls applied to the East European accession countries who joined the EU that year, and blamed the failure to listen on the 'decrease in respect for and tolerance of our immigrant communities'.[43] Part of the British Dream was very much an old Tory dream. Oliver Letwin as shadow chancellor spelled out the consequences of Howard's programme. 'Shrinking the state' meant making £35 billion worth of cuts to asylum seeker support, the military, transport and the courts system, with more money for 5,000 extra police officers, and more for health and education – contingent on greater competition within services.[44]

Despite Howard's rhetorical flourishes, this was not necessarily a break from Duncan Smith. Rather than the confusion of saying one thing but advocating the Thatcherite other, Howard was able to reconcile his predecessor's unhappy marriage of one-nationism and neoliberalism, and that result was more neoliberalism with a gloss of social concern. However, there were good reasons for Howard's lurch back to the right.

Not only was the BNP on the rise, but UKIP had broken through into popular consciousness. In January, the talk show host and *Daily Express* columnist Robert Kilroy-Silk had a column published titled 'We owe Arabs nothing', for which he was sacked from hosting *Kilroy* by the BBC. He defended his comments and denied he was a racist, pointing out that the piece had appeared previously and was reprinted in error.[45] The resulting furore ensured that issues around race and immigration attracted the headlines and the politicians, hence the new tough stance unveiled by Howard in February, but also provided propitious ground for other right-wing parties. Having returned its first MEPs in 1999, the United Kingdom Independence Party had built up a quiet but steady political presence via the television studios and Tory press as a pressure group on the Conservatives to keep them Eurosceptic. Capitalising on his new-found notoriety, Kilroy-Silk joined UKIP in February and was rapidly installed as the lead candidate for the East Midlands region. By May it was touted as a viable fourth party, doing better than the Liberal Democrats in one poll and attracting some celebrity supporters, such as self-described non-voter Joan Collins.[46]

The presence of an unexpected rival on the right flank and impending EU elections meant that Howard had no choice but to restate a hard line on Europe. His backbenchers would have been pleased, then, with his Berlin address, which emphasised British ties to the United States and the former colonies and dominions of the Empire, and the necessity for a two-speed Europe – one in which those countries wishing to integrate further can do so while those who do not, like Britain, continue with a picking and choosing of their opt-outs.[47] In April, launching the Tories' EU campaign at their Welsh conference, Howard promised a referendum on the Lisbon Treaty and attacked Tony Blair as 'un-British'.

Unfortunately for Howard, the voters were not listening. Heading to the polls on 10 June the Tories came away with 4.3 million votes, beating Labour's 3.7 million. However, they lost eight MEPs while Labour dropped six, and with 25.9 per cent of the vote based on a 38.5 per cent turnout, Howard's Tories performed worse than the catastrophic drubbing in the same elections Major received ten years previously. The real winners were UKIP, who increased their support by 2 million votes, returning twelve seats, including Kilroy-Silk, and beating the Liberal Democrats into third place. Further analysis of the UKIP vote showed that 45 per cent of them had voted Tory in 2001, as opposed to just 20 per cent for Labour.[48] The party also won two seats on the London Assembly, winning 156,780 votes (8.2 per cent) on the top-up vote, and their mayoral candidate won 115,665 votes (6 per cent). The consolation for the Tories was stasis – they kept their nine seats and their vote barely moved.

Faced with disappointing results, *The Times* argued that Howard 'not only needs to do nothing about the UKIP surge, but should say nothing about it. His colleagues need to be similarly Trappist', suggesting that the Tories' decision to fight the EU elections on a Eurosceptic platform allowed UKIP to outflank them based on a tougher but more easily understood programme of withdrawal.[49] Deny them the oxygen of publicity and they will go away eventually.

At first, this is exactly what Howard attempted to do by branching out into Labour territory and making big spending pledges on the NHS, with increased funding to the tune of £49 billion per year by 2009–10 and making choice the central plank of his health and education message. In that respect, what was new? The electorate were wondering as well and awarded him poor poll ratings and the Tories also-ran status in the Birmingham Hodge Hill and Leicester South by-elections. With traction weakening, Howard reshuffled his Shadow Cabinet with a view to a final relaunch at party conference, and Cameron and Osborne were promoted to policy coordinator and shadow Treasury minister respectively.

In July, Peter Mandelson, one of New Labour's architects, was appointed the EU Commissioner for Trade. This meant his resigning his Hartlepool seat, and a by-election which was held on 30 September – just days before the Tories met. Labour held on to the seat but with its majority slashed from 14,000 to just over 2,000. The Tories, who had habitually occupied the second position in the seat since 1974, crashed to fourth place as protest voters flocked to the Liberal Democrats, and UKIP came out of nowhere to claim 10 per cent of the vote.

The menace UKIP posed to the Tories at the next election became increasingly clear, especially as Kilroy-Silk had threatened to stand the party in every seat. Luckily, UKIP's celebrity MEP overreached himself after failing to oust party chair Roger Knapman in favour of himself and promptly resigned from the party to set up his own vanity vehicle, Veritas. The Tories then used conference to unveil a revamped logo with added red, white and blue, and their election pitch, which was a far from stirring mantra but one designed to capture the attention of the UKIP-curious, was 'school discipline, more police, cleaner hospitals, lower taxes and controlled immigration'.[50]

The conference speech itself was a retread of the British promise, with all the same themes recapitulated. Howard also chose the occasion to stress his Euroscepticism. A Conservative government would now seek to renegotiate chunks of the treaties the UK was signed up to. This meant removing the UK from the common fisheries policy, and, once again, opting out of the social chapter. In short, the party under Howard was more coherent and, on the surface, happier than in the days of Duncan Smith, but the policies offered and the positions taken had hardly changed. This was reflected not only in the policy content of his conference speech but also in the recycling of the same anecdotes from former keynote addresses.[51]

As the general election approached, Howard was more determined to prove that there was something of the right about him.

To head off the UKIP challenge, the Tories embarked on a billboard campaign that asked, 'Are you thinking what we're thinking?,' which was immediately followed with, 'It's not racist to impose limits on immigration.'[52] Howard's pre-election press conference put forward a seven-point plan targeting travellers and criminalising trespass, and promising an end to political correctness, more prisons, stiffer sentences and more British border guards to keep people out. The unveiled manifesto synthesised all these themes, talking the inclusive language of the one-nation-sounding 'British Dream' one moment and then the authoritarian and traditionalist talking points the next. At least it was coherent and consistent with everything Howard had said over the previous eighteen months. It is just that what he said was neither innovative nor appealing.[53]

When it came, the election was a foregone conclusion. It was not a question of whether Labour would win, but of what size its (reduced) majority would be. The Tories increased their seats by thirty-three on 8.8 million votes or 32.4 per cent, a feeble rise of 0.7 per cent on the 2001 debacle. What made the result look less appalling was the slide in the Labour vote, with just 800,000 separating them from the Tories but, thanks to a more efficient distribution of votes, a majority of sixty-six. UKIP, for its part, stood 496 candidates and polled 606,000 votes (2.2 per cent), a result that surely cost the Tories a handful of extra MPs. The turnout bumped along historic lows with just 61.4 per cent of the electorate choosing to vote.

For his part, Howard said that the party could hold its head up about the results but added that he had not achieved what he set out to do. Instead of resigning he said he would not lead the party into the next general election, and would stand down after the party had had a period of reflection – 'I intend to stay as leader until the party has had the opportunity to consider whether it wishes those rules to be changed and if so how they should be changed,' hinting that perhaps the party might like to renege on its recent foray into managed membership democracy and the leadership election be taken back in-house.[54] As a means of leading this reflection, he promoted Cameron and Osborne again to shadow education secretary and shadow chancellor respectively.

Eight years in opposition and the Tories did not have a lot to show for it. In absolute terms they had a million fewer voters than in 1997 and as a proportion of the voting electorate it had grown by just 1.4 percentage points, yielding them just thirty-four extra MPs compared with their nadir. In Scotland they had recovered one seat, and in Wales, in 2005, they managed to add three. But overall, 2005 painted a picture of a party with nowhere to go.

Blairism had successfully incorporated the authoritarianism and pro-market settlement of the Thatcher years, while also increasing funding to and improving the quality of public services (and simultaneously expanding on Major's Citizen's Charter as the blueprint of its reforms), extending individual rights in the workplace, making important democratic reforms with a new constitutional settlement and legislating against inequalities and discriminations – moves the Tories set their faces against. When Hague, Duncan Smith and Howard tried contesting this terrain with promises of more choice the broader electorate, particularly those who had voted Tory in the past and were receptive to these messages, stayed with Labour because it was implementing policies of this character. When the Tories tried outflanking Blair on issues like law and order and immigration, the authoritarianism of his government meant that anything else was flirting with the fringes.

There was perhaps mileage in compassionate conservatism but none of the three leaders were particularly sympathetic characters, and especially so Howard, whose record in government was happily flagged up by Labour in its 2005 campaign. Nor did the Tories take this seriously. They showed that you have to match words with deeds – a party, especially a 'nasty party', will have a hard time convincing an electorate of its inclusive credentials if it is stirring the pot on asylum and immigration and sounding xenophobic when it comes to matters European. Returning to John Ross's thesis, they appeared to be at the end of a process that had been accumulating for seventy years and were at last supplanted by a party as dominant as they had been during their 1980s heyday.

This incoherence at first might have resulted from exhaustion and a shattering defeat where chunks of the Thatcher–Major coalition went over to the enemy, but under Howard's tenure it was baked into the strategic thinking of the party. The rise of UKIP in 2004 put the Tories in the novel situation of facing a viable competitor to their right in second-order elections.

Naturally, UKIP dropped back in the general election, but polling 600,000 votes when Labour only had a 800,000-strong lead flagged up the importance of neutralising the new challenger, in terms of both preventing any of the existing voter coalition from going over to them and making sure UKIP support would come back. This meant that any touchy-feely strategy allied to moderation on Europe could leave the right flank vulnerable to populist agitation on immigration and the EU.

Therefore, in 2005 it appeared that the Tories were in an even more disadvantageous position than in 2001, hemmed in by New Labour occupying the ground of managerial politics and the possibility of vote-catching via populist agitation circumscribed by UKIP, which could do it more convincingly and was not constrained by the necessity of appearing as an alternative government. The path back therefore meant the assembly of a new coalition with a consistent theme that did not try to face both ways, and this is what the next phase of the party's development elected to pursue.

5

The Rise of Liberal Toryism

When Michael Howard gave notice of his resignation on the morning of 6 May 2005, he called for a period of reflection to consider at length the lessons of the recently lost general election. He urged a reconsideration of the leadership rules as well as a new leader. Unfortunately for his legacy, Howard's end bequeathed no such rule change. He favoured amending the threshold for nomination by replacing the proposer/seconder system with the backing of 10 per cent of Tory MPs. Successful candidates would then address the National Convention, which would form the basis of a consultative vote of the membership. This would be taken into consideration as MPs voted through different rounds, eliminating the lowest placed except for the choice of the convention, which would have a reserved place at each stage of voting. This most indirect expression of members' democracy was able to muster initial support at the 1922 Committee, but not in the wider party, and so the Hague reforms remained unaltered.[1] The five-month-long contest did, however, yield a new leader somewhat at odds with the previous forty years' worth of predecessors.

In July, the 'modernising' Conservative think tank C-Change published its findings about the general election. It found a fall-off in the number of women supporting the party when, historically, the party could count on their disproportionate support (falling from 45 per cent in 1992 to 32 per cent in 2005) – the chasm was particularly acute among younger women.

Nor were seats won thanks to a groundswell of enthusiasm for the Conservatives – the Liberal Democrats taking votes from Labour as well as Labour voters tending to stay home in anticipation of another foregone conclusion had much more to do with it. And only 28 per cent of non-Tories thought that the party was on the right track. The solution? Sticking to some core conservative principles, such as tax cutting, but emphasising compassionate conservatism for reaching out beyond the core vote.[2] Also worrying for the Conservatives was the continued downward spiral of the membership. The leadership election reported a 78 per cent turnout, indicating in a party of 254,928 members a fall of over a fifth in just four years.[3]

Seven men indicated their interest in contesting the leadership but only four put their names forward – David Cameron, Ken Clarke, David Davis and Liam Fox. Campaigning all summer before the MPs met in October for the gatekeeping rounds of voting, Cameron and Clarke put themselves forward as the natural choice for Tories seeking to move the party more towards the centre on social issues and Europe. Davis staked out a more right-wing position, with concessions on social liberalism and the emphasis on his humble background. His 'modern conservatism' pitch came unstuck following a number of gaffes, which involved wandering around the year's party conference with a posse of young women in tight-fitting 'It's DD for me' T-shirts and indicating a preference for blondes over brunettes during a *Woman's Hour* interview.[4] For his part, Liam Fox offered the comforting nostrums of the leaders of the recent past – entrepreneurialism, low taxes, distance from a stagnating EU. What did single him out and showed a possible avenue for a more compassionate conservatism was a stress on mental health problems and a forthright attack on domestic violence.[5]

In the first round of voting on 18 October David Davis came first with sixty-two votes, followed by Cameron on fifty-six, Fox on forty-two, and Clarke eliminated on thirty-eight. In the second round, Davis unexpectedly fell back to fifty-seven with Cameron surging to ninety, and Fox polling fifty-one. On 6 December the membership voting saw Cameron win convincingly with 134,466 votes (67.6 per cent) to Davis's 64,398 (32.4 per cent). Nonetheless, this was not a foregone conclusion.

Conservative commentators observed how Cameron's campaign was visibly faltering prior to conference season. The turning point was his speech to conference, which impressed the audience with its impeccable polish, delivered without any notes. Cameron argued that it was necessary for the Tories to hold on to core ideas, but these need not be a barrier to winning voters back from Labour. The task for the Tories was persuasion, not hoodwinking or gimmicks. As one Tory commentator put it,

> My straw polls tell me that few Tory members can now remember very much of what David Cameron actually said in his Blackpool speech. What they can remember is that they liked him from that moment on. They weren't convinced by great arguments. They fell in love. He is the kind of man that mature Tory ladies have always hoped that their daughter might bring home. By contrast, the same ladies saw the Davis team as the kind of bunch of they wouldn't want their sons to fall in with.[6]

It was not only the consistency of Cameron's message that marked him out from his immediate predecessors; also he was the first Tory leader since Alec Douglas-Home not to have hailed from a working-class or petit bourgeois background. Yet despite this, Cameron otherwise fitted the mould of Wheatcroft's 'new men' much better than previous leaders. Having attended Eton and Oxford, between 1988 and 1994 Cameron held a variety of jobs working for the party's research department, including adviser to Downing Street charged with preparing John Major for Prime Minister's Questions. He was latterly a special adviser to Norman Lamont, and then the same for Michael Howard.

Sensing a period working outside politics would be useful for his career, Cameron was appointed director of corporate affairs at television studios Carlton Communications – a job he acquired through his connections.[7] All the while Cameron searched for a seat, notably losing heavily after running for Stafford in 1997, before getting selected for safe Witney in Oxfordshire in April 2000. Therefore Cameron was unusual in the sense of having only sat in Parliament for one term before running for the party leadership, a feat matched by his later opposite number, Ed Miliband, and exceeded by his future coalition partner Nick Clegg, who became the Liberal Democrat leader in his first parliamentary term.

Modernisation

Cameron's large mandate and favourable relationship with the press granted him significant room for manoeuvre, and this enabled him to pick up the compassionate conservative themes and apply them more consistently. Bale likens this approach to decontamination, involving a studied silence on the 'Tebbit trinity' – tax, immigration and Europe.[8] His victory speech spelled out the line of march: a more gender-balanced party; one that cares about improving public services, not inducements for opting out of them; caring about the environment and taking carbon emissions seriously; the usual toughness on law and order; and arguing positively for social justice. Foregrounding the orientation to come, he signalled his post-Thatcherite credentials by noting that 'there is such a thing as society, it's just not the same thing as the state', and talked about our responsibility to each other.[9]

Indeed, over the Christmas period Cameron made a number of interventions around the NHS, tacking poverty, immigration and the environment, where he was memorably pictured in the Arctic Circle driving and cuddling Huskies, to quickly build up an image of a new kind of Tory. In the New Year he explicitly repudiated Thatcherism and emphasised the importance of the centre ground to win over former Tory voters.[10]

Establishing distance from Thatcherism, he moved towards Labour on certain issues. Tory positions on the NHS, grammar schools and tuition fees were discarded in favour of accepting Labour's positions. Policy reviews were also announced in April, due to report during the summer. Already confidence was returning to the Tory camp. Not only were donations on the increase again, but polling was looking more favourable. Until late April, both parties routinely swapped positions in the polls, and then consistent Tory leads began to be reported, at first modest and then occasionally double-digit before settling down to more modest but sustained leads by the summer.[11]

Cameron was also blessed with better approval ratings than Tony Blair, peaking at +14 per cent versus the prime minister struggling with −30 per cent that March.[12] The change message was cutting through to significant swathes of voters, though the year's local elections must have come as a disappointment. Despite the grand hopes, there was no advance in vote terms on the previous contest, polling 40 per cent of the vote while Labour languished at 26 per cent, with the Liberal Democrats a close third on 25 per cent.

Some of this reflected the campaigns the two parties were running. The Tories were showcasing their freshness and their press launch centred on green issues, with the new slogan 'Vote blue, go green'.[13] Labour's strategy centred around a poster campaign featuring 'Dave the Chameleon'. The Tories came away with a net increase of 316 seats and eleven councils, while Labour lost 319 councillors and seventeen councils. With one council and two net gains for the Liberal Democrats, it appeared that they had reached a natural limit targeting the Labour vote.

Modest success for Cameron was overshadowed by a much more modest breakthrough in local government by the BNP. Its thirty-three-seat gain attracted disproportionate press coverage and established it, in local government, as the most major of the minor parties. UKIP, by contrast, returned just one councillor. Disappointment also followed the Bromley by-election that June, following the death of right-winger Eric Forth. Despite the new image, the Tories were only just able to hold the seat, having their majority slashed to 663 from 13,342 at the general election by the Liberal Democrats: a setback that, for the leadership, indicated the need to go further and faster on moderation.

The findings of the policy reviews were condensed into the *Built to Last* document, which was to serve as a restatement of Tory principles in the post-Thatcherite era. Cameron's own foreword stated four key positions, or 'revolutions', as he styled them: personal responsibility and the support to be able to exercise it, professional responsibility (the freedom to best serve one's vocation – in public service), civic responsibility (community empowerment) and corporate responsibility (an emphasis on businesses' role in enhancing personal wellbeing and the environment).[14] Clustered around eight subsections covering economy and enterprise, social injustice, the environment, public services, global poverty, constitutionalism, communities and local government and diversity, this had the merit of rhetorically breaking with previous iterations of conservatism and contesting New Labour on some of its chosen ground. As Peter Dorey and his colleagues noted, it allied Tory values to a critique of the target-driven governance of public services that Blair took over from John Major.[15]

In a show of engagement with the party, Built to Last was put to the party for ratification in September, the document being endorsed by 60,859 to 4,787 on a 26.7 per cent turnout (indicating a membership of 245,865, a fall of 10,000 since December's leadership election).[16] This turn to social liberalism did not sit easy with the political outlook of the parliamentary party. Polling undertaken in 2007 found that 54 per cent of Tory MPs believed that same-sex couples should not have the same statutory rights as heterosexual couples, and 80 per cent believed that multiculturalism was not a good thing. This found its echo among the commentariat, with conservative columnist Peter Hitchens bemoaning the 'doom' of the Tory Party as Cameron's adoption of social liberalism was tantamount to capitulating to the left; it allied Tory values to a critique of the target-driven governance of public services that Blair took over from John Major.[17] Veteran backbencher Edward Leigh also argued that steering clear of immigration and Europe ceded the field to UKIP and the BNP.[18]

Cameron, however, remained undaunted. His first conference speech as leader suggested that equal marriage between same-sex couples was under active consideration, but he used the occasion to emphasise the importance of the NHS. To lance the boil of the notion that the NHS was not safe in Tory hands, Cameron talked about his severely disabled son Ivan. He recalled constant visits to the hospital and night-time vigils in his bedroom. He was able to show that he shared the experiences of millions of others and had a vested interest in making sure the NHS was properly funded and well run. Oddly, however, this intervention did not have much effect on the polls. If anything, the margin of Tory leads narrowed, which was disappointing given the political distance travelled.

Come the New Year there were reasons to be cheerful. Between January and May 2007, the Tories enjoyed consistent poll leads of eight to nine points. Cameron was also gifted an opportunity to stress how much the party had changed following the frank comments from Patrick Mercer, a former colonel turned Tory MP. He described institutionalised bullying in the military, and that black soldiers could expect to be racially abused as a fact of life. He went on to say, 'I came across a lot of ethnic minority soldiers who were idle and useless, but who used racism as cover for their misdemeanours.'[19] Cameron immediately sacked Mercer from his homeland security brief and later prevented him from standing again for the party. After the rough came the smooth. At March's spring forum Cameron announced his intention to introduce green taxes on pollution to cut taxes elsewhere and discourage 'unnecessary' aviation.[20]

Therefore, as the May local elections and parliamentary and assembly contests in Scotland and Wales approached, the Tory leadership must have been eager to see whether eighteen months of their liberal rebrand was about to pay off in electoral terms. In Holyrood the Tories stood still, gaining an additional constituency seat but losing two regional seats and 50,000 votes compared to the supposed nadir of 2003. Wales saw a modest improvement, winning four more constituency seats but losing three on the top-up. However, while their vote in both sections increased by 2.5 per cent and 2.3 per cent, it did put them above the second-placed Plaid Cymru in popular-vote terms. For the local council elections, the Tory vote held steady for the third year running at 40 per cent, but this belied the victory in seats; the Tories won control of thirty-nine councils and gained an extra 932 seats. Little headway in the nations, but a solid performance in England, suggested that the 'new' Tories were gaining traction. Pleasingly for Cameron, UKIP and the BNP performed modestly. It now appeared that neither was a threat to the Tories and, if anything, it was the BNP which might pose Labour the biggest threat in its neglected heartlands.

This visible progress was marred by two setbacks. On 26 June, the eve of Gordon Brown taking over from Tony Blair, the Tory MP for Grantham and Stamford, Quentin Davies, defected to Labour. Cameron was guilty of 'superficiality, unreliability and an apparent lack of any clear convictions', comparing him unfavourably to Brown, whom 'I have always greatly admired, who I believe is entirely straightforward, and who has a towering record, and a clear vision for the future of our country which I fully share'.[21]

There was also an opportunity to test how well Cameronism played in a safe Labour seat following the death of Piara Khabra. The by-election for Ealing Southall, called for 19 July, saw both main parties mired in controversy. First, as Khabra had previously announced his intention to stand down at the next election Labour imposed an all-women shortlist for the seat – a decision later rescinded in favour of a standard selection. This was followed by the defection of five local Labour councillors to the Tories.[22] The Tories, however, were afflicted with difficulties of their own. Their candidate was Tony Lit, a local businessman with approximately two weeks of Conservative membership to his name. His selection provoked the defection of the association's deputy chair to the Liberal Democrats. This was compounded after it emerged that Lit had been at a Labour fundraiser and donated the party £4,800 just eight days prior to taking out Tory membership.[23] There was further embarrassment when campaign coordinator and shadow housing minister Grant Shapps was caught apparently impersonating a local Liberal Democrat activist on YouTube.[24] In the event, neither mid-term blues for Labour nor embarrassing difficulties for the Conservatives made much difference; the seat was held comfortably with a 5,000-strong majority, with the Liberal Democrats second with 10,118 votes and the Tories third on 8,230 – an increase of just 0.9 per cent on 2015. The Sedgefield by-election, taking place on the same day, was even less encouraging. Labour conceded vote share to the Liberal Democrats, but still managed to win the seat comfortably. The Tories, however, managed 4,082 votes, a 0.2 per cent-point increase on the general election.

The difficulty the Tories now faced was one of a 'new face' fronting up the government, despite Brown being a familiar New Labour presence. Taking office on 27 June, Brown announced that his government would be of 'all the talents', signifying that he stood for change. These 'talents' included the former head of the Confederation of British Industry, Digby Jones, who was given a life peerage so he could take up his trade position.[25] There were also (purposely leaked) offers of the Northern Ireland Cabinet post to former Liberal Democrat leader Paddy Ashdown, designed to create a serious, if not post-party politics, managerial image for Brown.

The immediate consequence of Labour's new leadership was a turnaround in the polls, with consistent leads running all the way from the end of June to early October. The response of the Tory right was to make public their grumbles, with a handful of no-confidence letters going to the 1922 Committee and open criticism of the modernisation project.[26] Unfortunately for Cameron, he was invisible when floods hit central and northern England and mid-Wales as he was in Rwanda promoting the new Conservative position on foreign aid. This gave Brown political space to establish himself as a hands-on prime minister and a substantial figure who was reliable in a crisis. Brown also weathered a series of one-day strikes in Royal Mail without difficulty. Luckily for Cameron this was not to last.

At a crunch meeting in July, Cameron had promised his back-benchers a turn towards more traditional messaging in the autumn. On 22 August eleven-year-old schoolboy Rhys Jones was walking home from football practice and was shot dead in an unprovoked attack. This was used by Cameron as an opportunity to expound on a traditional Tory strength. Having had his law and order position caricatured as 'hug a hoodie', Cameron attacked Labour's record as being soft on crime and touching on ground he would later return to with his notion of 'Broken Britain'.[27] The second opportunity was the collapse of the Northern Rock bank. An early casualty of the brewing financial crisis, the bank had borrowed heavily to lend money for mortgages which, in turn, were then sold on. Northern Rock went into crisis when it could no longer sell its loans as markets were realising the risk attached to buying them.

This crisis and the emergency intervention of the Bank of England caused a run on the bank as depositors queued up to retrieve their savings – exacerbating the Rock's cash crisis. On 18 September Brown moved to guarantee all the deposits to calm an increasingly jittery market, and guaranteed its liquidity while the bank was restructured in the hope it could be sold as a going concern.[28] When these schemes fell through the government was forced to nationalise Northern Rock the following February. Brown's rescue package was a clear break from the governing common sense that New Labour and the Tories subscribed to, though this was promptly forgotten by Cameron in his response. He blamed Brown for the difficulties because Labour had presided over a careless expansion of private and public debt. In other words, government irresponsibility and Labour profligacy were the root of the crisis – a return to well-worn Tory themes. The polls, however, disagreed, and going into the party conference season Labour was still enjoying double-digit leads. It was to be short-lived.

The Tory conference was the turning point, in which several eye-catching proposals were unveiled. These included an emphasis in combating public and private debt, cuts to inheritance tax, the abolition of home information packs (a package of documents that made the selling of houses more time-consuming and costly) and the abolition of stamp duty for first-time buyers. Cameron also goaded Brown into calling an election in his conference speech, even though the Tories were badly trailing Labour.[29]

There was meat for the traditional Tories too, with a pledge to build more prisons and force down the rate of immigration. The polls after conference showed slippage in Labour's lead and contributed to a panic. Throughout summer speculation about an autumn election had been rife, backed by leaks, trade unions readying phone banks and even the unveiling of the 'No Flash, Just Gordon' billboard campaign. The obvious preparations were rowed back on 6 October as Brown categorically ruled out an election. The effect was compounded by Alastair Darling announcing three days later that Labour was cutting inheritance tax, making it appear as if the government was running scared of the Tories.[30]

As we have seen, Thatcher and Major were destroyed once their authority slipped away from them. While the election that never was pinpointed a change in Brown's political fortunes, it was not necessarily the case that the situation was unrecoverable; this was hardly a poll tax or a Black Wednesday moment. What we saw, and what the Tories benefited from, was a series of decisions, scandals and latterly in-fighting that proved as calamitous to Labour's hopes as the pit closures programme and VAT on home fuel bills did for Major.

The first of these difficulties was questions raised over Labour's commitment to the armed forces, with leading military figures and Cameron and Nick Clegg combining their efforts to accuse Labour of abandoning the military covenant, a criticism often made of Tony Blair for not supplying personnel with adequate equipment in the field or the required support when they returned home.[31] Furthermore, a series of financial scandals refused to go away.

Prior to his departure from office, Blair was dogged by a loans-for-peerages scandal that funded the party to the tune of £14 million and saw him interviewed under police caution.[32] In November, it emerged that property tycoon David Abrahams had donated £600,000 to Labour through intermediaries, which invited a second police investigation and saw the resignation of Peter Watt, the party's general secretary.[33] In January 2008 this line was compounded after it was revealed that Peter Hain, the Wales and DWP minister, had neglected to declare £103,000 raised for his deputy leadership campaign in the previous summer; he resigned amid a police probe into his funding.[34] Adding to Labour's woes was the loss of child benefit data of 25 million people in the same month, and finally in February, after six months of failing to find a purchaser, the government nationalised Northern Rock – upending the economic management dogma of the previous thirty years.[35] Vince Cable, then the acting leader of the Liberal Democrats, keenly summated the woes bedevilling Brown when he described his 'remarkable transformation in the last few weeks from Stalin to Mr Bean'.[36]

Cameron was not without difficulties during this period. The Tories were also dragged into the money quagmire when it emerged the backbencher Derek Conway had paid his son £40,000 over a three-year period as a member of his parliamentary staff but without his doing any work. To forestall any damage, Cameron quickly moved to remove the whip.[37] The Tories also saw Bob Spink, another backbencher, resign the whip following moves by his association to deselect him – he then subsequently sat for UKIP.

While these were no more than embarrassments, the Tories escaped any polling sanction as a new Labour crisis erupted. In the 2007 Budget, Brown had announced that the government would be scrapping the 10p tax band for low earners and would see them begin paying income tax at the rate of 20p in the pound, due to be implemented in April 2008. This was projected to cost low-paid workers and pensioners an additional £230 per year. On the eve of its coming into force, the long-standing cut exploded as a political issue. Alistair Darling scrambled to come up with a compensation package for those due to lose out, undermining the point of the measure in the first place, and afforded Cameron the opportunity to affect a concern for the poor.[38] Its mishandling underlined a disastrous six months, and impacted directly on the local and devolved elections.

In popular-vote terms the Tories commanded 44 per cent of the popular vote, winning a further 256 councillors and control over twelve more councils. Labour's vote share plunged to 24 per cent, a percentage point behind that commanded by the Liberal Democrats. On the further right UKIP gained three councillors and the BNP ten. More significantly, while the Tories topped the poll for the London Assembly and became the largest party, the election also saw Richard Barnbrook returned for the BNP, then its biggest electoral success.

The real prize of the night for Cameron was winning the London mayoralty as Boris Johnson defeated Labour's Ken Livingstone. Rubbing the result in was the disaster – for Labour – of the Crewe and Nantwich by-election, held on 22 May. In a campaign characterised by complacency and ineptitude, Labour selected as its candidate Tamsin Dunwoody, daughter of the recently deceased incumbent, Gwyneth Dunwoody, in a move that looked like the party was banking on name recognition. Labour's campaign also indulged a crass faux class war demonisation of the Tory candidate, Edward Timpson, as a toff. It was a campaign roundly mocked and criticised in the press.[39] In the event, the Tories won the by-election handsomely, turning over 7,000 votes and establishing a new majority 7,860 votes strong – the first time the Tories had taken a seat in a by-election since 1978.

With increasing confidence, Cameron began asserting more traditional concerns. In November Alan Duncan, the shadow secretary for business, and Jonathan Djanogly published *Labour and the Trade Unions: An Analysis of a Symbiotic Relationship* for the Centre for Policy Studies, which argued that increased trade union rights under New Labour had placed 'significant extra burdens' on employers. They unveiled measures specifically aimed at curbing or hampering the deployment of union political funds.[40]

This implied that the Tories could be expected to take further action against trade unions while targeting a key source of Labour Party funding. In January Cameron himself focused on the imaginary 'something for nothing' culture and called for compulsory workfare schemes for the unemployed.[41] This was followed several months later by the DWP shadow Chris Grayling unveiling traditional-sounding policies on social security. He made the argument that the root of unemployment was not the lack of jobs (i.e., vacancies always trailing the number of people out of work) but 'dependency culture', which was cultivated by the welfare state itself.

To this end the Tories would force eighteen- to twenty-one-year-olds to undertake compulsory work assignments on pain of losing support, and time-limited access to social security. There were to be obligations attached to accepting job offers, and the back-to-work process would be contracted out to private providers on a payment-by-results basis.[42] These steps were calibrated to be in tune with public opinion as well as an attempt to steal the initiative back from Labour, whose approach had proven as conditional as Thatcher's and Major's. No votes were to be lost from benefit bashing.

Moving more confidently back on to Conservative terrain was the opportunity presenting itself when the stock markets imploded early in the autumn. The collapse of the major investment bank Lehman Brothers and the US nationalisation of mortgage lenders Fannie Mae and Freddie Mac also saw Britain – with the City of London the pre-eminent hub for international banking and finance – badly hit. In the UK, the government oversaw the enforced buyout of Halifax Bank of Scotland by Lloyds TSB, nationalised the mortgage book of Bradford and Bingley and recapitalised the banks to the tune of £37 billion while providing deposit guarantees on accounts up to £50,000. The government also took direct stakes in several banks in order to prevent implosion, cut VAT by 2.5 per cent to stimulate consumer spending and reduced interest rates to negligible levels to forestall a crisis of defaulted mortgages and home repossessions.

This decisive action initially caught the Tories off-guard, their opposition to part-nationalisation and emergency Keynesianism viewed as an unwillingness to do what was necessary to save people's livelihoods and, worse, as dithering. The consequence was a revival in Labour's polling. At the beginning of September, it had been nineteen to twenty points behind the Conservatives'. By Christmas the deficit was reduced to between five and seven points. It is easy to see why. Previewing that year's conference speech on the *Andrew Marr Show*, Cameron argued that nationalisation should not be the 'stock response' to banking failure. His speech saw a Tory return to 'sound money' and a polemic against

'Labour's spendaholic culture', which meant reforming 'inefficient' public services. As a panacea, Cameron promised lower taxes and more enterprise. He also ruled out more state control, arguing not for a 'bigger state' but more 'efficient government.'[43] Thankfully for Cameron, the Labour poll bounce was only short-lived and come the new year the gap widened again.

What solidified polling divergence was the MPs' expenses scandal, following ongoing legal wrangles from a freedom of information request regarding expenses claimed by some MPs. In January, the government tried blocking the disclosure of information and enforced a three-line whip in the Commons to this end, a move the Opposition parties opposed. In the face of a media storm, Labour retreated, and publication of expenses was scheduled for July. However, details were trailed throughout 2008 and 2009.

On 13 March, it was revealed that MPs had made claims for up to £10,000 for new kitchens and bathrooms, and at the end of the month Commons Speaker Michael Martin was found to have spent £700,000 renovating his official residence. In April, the Speaker released details of senior Labour politicians' claims and early in 2009 it was revealed that several ministers were making creative claims under the system. Chancellor Alistair Darling was shown to be claiming 'second home' mortgage payments for his constituency address and living rent-free in Downing Street, while renting out his former London address, for instance.

On 8 May, the *Daily Telegraph* published all the claims made by MPs for the previous four years.[44]

The scandal bit deep. The public reacted angrily to politicians preaching austerity and sacrifice as they helped themselves to luxury goods and generously subsidised mortgages. The Tories were far from exempt from the scandal, which was best symbolised by the (rejected) expense claim for a duck house by Gosport MP Sir Peter Viggers, and the (successful) claim by Douglas Hogg for having his moat cleaned.[45] In these cases and others involving the abuse of the mortgage claims process, Cameron compelled them to stand down at the next election.

Speaking after the scandal broke, he said that many of the claims were wrong and apologised on behalf of his party. He also expected Tory MPs to pay back 'excessive' claims, and any refusing to do so to be expelled. His rules for future claims would only cover costs for rent and utilities for second homes.[46] As such the appearance of decisive action spared the Tories some of the damage.

The government was not so lucky, and the calamities carried on piling up. For instance, Labour suffered a high-profile defeat by a media-confected campaign led by the actor Joanna Lumley over the rights of retired soldiers from the Nepalese Gurkha regiment to settle in Britain. There was also a widely derided appearance by Gordon Brown on YouTube, 'unhelpful' articles by former ministers Charles Clarke and Hazel Blears and resignations from the Cabinet by James Purnell and Caroline Flint. Labour MP for Norwich North Ian Gibson resigned from the Commons after being told he would not be able to stand for Labour at the next election following the expenses scandal. It appeared that the government was drowning in calamity and misfortune, much of it unnecessary and self-inflicted.

The local elections proved a catastrophe for Labour as it slumped to 23 per cent of the popular vote, well behind the Liberal Democrats' 28 per cent and the Tories' 38 per cent. The latter gained 244 councillors and the control of seven extra councils, including the remaining English county authorities under Labour control. If anything, the EU elections held on the same day were even worse for Labour. The government again was in third place, losing five MEPs and polling only 15.2 per cent of the popular vote – behind UKIP's 16 per cent and heavily trailing the Tories on 27.4 per cent.

Despite topping the poll and winning the lion's share of seats, returning twenty-six MEPs, what should have been a pre-general election triumph was shunted aside by the more newsworthy success of UKIP. The party returned thirteen MEPs on its explicitly anti-EU platform but, more controversially, the BNP also won two seats. Its 6.3 per cent saw party leader Nick Griffin elected in the North West region, and Andrew Brons for Yorkshire and the

Humber. While the Tories were expecting punishment for the expenses crisis too, the rise of two viable parties to their right suggested that there were limits to how far Cameron's liberalising project could go – but he nevertheless interpreted the results as heralding an imminent majority at the next election.[47]

If there was any doubt at all, the by-election for Ian Gibson's seat was held on 23 July and, again following the Crewe and Nantwich debacle, Labour's majority of 5,500 evaporated as the Tories' Chloe Smith took the seat with ease, securing a 16.5 per cent swing and a new majority of 7,348. Another triumph, but one tempered with a slight degree of unease – UKIP was able to poll 4,068 votes, or 11.8 per cent of the vote. This was an indicator that while it may not be in the running for any seats in 2010, there was the possibility it could stymie the Tory advance in some marginal seats.

Fortunately for Cameron, things appeared to go well for the moment. At the 2009 party conference, he reasserted the spending-beyond-our-means narrative and argued that Labour's love for big government was the original sin responsible for the harsh judgement of the rapidly contracting market. Treading carefully, his speech avoided overt Thatcherite framing of Tory spending plans:

> So I say to the Labour Party and the trades unions just tell me what is compassionate, what is progressive about spending more on debt interest than on helping the poorest children in our country? The progressive thing to do, the responsible thing to do is to get a grip on the debt but in a way that brings the country together instead of driving it apart . . . It means showing that we're all in this together which is why we'll freeze public sector pay for all but the one million lowest paid public sector workers . . . for one year to help protect jobs. And it means showing that the rich will pay their share which is why for now the 50p tax rate will have to stay and Child Trust Funds for those on middle and higher incomes will have to go.[48]

Burnishing the progressive credentials further, Cameron attacked Labour from the left by highlighting pensioner poverty and the

'broken society' of benefit caps, youth unemployment and gallop-
ing inequality. This was married to more traditional Tory messaging
on crime, schools (more discipline, more parental choice), patriotism and meritocracy. In effect, it was little different in substance
from either of the speeches made by Gordon Brown and Nick
Clegg.

Cameron did have another reason to be cheerful. As the self-
styled talisman of successful political leaders, the *Sun* declared it
was switching its support back to the Tories in a move timed to
discombobulate Labour as it met for its conference.[49] Cameron
also had the advantage of Labour in-fighting to fall back on. With
dismal polling figures continuing through to Christmas, in the
New Year former ministers Patricia Hewitt and Geoff Hoon, both
of whom were being forced to stand down following expenses
revelations, circulated a letter among MPs calling for a secret
ballot of the PLP to replace Brown with a yet-to-be-determined
figure.[50] Their new prince did not step up, and so the attacks on the
prime minister continued. In February, Brown was dogged by allegations that he bullied Downing Street staff in claims made by
the National Bullying Helpline.[51] And so the scene was set for an
election that appeared nothing less than a foregone conclusion.

Yet it did not turn out that way. Two polls published on 6 April,
the day the general election was finally called, put the Tories on 40
per cent (YouGov/*Sun*) versus Labour's 32 per cent, and the Liberal
Democrats' 17 per cent. The other (Harris/*Metro*) recorded the
parties on 37 per cent, 28 per cent and 20 per cent respectively. The
Tory manifesto, *Invitation to Join the Government of Britain*,
repackaged liberal conservatism, 'progressive' austerity and a
softer framing of Tory staples around crime, immigration and the
EU in a lavish hardback cover and graphic design redolent of 1950s
politics posters.[52] Yet politics did not dominate the campaign as
such, considering the real differences on economic management
and public spending. It was more focused on personality.

In April, British television channels collaborated to host three
leaders' debates between Cameron, Brown and Clegg. With seemingly nothing to lose, Labour hoped that what the prime minister

lacked in public relations he could make up with intellectual heft and substance. Cameron would get the chance to display showmanship skills honed through years of speechifying and Commons appearances, and as Westminster's third party the Liberal Democrats could only benefit from introducing their largely unknown and unnoticed leader to wider audiences.

Having prepared the ground with a considered strategy, the television debates threw the Conservatives off course. While they were ostensibly about policy, the media treated them as pointscoring contests, concentrating on Clegg's eye contact, Cameron's smoothness and Brown's clunky delivery. Under these circumstances, Clegg stole the shows. As the outsider, he pitched himself as the real change candidate. So-called Cleggmania saw the party surge in the polls, often eclipsing Labour and on four occasions leading voter intentions. Appearing as a 'young people's' candidate thanks to youth-friendly policies, including abolishing university tuition fees and being apart from the corrupt, established 'old parties', there were reports of surging electoral registrations and anticipation of a record turnout among the eighteen- to twentyfours. However, by polling day, the mania had subsided, not least thanks to scurrilous attacks on Clegg's origins and lack of patriotism led by CCHQ, and by the last debate Cameron had found his feet again.

Matters around personality were compounded further when Gordon Brown had a chance encounter. On 28 April he had an altercation with Gillian Duffy, a Labour-supporting pensioner, who complained about access to benefits and immigration. Once back in his car Brown complained about being ambushed by a 'bigoted woman'. Unfortunately, his Sky News microphone was live and when he appeared on radio shortly afterwards this was played back to him. There followed a media circus and a grovelling apology to Mrs Duffy, who subsequently had a career as a celebrity working-class woman to whom leading Labour politicians and the Westminster circus paid homage – until she left the party in 2016.[53] Remarkably the episode did not appear to erode Labour's support any further.

Come the general election itself, the clamour for Cleggmania fell somewhat short of polling. The Liberal Democrats managed 23 per cent but returned only fifty-seven MPs – five fewer than the high-water mark under Charles Kennedy. Labour plunged to 29 per cent of the vote, sustaining a net loss of 91 seats – its worst result since 1983. The Tories, however, fell short of expectations and did not return a majority. At 306 seats (minus the Speaker), the Tories made no progress in Scotland but gained five seats in Wales, taking its overall total there to eight. More significantly, however, Cameron was nineteen seats from an overall majority. He therefore sought and entered a power-sharing coalition with the Liberal Democrats.

Despite their forming the largest party, it was a disappointment considering the ideological contortions the Tories had performed, the backing of virtually the entire press (only the *Mirror* backed Labour, while the *Guardian* and the *Independent* backed the Liberal Democrats – even the *Financial Times* urged support for the Tories). Brown's repeated and oft-highlighted blunders and Labour disunity were too much for the party's erstwhile allies in the fourth estate.

Among Conservatives, one unnecessary failure of the Tory campaign was the nebulous 'Big Society' concept. Growing out of Cameron's speeches, this notion repositioned the Tory critique of New Labour. Instead of simply denouncing the 'nanny state' and 'broken Britain', it laid stress on the state getting out of the way of civic initiatives and building cohesive communities. It was communitarian in character, emphasising responsibilities, but not at the expense of Cameron's socially liberal rights agenda.

Activists and Tory politicians claimed that this was proving hard to sell on the doorstep, with one going so far as to say that the confusion it caused cost the Tories their majority.[54] Given that neither Blair nor Brown tried using their so-called 'Third Way' to muster electoral support, perhaps the Tories were confused about the purpose of a few insights strung together in a cod philosophy. The 'Big Society, not Big Government' slogan was used and flanked several of Cameron's campaign set pieces. According to

ConservativeHome's review of the election, 62 per cent of Tory Party members thought the campaign was poor. Allowing the Liberal Democrats equal footing in the leaders' debates undermined the change message (91 per cent of a 109-strong sample of Tory candidates agreed with this). Others felt that the leadership should have adopted anti-politics positioning (presumably to prevent support bleeding to UKIP) and should have gone for more negative campaigning. The review claimed that the party needed just 16,000 extra votes spread across nineteen constituencies to have won an outright majority and blamed a poor campaign and broadcast media bias for not winning one.[55]

A more balanced review was provided by Lord Ashcroft the following September, arguing that the Tories' managing to win so many seats and come out as the biggest party while the electoral landscape was stacked against them was a considerable achievement. For instance, Labour won ninety-two more seats in England than the Tories in 2005 despite the latter winning the popular vote – though in 2010 they won 297 versus Labour's 191 seats. Crucially, in addition to the increased Liberal Democrat vote a significant proportion of swing voters were unconvinced by the Tories and were prone to the scaremongering campaigns run by opposition parties.[56]

Considering the demographics underlying 2010's voting, Ipsos MORI polling for the *Observer* found that Tory support outstripped Labour in all categories save the working class. Labour also tied for the support of C1s ('routine white collar') with the Liberal Democrats and trailed them among the C2s ('skilled working class'). The same polling found significant differences by gender and age. For example, the Tories led among men of all age groups but by progressively shorter margins as one went down the age ranges. For women, Labour had big leads among the under-thirty-fives.[57] The Tories recorded increased support across all age/gender cohorts, though one can suppose for different reasons. The destruction of Gordon Brown's authority, the visible exhaustion and infighting of Labour in office, and its reputation for callous incompetence concerning the 10p tax rate and MPs' expenses crowded out its chief strength – the swift response to the 2008 crash – which was turned by the Tories into a narrative of profligacy with the public finances. This messaging was more likely to chime with older voters who had supported the Tories between 1979 and 1992 but switched to Labour in 1997. For younger voters (the under-thirty-fours), Labour was the only government most had known as adults and so would be penalised by an incumbency disadvantage considering its policy mix, particularly on age differentials to the minimum wage, social security eligibilities, tuition fees, the property market and bearing the brunt of the economic crisis.

Therefore Cameron's campaign of detoxification and moving his party in the direction of social liberalism undoubtedly assisted the increase in support for the Tories among younger voters – particularly among men in the 25–34 bracket.

The Liberal Democrats also experienced a rise in support from these layers. While men aged eighteen to twenty-four declined versus 2005, this was more than made up for by women of the same age, whose support surged by ten points. Therefore, among the lowest age group, the non-Tory vote between 2005 and 2010 remained static at 49 per cent for men and 69 per cent for women – with movements taking place away from Labour to the Lib Dems.

The extremely modest upticks in support for the Tories largely came from elsewhere. For the next age cohort up, support declined from 60 per cent to 55 per cent for men and for women from 71 per cent to 62 per cent, indicating that the Tories enjoyed more success winning over support from the people in their early to mid-careers, but still trailing badly. Overall, there was a tendency for women voters to support the Tories as one progressed up the age ranges while the picture was more mixed for men, whereas older men were more prepared to vote for someone other than the three main parties.

This pointed to several conclusions. Cameron was successful in putting the Tory coalition back together only in part. The bedrock of (older) women was successfully won over, as well as a plurality of early-career men. However, older men were more muted in their enthusiasm for the Tories, and for Cleggmania for that matter.

The comparatively large support for other parties could conceivably be claimed by UKIP and the BNP, which polled 919,000 and 564,000 votes respectively. As the more unreconstructed Tories warned, the possibility that a socially liberal Tory Party could drive away some of its former support proved accurate. However, by the same token, would the party have polled as well among undecided voters had matters remained the same as before 2005? The figures still demonstrated that the youngest cohort were most resistant to the charm offensive, while the eldest were unconvinced by the progressive agenda. This was a pattern that would only widen over the coming decade.

6

Liberal Toryism in Office

With only 36.1 per cent of votes cast, David Cameron entered Downing Street with the second-lowest share in British political history – only managing marginally better than Tony Blair in 2005. Despite having to rely on the Liberal Democrats as coalition partners the 2010–16 governments used the economic crisis as a pretext for deepening the neoliberal settlement even further. The period was marked by a further consolidation of Citizen Charter-style governance with greater monitoring of public sector staff and those accessing these services. Social security, health and education underwent radical restructuring consistent with neoliberal common sense, and, like his predecessors', Cameron's time in office saw the authoritarianism of the state retrenched. This was made more galling by the woollen mitten covering the iron fist. Brutal cuts to the income of Britain's poorest were alibied by appeals to self-responsibility. The closure of community infrastructure, like meeting halls, libraries and service hubs run by local authorities, was an 'opportunity' for the new wave of volunteering and civic pride Cameron sought to encourage. These six years were a test for liberal Toryism, and the result was little different to the divisions that Thatcher and Major left in their wake.

Cameron's premiership was characterised by ritualistic evocations of the deficit, a slapdash approach to day-to-day issues, extreme short-termism in pursuit of favourable headlines and a series of increasingly risky gambles for diminishing returns. The interim Coalition Agreement, once leaked, showed that the Liberal Democrats had abandoned their dovish and semi-Keynesian policy stance and agreed with the Tories on 'a significantly accelerated reduction in the structural deficit over the course of a parliament, with the main burden of deficit reduction borne by reduced spending rather than increased taxes'.[1] Indeed, the coalition justified its existence in the terms of two parties coming together in the face of an unprecedented national emergency. To this end the new government was committed to an emergency budget within fifty days of entering office and a comprehensive spending review in the following autumn.

In a seeming success for the Liberal Democrats, with spectacularly unintended results, the government pledged to 'restore the earnings link for the basic state pension from April 2011 with a "triple guarantee" that pensions are raised by the higher of earnings, prices or 2.5%'. There were also pledges on raising the tax threshold, thereby taking the lowest paid out of income tax, and several constitutional reforms. These included fixed-term parliaments, a limited right of recall to force a by-election where an MP had committed a crime or was egregiously in breach of rules and a referendum on first-past-the-post for Westminster elections. There were also a series of minor pledges, which in the event were not taken too seriously, on civil liberties and environmental issues.

In sum, while the hawkish line of public sector cuts was draped with language around protecting the most vulnerable, the coalition lash-up – awarding Cameron a seventy-eight-seat majority – ensured that there was considerable wriggle room for ignoring the Eurosceptic right of the party and, ironically, gave him a programme much more in tune with previous pronouncements than might otherwise have been the case. There was some discontent among the Tories that all the policy sacrifices begrudgingly accepted had not awarded them the majority promised. The reservation of five cabinet posts and twenty ministerial and junior governmental positions to the Liberal Democrats did little to ameliorate the grumbles.

Cameron's time in office is punctuated by the small, unexpected majority he won at the 2015 general election, but despite the annihilation of his former coalition partners there was no qualitative break between the long and short periods of the Cameron governments. The Liberal Democrat cushion provided insulation from internal politicking and disgruntlement. In the wider country the collapse of the BNP and increasing disenchantment with Cameron, particularly following moves to push equal marriage between same-sex couples through the Commons, saw UKIP become a more menacing force. During 2014 and after, his strategy was more explicitly concerned with winning back these voters and his instrument was the pledge to hold a referendum on EU membership – a measure to spectacularly backfire and destroy his political career. Therefore one can see a continuity of strategy running through Cameron's two governments, which makes the case for separating them out on grounds of anything other than chronological and political arithmetic difficult to sustain.

Unlike Thatcher and Major, the period of neoliberal consolidation between 1992 and 2010 ensured that class politics in the sense of an open confrontation with and defeat of the workers' movement was unnecessary. However, another common theme running through the coalition's 'liberalism' was not just the stress on the atomised, rational choice-oriented individual, but a politics of us-versus-them-ism: the creation of new scapegoats to justify policy changes and, crucially, undermine nascent forms of solidarity. This is not to say that the Cameron governments did not provoke opposition, some of which was militant, but this largely failed to find sustained political expression (in England and Wales) until Jeremy Corbyn won the 2015 Labour leadership election. The Cameron governments then presented themselves explicitly in economic and state-order terms; get the economy moving again, and deal with the debt crisis of the state by reforming it, reconfiguring it and cutting it.

This distinction is an analytical separation. As became increasingly clear, the Tory agendas for the economy and the state were frequently used as synonyms for one another. Cutting budgets and reducing the public spending deficit became a sign of economic competence, while stagnant GDP figures – at least in the coalition's early years – were played down as the relevant signifier of efficacy.

This was also the period in which the policy legacies of Thatcher and Major 'matured' and consolidated the rising political fortunes of the Tories. While the organisation of the party continued withering on the vine, Cameron's decision to protect pensioners' incomes and exempt them from changes to social housing, encourage a burgeoning of second and third home ownership to rent and concentrate Tory energies on winning over older voters foregrounded the political polarisation of the EU referendum and the 2017 and 2019 general elections. Such was the outcome of blind, short-termist and decadent political leadership.

The Economics of Austerity

The threefold objective of the Tory-led coalition was cutting the deficit, managing the growing debt and building a 'new economy' characterised by 'balance'.[2] For George Osborne, Germany provided the model for the sort of advanced economy Britain should aspire towards, with a strong finance sector allied to world-leading manufacturing and export-led growth. To reach this destination, redistributing economic opportunity outside London and the South East was a priority. Vapid soundbites referring to the 'Northern powerhouse' and 'Midlands engine' peppered Osborne's speeches, the flatteries of backbenchers smarming their way up the career ladder and the Tory stable of nodding client journalists. 'Balance' was also to be achieved by making the UK less dependent on financial services and encouraging industry. And lastly, the map of the economy was to be redrawn by peeling back the public sector to allow private enterprise to fill the gaps in the state's provision.

Among the new government's first moves was setting up the Office for Budget Responsibility (OBR), ostensibly to prevent chancellors now and in the future from fiddling growth forecasts and as a means of disciplining central government. As George Osborne put it, the OBR would

> remove the temptation to fiddle the figures by giving up control
> over the economic and fiscal forecast. I recognise that this will

create a rod for my back down the line, and for the backs of future chancellors. That is the whole point. We need to fix the budget to fit the figures, not fix the figures to fit the budget.[3]

Preparing the ground for the emergency budget on 22 June, Cameron took to the airwaves to claim that the budget position of the government was worse than he had been led to believe and that 'the taxpayer' would be paying £70 billion a year in interest payments by 2015 unless something drastic was done.[4]

When the Budget arrived, it clearly fell far from the all-in-it-together rhetoric. Osborne's plan had two aspects: extend tax relief on the first £5 million of capital gains tax, a 1 per cent year-on-year reduction of corporation tax from 28 per cent to 24 per cent and reduced taxes for small businesses. Presumably allowing businesses to keep more money might free up extra funds for investment. Also, shielding business from the cost of raising low pay, the Tories raised the income tax threshold by £1,000, which would take a projected 880,000 out of paying tax and worked as a personal tax cut for everyone else of around £200/year.

These carrots were accompanied by a large stick. There was a VAT increase from 17.5 per cent to 20 per cent, an increase in the pension age, the freezing of public sector salaries for two years except for those earning below £21,000, cutting housing benefit for unemployed people out of work for more than a year, reductions to housing benefit claimants for those living in council and social housing properties larger than their needs (what later became the bedroom tax; see below), capping payments at £400 a week, cuts in grants to pregnant women and linking benefits to the consumer price index. Government departments were expected to shoulder budget cuts of up to 25 per cent.[5] The overall aim was to reduce spending to the point where, in terms of day-to-day spending, the government would run a surplus by 2014–15 – coincidentally in time for the election.

The coalition followed its emergency budget up with a spending review in the autumn. For Osborne, the principles underpinning his strategy were 'reform, fairness, and growth'. There was to be

£6 billion worth of cuts to Whitehall and the loss of 490,000 jobs from the public sector over the following four years. Osborne was keen to stress that most of this would be met by natural turnover, such as retirement and not replacing staff who leave, but also believed that the impact would be cushioned by job creation in the private sector. Citing the 178,000 jobs created in the previous quarter, Osborne was silent about whether they were like-for-like replacements and offered similar levels of remuneration.

He also set out the reduction in government grants for councils, starting with a 7.1 per cent cut from 2011 and a reworking of the funding formula, stripping out additional needs and local circum-stances and 'equalising' funding on a per-person basis. This meant cuts falling hardest on local authorities with the highest poverty indices. Increased National Insurance contributions were announced as a means of boosting the state pension, a bonfire of the quangos to satisfy a 15 per cent cut to the Culture department, and the identification of £5 billion supposedly lost to social secu-rity fraud and a set of tough measures to deal with it.

In terms of stimulus, the capital spending budget was projected to be £51 billion, £49 billion, £46 billion and £47 billion until 2014–15. But overall this was the only spending earmarked for that purpose. Some £1 billion was committed to carbon capture and storage pro-jects. Another £1 billion was committed to offshore wind farms and a further billion for a green bank and 'Green Deal' incentives. The NHS budget was given above-inflation rises but the schools budget was to rise from £35 billion to £39 billion, a static spend in real terms. In short, despite Osborne's ambition to rebalance Brit-ain, the Budget and the spending review were destructive and illiterate if the Chancellor was determined to build a 'growth-led' economy. This was a recipe for dampening demand, informed by a (not entirely good faith) belief that public sector cuts magically create space for market economics.

Hope was not enough to bridge the gap between deeds and words. At the end of 2010 unemployment had risen to 7.9 per cent, or over 2.5 million people. In 2011 it peaked at 8.1 per cent before coming down slightly to 8 per cent in 2012 and 7.6 per cent in 2013.

Afterwards the recovery in the job market was rapid, but there were three full years in which fiscal contraction meant that the economy was not as buoyant as might otherwise have been the case. Wages and salaries saw sluggish growth while real wages fell between 2010 and 2015.[6] On GDP growth, after reporting 1.9 per cent growth for 2010, for 2011 and 2012 it stagnated at 1.5 per cent before experiencing a fillip in 2013 when it climbed to 2.1 per cent. It also meant that Osborne's deficit targets were missed, with the Office for National Statistics (notably not the Treasury) reporting the final achievement of a surplus in November 2017.

Despite the missed targets and tardy growth, the Tories did find the time to make further inroads into workplace rights. From April 2012 the qualifying period for claims of unfair dismissal was extended from one year of employment to two, and the composition of employment tribunal panels was at the discretion of the presiding judge, who could now either hear them alone or appoint lay members from business and the trade unions – this was previously automatic.

The Tories' economic strategy was forced to face reality following Osborne's 2012 speech, which was subsequently dubbed the 'omnishambles budget' by Labour leader Ed Miliband, himself channelling *The Thick of It*, the popular satirical sitcom (especially within Westminster circles). Osborne again raised the threshold for the basic rate of income tax from £8,105 to £9,205, saving tax payers £220 a year. He also lowered the threshold at which the 40 per cent band was applied from £42,475 to £41,450 and cut the top rate of tax to 45p from 50p. Changes to income tax allowances on pensions would see 4.4 million over-sixty-fives worse off by £83 a year.

There was also an immediate cut in Corporation Tax to 24 per cent, two years ahead of schedule, with a further deduction pre-announced for 2014 to see it reduced to 22 per cent. Unsurprisingly, Labour attacked it as a millionaire's budget, albeit balanced at the expense of the 'squeezed middle'.[7] These criticisms stung as Osborne pitched towards championing 'working families' during the following year, outlining his intention to raise the tax threshold to £10,000 a year earlier than planned while cracking down on social security by introducing a cap on benefits. It also became apparent to Osborne that these efforts were taking demand out of the economy, and so the following December's Autumn Statement outlined a Keynesian-lite package of policies. These included increased spending on flood defences, another £1 billion for roads, the rolling out of ultra-fast broadband in a dozen cities, a £600 million fund for science, and a commitment to maintaining the annual £33 billion infrastructure investment bill. A further £1 billion was available for new schools too, which meant more money for the semi-privatised academy chains and the free schools Tory pet project.[8]

These meagre stimulus measures were packaged with another attack on workplace rights. In the Growth and Infrastructure bill, which began its passage through the Commons that December and was pre-announced by Osborne at the Tory conference, employers would have the right to offer a buyout of their workers' statutory rights in return for a package of shares worth between £2,000 and £50,000. This could be offered to prospective employees from day one in lieu of established protections. Presumably, to Osborne's mind, over-mighty shop stewards and workplace union branches were holding back growth. As Justin King, the chief executive of Sainsbury's, put it in response, 'What do you think the population at large will think of businesses that want to trade employment rights for money?' Mike Emmott, an employment adviser at the Confederation of British Industry, said, 'employees have little to gain by substituting their fundamental rights for uncertain financial gain and employers have little to gain by creating a two-tier labour market'. Of 200 businesses contacted by the government in its consultative exercise, only five expressed an interest in the scheme. To try and sugar the plans, the following March Osborne promised that the first £2,000 payment to workers would be tax-free.[9]

Underlining the weakness of Osborne's newly found fondness for stimulus measures was his announcement in March that he was extending the public sector pay rise cap of 1 per cent for another year. There was also an introduction of a house buying scheme where purchasers could access a low-cost loan covering 20 per cent of a property's value provided they could find 5 per cent of the value as the deposit, and the loan only became payable once the house was later sold on. Designed not to come into force until 2014, it was a transparent election bribe. Osborne's 2013 Budget also wanted to do more to rebalance public and private sector employment and pledged the partial privatisation of Royal Mail and selling off the Student Loans Company.

Confirming fears about the quality of the jobs replacing those lost by the private sector, the previous three years had seen a surge in zero-hour contracts.[10] There were also further attacks on workers' rights. These included a diminution of consultation over redundancies, capping awards for successful employment tribunal cases at one year's salary to a maximum of £74,200 and the introduction of tribunal fees. This was ostensibly to ward off vexatious claims, but in practice the package of changes consolidated the already strong position of the employer even further.

As 2013 saw the turn to renewed growth and paid employment resumed its upward trend, a chronic feature of the British economy reasserted itself: underproduction. According to Office for National Statistics productivity measures, output fell from 103.4 per worker in May 2008 to 99.1 in the fourth quarter of 2013. Instead of investing in new technologies, employers took advantage of mass unemployment and stalling wages to simply take on more workers – by June 2014 the number of people in work stood at 30.5 million, a then all-time high.[11]

Adding to what became known as the productivity puzzle were millions of self-employed people who had entered the market thanks to a relative scarcity of suitable vacancies. In other words, the apparent stagnation was a consequence of productivity becoming disarticulated from the numbers deemed economically active, itself a result of the Tories' failure to invest properly.

This typified the Tory approach to fracking, for example. Forgetting the previous decade's worth of greenwash, the 2014 parliamentary opening saw the Tories considerably liberalise the rules governing the extraction of shale gas. This was despite the possibility for localised micro-earthquakes and the contamination of the water table, as seen from multiple drills across the United States. The new rules allowed fracking companies to commence operations without informing landowners first, granted them permission to drill under businesses and homes regardless of the consent of the owners of these properties and removed the right to consultation with local people. This unseemly rush was about consolidating what was then the fastest-growing economy in the EU, and ticking several of Osborne's boxes around cheaper energy, economic rebalancing, jobs in 'proper' industry, exports and GDP figures. Close Tory links with fossil fuel lobbyists were entirely coincidental.[12] Unfortunately for the government, these measures came into force just as oil prices collapsed, ensuring the hoped-for boom in shale gas was a non-starter.

Going into early 2015 with the election due, the Tories were able to claim the high ground of economic competence by eliding economic recovery with deficit reduction and talking up the employment numbers and GDP growth. This formed the bedrock of their strategy and enabled them to win a majority, even if it meant annihilation for their Liberal Democrat partners.

On returning to office, Osborne moved very quickly to commit the state to running a budget surplus. 'In normal times, governments of the left as well as the right should run a budget surplus to bear down on debt and prepare for an uncertain future.'[13] In other words, this was another disciplinary mechanism designed to curb future state spending and would, according to his calculations, politically cost any government daring to repeal it. This party-political posturing informed the rest of Osborne's victory Budget.

He rebranded the minimum wage the National Living Wage for workers aged over twenty-five and outflanked Labour from the left; the Tories originally projected a £9/hour wage by 2020 whereas Labour were calling for £8, but also announced continued freezes for public sector pay and tax credits. These were traps designed to influence Labour's leadership contest, and indeed caused a split in the party when acting leader Harriet Harman demanded MPs abstain on the first reading of the bill while many MPs, not all of them left-wing, rebelled and voted against.

Luckily for Osborne his edging away from the low-stimulus budgets of his recent past and back to the comfort zone of pre-2012 did not cause too much controversy thanks to the OBR's strong growth projections. This was underlined in October when Britain's steel industry largely collapsed, and no state aid was forthcoming.

Before Osborne's departure from office following the EU referendum, the Tories' final piece of significant legislation was another assault on trade unions. Sponsored by self-confessed Ayn Rand supporter and short-lived future Chancellor Sajid Javid, the Trade Union Reform Act 2016 was partially watered down as a quid pro quo between David Cameron and the TUC to compensate it for supporting Remain in the referendum. It introduced turn-out thresholds of 50 per cent for successful industrial action votes. In the public sector a threshold of 40 per cent of all eligible members, whether they turned out or not, was specified for lawful action to proceed. It imposed time limits on disputes, which meant that a fresh ballot was necessary at six-monthly intervals and the ending of free payroll deductions of union dues by public sector employers. It was clearly a set of measures designed to further tie union organisation up in compliance issues and frustrate their efficacy, even though the level of disputes was at a historic low. In other words, it was a class-conscious effort by the Conservative government to mute potential future industrial opposition to its schemes.

Osborne's economic programme, in sum, was as short-termist as it was arbitrary. The targets for deficit reduction and debt were governed by the timetable of the 2015 general election, and GDP was reified as the sole index of economic wellbeing once the numbers reported turned healthy. This meant consciously turning a blind eye to the drop-off in the quality of jobs, as wellpaid public sector roles were replaced by a preponderance of poor-paying occupations. Nor was Osborne particularly interested in the surging number of part-time jobs, stagnating wages or the overheating housing market. What mattered were headline figures where the chancellor would announce the continual uptick in economic activity measures while a stream of slavish backbenchers at Prime Minister's Questions and other Commons debates heaped praise on his 'long-term economic plan'. There was no such plan.

Was this just a question of poor leadership? The tolerance of mass unemployment, and its later subsumption by low pay, precarity and underemployment, refute any notion that Osborne and Cameron's primary concerns were economic growth. For them, the 2008 crash presented an opportunity, and once in office and with varying degrees of skill they set out to consolidate a neoliberal response to the crisis. This meant reinforcing the power of the market through deregulation, extending market logics to more areas of the state, stripping back protections, reducing the meagre powers of trade unions even further and protecting the vested interests that the Tory Party rests on and articulates. Their plan was driven by class interests rather than the technocratically defined needs of capitalism to secure sustainable growth or strike a well-balanced equilibrium. This was economic-order politics steered by class politics, which had the happy by-product, for them, of consolidating the Tories' 2010 electoral coalition and expanding it.

Social Security

Despite David Cameron's soothing language in opposition, it quickly became clear that social security was going to be a political weapon to meet two objectives. The first was to complement austerity economics by undermining lingering notions of solidarity between the in-work and the out-of-work, individuating the experience of unemployment and making a claim more difficult. The second was to undertake a campaign of demonisation and scapegoating against those fallen on hard times – a return to the two-nation Toryism of the Thatcher and Major years.

Nick Clegg, as deputy prime minister, characterised the coalition government's assault on welfare as speaking up for 'alarm clock Britain'.[14] Osborne preferred to talk explicitly about the 'strivers versus the skivers' and 'workers, not shirkers'.[15] When a less strident tone was required, Cameron himself referred to their social security programme as a moral crusade. For example, responding in 2014 to criticisms of his programme by the Catholic Church, he said,

> Our long-term economic plan for Britain is not just about doing what we can afford, it is also about doing what is right . . . Nowhere is that more true than in welfare. For me the moral case for welfare reform is every bit as important as making the numbers add up . . . That means difficult decisions to get our deficit down, making sure that the debts of this generation are not our children's to inherit . . . But our welfare reforms go beyond that alone – they are about giving new purpose, new opportunity, new hope – and yes, new responsibility to people who had previously been written off with no chance . . . Seeing these reforms through is at the heart of our long-term economic plan – and it is at the heart too of our social and moral mission in politics today.[16]

This dovetails with the 2010 manifesto. During opposition the Tories gingerly inched towards something like a reassertion of Thatcherite attitudes to social security. In their programme, welfare was positioned under 'Get Britain working again'. The Tories pledged to create a Work Programme for all unemployed people while offering individualised and tailored help to get back into work; workers would be compelled to accept job offers on pain of withdrawn payments and those unemployed in the long term would participate in compulsory work schemes. They also promised to 'reassess all current claimants of Incapacity Benefit. Those found fit to work will be transferred onto Jobseekers' Allowance'.[17] Once in office, however, the changes made to social security were more far-reaching.

The key to the Tories' restructuring of welfare reform was the Work Programme, which extended and replaced a series of measures developed by Labour to address long-term unemployment, but even by 2008 a number of questions had been raised about the efficacy of these schemes. Based on the assumption that so-called cultures of worklessness were the root of social security claims, as opposed to the lack of jobs, those entering the programme – who had been on JSA for over nine months – were taken on by participating employers and represented a cut-price workforce without entitlement to the minimum wage and other employment protections.[18] As Page notes,[19] administering the scheme was put out to competitive tender and projected to cost £2.8 billion between June 2011 and March 2016. Humiliatingly for the government, by November 2012 it was found to be worse than useless. Whereas 5 per cent of long-term recipients could expect to 'naturally' find a job without job centre intervention or coaching, the Work Programme's success rate (measured in subsequent employment lasting for more than six months) was 2.3 per cent.[20]

A dismal record was no barrier to introducing more conditionality. From October a new series of sanctions came into force covering unemployment benefits. For JSA, there were three penalty tiers for claimants if they did not attend a job centre interview; did not participate in its compulsory Employment, Skills and Enterprise programme (a package of sub-schemes offering skills training, including 'job-seeking'); and did not comply with a 'jobseeker direction' (i.e., being directed to apply for certain vacancies); or refused to take up an offer of a place on a training course.

Failure to comply meant that a 'customer', as the guidance labels clients, loses four weeks' payments on the first offence and thirteen weeks' for subsequent breaches. Recipients who do not 'actively' seek work are liable for the same range of penalties over a fifty-two-week period. High-level sanctions came into play if a claimant is fired due to misconduct or voluntarily leaves their job, does not participate in mandatory work activities, is not available for a job or refuses or fails to apply for a suitable job as determined by their adviser. Penalties ranged from thirteen weeks for the first failure to twenty-six weeks for the second and three years for the third.

This punitive system devolved discretion to job centre advisers, and the appeals process often featured applicants who missed an appointment due to a medical emergency or were at a job interview. Iain Duncan Smith as the DWP secretary was later forced to deny evidence presented to the Commons that job centre managers had a culture of sanctions targets and that advisers were pressured to hand as many out as possible.[21] Up to 2014, this meant that over a million unemployed people had received sanctions – 28.7 per cent of the those in receipt of the benefit.[22]

Part of the same package were changes to Employment Support Allowance (ESA), a form of income support available to disabled or chronically ill people unable to work. In line with the review of all Incapacity Benefit cases, the Tories wanted to move all of them onto ESA. Introduced by Labour in 2008, its objective was to sort between claimants who were capable of some form of limited work and those who were not.

This entailed an in-person Work Capability Assessment in which the claimant was put through a battery of non-medical tests of mobility, eyesight, comprehension and mundane physical activities. Under the Conservatives, those scoring over fifteen points were placed in the Support Group and would be retested in the future, even if the illness or impairment was chronic and/or terminal. Those scoring fewer points were assigned to the Work-Related Activity Group. As a condition for receiving the benefit there was a compulsory 'work-focused' interview and, where appropriate, mandatory training as per JSA, including a similar sanctions regime. If zero points were scored, ESA was denied altogether, and unsuccessful claimants were invited to apply for the standard dole.

The Work Capability Assessment came to be criticised as arbitrary, cruel and Kafkaesque as people with severe physical maladies and mental health problems were routinely found fit for work; it was at the assessor's discretion whether to pay attention to medical evidence an applicant brought along to their test (the findings of each test were passed to a DWP decision maker). Many did not and, as a result, success at appeals was very high. In 2013, decisions were overturned in 37 per cent of cases, mushrooming to 72 per cent by 2018.[23]

Another great Tory crusade was against housing benefit, which for reasons of electoral expediency Cameron chose not to label the landlords' subsidy. A fruit of the 2012 Welfare Reform Act, central to the Tory changes was a desire to cap payments and re-engineer the occupancy of the UK's social housing stock. Duncan Smith's first move was to make cuts of between £10 and £20 for low-paid and long-term unemployed recipients, arguing it was 'unfair to the people on benefits living in accommodation that they could never afford to maintain if they entered work'.[24]

The second line of attack involved what became known as the bedroom tax, which the Tories consistently referred to as the 'spare room subsidy'. Modelled on the approach to private tenants that Labour had previously engineered, housing benefit claimants in social or council housing were assessed according to whether they 'under-occupied' the property. For example, if a single person occupied a two-bedroom house or a couple had a three-bedroomed home, they were 'under-occupying'. Their housing benefit would be reduced by 14 per cent if a tenant was under-occupying by one room and 25 per cent by two. The 2012 Act did not specify a definition of a bedroom, leaving it up to the landlord to define it according to the tenancy agreement.

Theoretically, councils and housing associations could rewrite these documents to help tenants dodge the reduction, but in practice such an exercise would have affected their asset base and ability to borrow money. As far as the Tories were concerned this was a fair policy because it freed up properties for larger families on social housing waiting lists. The obvious problem was that after decades of public housing sell-offs there were few suitable properties for tenants to move into to avoid the reduction.

Punitive changes to Council Tax benefit came into force simultaneously. Under these rules, the administration of the benefit was devolved to local authorities but top-sliced by the government by 20 per cent, meaning that claimants would normally be expected to find a minimum 20 per cent of the bill. In another of Osborne's political traps, local authorities were given the discretion of funding the benefit shortfall themselves but in practice this was impossible thanks to government-mandated cuts to the local government grant. It also eroded the Council Tax base for several councils who were left out of pocket by the reduction and had little chance of recovering monies owed by pursuing claimants through the courts.

The last big change to come out of the 2012 Act was the benefits cap, which was set at £25,000 a year. Exempting pensioners, like all the other welfare changes, the cap took all benefits into consideration, including housing benefit. While projected only to affect a small number of people (the DWP issued only 20,000 letters),[25] its impact was set to fall most heavily on London and the South East and effectively price those on low incomes out of the capital.

Coincident with these changes was the introduction of Universal Credit. A pet project of Duncan Smith, it aimed to combine all benefits into a single payment, thereby leaving out the need for duplicated administration and separate application procedures. Additionally, the level of payments would automatically adjust itself if one were in work but with variable hours. Working tax credits – a Gordon Brown innovation designed to subsidise low wages – would take up the slack when hours were thin on the ground, but payments would pare back when certain thresholds were crossed. However, the timetable for its introduction constantly slipped back and it proved incredibly complex to run, with errors in the amounts owed and delays in payments.

The Tories' return to a Thatcherite welfare position met half-hearted opposition from the Labour Party. The bedroom tax changes were only formally opposed six months after its introduction, while the party was formally committed to being even tougher on welfare than the Tories.[26] With no political costs attached to welfare, the Tories went into the 2015 election pledging to lower the benefits cap to £23,000 and introduce sanctions for chronically ill recipients who refuse treatment.[27]

In the event, it was an unplanned welfare attack that caused the Tories most political pain. To phase in Universal Credit, after the election Osborne announced the abolition of working tax credits from April 2016, which would have amounted to a £4.4 billion cut. This provoked opposition among the Tory benches and the press, with Osborne forgetting how low-paid workers were considered in the popular imaginary among the 'deserving' poor.

This plan was reversed in his autumn statement but reintroduced prior to the March Budget. Osborne then announced a change to how Personal Independence Payments, the non-work-related disability benefit, would be calculated. This meant that up to 600,000 recipients would no longer be eligible for 'enhanced' payments and, coincidentally, would save the Treasury the £4.4 billion Osborne had earlier been forced to abandon.

Making matters worse was his simultaneous announcement that the threshold for the 40 per cent income tax rate was rising again, saving the upper levels of the middle-class salariat a further £500 per annum. The fallout was greater than the omnishambles budget. Duncan Smith resigned as DWP secretary, protesting that he was 'unable to watch passively whilst certain policies are enacted in order to meet the fiscal self-imposed restraints that I believe are more and more perceived as distinctly political rather than in the national economic interest'.[28] The storm of criticism saw Osborne disappear from public view for several days, before returning to the Commons to announce that he was withdrawing the disability cut.

Social security, then, was a weapon in the Tories' efforts to embed two-nation politics. Building on the approach to welfare of the Thatcher and Major years, benefit recipients were cast as unpeople scapegoated for high public spending and unemployment, and footballs to be kicked around for favourable headlines. The onerous new conditions attached to accessing the system were designed to put people off from applying, and each applicant was treated with institutionalised suspicion. To rely on social security was, by design, an atomising experience in which the responsibility for getting back into work and/or improving one's lot was down to individual effort. In turn, this helped reinforce the Tory narrative of economic recovery; these measures were justified and hailed as underpinning the so-called jobs miracle, as if punitive measures themselves were spontaneously and magically creating the low-skilled, low-waged jobs millions of people were shuffling into.

It helped ensure that Labour's responses to welfare reform, particularly prior to summer 2015, were characterised by catch-up and pandering. Challenging Tory moves was not uncontroversial in the party, and some even found opposing the bedroom tax a step too far. This attitude helped inform the immediate debate following the 2015 election loss. Labour was, apparently, no longer on the side of 'aspiration' and Harriet Harman as acting leader justified the party's abstention on the first reading of Osborne's cut to working tax credits as 'listening' to the message the electorate had sent. Without Labour contesting the ground the Tories had pitched on, it looked like Cameron and Osborne were on the brink of consolidating the neoliberal response to the economic crisis as a rejuvenated iteration of the Thatcherite settlement.

Health

Like John Major's government, Cameron's Tories were keen to reinforce neoliberal discipline on state institutions, and this was particularly the case with the NHS. This was the subject of their most complex piece of 'successful' remodelling of state institutions during the 2010–15 parliament. The Tory manifesto gave little clue about what was to befall the NHS, with the rote talk of patient choice, decentralisation, transparency and preventive medicine. It talked about patients in charge of their own healthcare, combined with a 'rate your doctor' system along the lines of 'customer' satisfaction surveys rampant across public services and higher education. It promised a war on bureaucracy at clinical need's behest, with the projection of reducing administration budgets by a third. Interestingly the manifesto contained no spending commitments for the NHS.[29] Likewise, the Coalition Agreement was innocuous, committing both parties to real-terms increases in funding while excluding the reorganisation of the NHS as a matter for consideration. Despite this, in July Health Secretary Andrew Lansley presented a White Paper committing the government to an ambitious and complex reorganisation of the health service, often described as the most far-reaching since its establishment in 1948.[30]

Under Labour, funding to the NHS was substantially increased and new estate was built or refurbished via private finance initiative contracts. This said, it did not depart substantially from the structure bequeathed Labour by John Major. Despite pledging to abolish the internal market prior to 1997, following Labour's re-election in 2001 there was a push to outsource more NHS-provided services to the private sector, but also to take on more staff and to focus on patient choice and rights and, crucially, on incentives provided for meeting targets. The service overall was overseen by a succession of regulatory bodies. This meant that NHS performance indicators substantially improved with the rate of deaths in hospital falling alongside waiting lists for operations and at Accident and Emergency.

The targets culture did in some instances generate perverse incentives. For example, the excess number of patient deaths at the Mid Staffordshire NHS Trust revealed a staff culture marked by indifference, alienation, bullying and a concern for targets to the exclusion of all else, including clinical need.[31]

Andrew Lansley's proposals, which the 2012 Health and Social Care Act legislated for, departed radically from Labour's tinkering and were even more ambitious than anything Major's Citizen's Charter conceived. Effectively, the proposed restructure removed any role for the health secretary and the Department of Health and let the market run amok.

The new structure retained its free-at-the-point-of-need ethos, in most cases, but the NHS was reduced to a label adhering to a market of private, public and charitable health providers competing for state-funded clinical delivery contracts. Taking the principles from the Tory manifesto as its jumping-off point, the new Act abolished primary care trusts (PCTs) as the vehicles by which funds were allotted and replaced them with smaller clinical commisioning groups (CCGs). Monies were handed to these general-practitioner-run bodies, who then purchased services from any willing (and, as determined by the tendering process, capable) provider. Therefore hospital trusts might compete with private consortia for contracts pertaining to all areas of medicine: cancer services, physiotherapy, counselling, immunisation. This met the objective, at least on paper, of putting funding decisions in the hands of medical professionals, but also succeeded in fragmenting the health service further. Whereas 152 PCTs distributed the finance of the NHS pre-2012, afterwards some 200 CCGs existed and covered around 226,000 patients each over a much smaller geographic area.

Lansley's scheme was the direct successor to Thatcher's reforms. It shared her assumptions that competition was the driver of quality and that where the market abides services tend to be better and cheaper. The practice, however, did not match the theory and did not make for a more efficient service. The cost of the reforms was priced at £1.5 billion, and while the government claimed that this had been recouped in cumulative savings following the abolition of PCTs, the National Audit Office was sceptical.[32] What was certainly fanciful was the notion that administration costs would be cut by up to one third. Managers and accountants were kept on the payroll to put in bids for services, monitor market signals and lobby funding bodies. If anything, more markets was just the recipe for more bureaucracy.

Reflecting on these reforms in 2015, the head of the King's Fund, Sir Christopher Ham, said that these reforms did not privatise the NHS, but the government had succeeded in introducing thoroughgoing marketisation at the cost of fragmentation, generated a confused and confusing system and produced an unnecessary distraction to tackling long-term health challenges, especially around the integration of health and social care – the latter of which was the province of local authorities and subject to the swingeing cuts the Tories were imposing on councils.[33]

The other intended consequence of the legislation was an effort to depoliticise yet another area of state responsibility. As Nigel Lawson attempted to subordinate economic policy to the pound's position on the international exchange markets, and as Gordon Brown turned interest rate policy into a technocratic as opposed to a political decision by handing the responsibility to the Bank of England, Lansley's reforms set about establishing the independence of the NHS. The secretary of state was no longer responsible for strategic decisions, nor, according to its organisational diagram, were they accountable for its performance. Working with the

Treasury, their responsibility devolved to securing funding – they (theoretically) did not have input on how the money was spent, or on the strategic decisions that increasingly came to be guided by NHS England, or the Scottish and Welsh governments.

Despite the reforms, practice has necessitated that CCGs and providers work around the rules imposed by the government. They were becoming more cooperative, collaborative and integrated, culminating in the NHS Long-Term Plan published in 2019 which highlighted NHS England's strategic goals and its apportioning of funds to meet these objectives.[34] Interestingly, a series of reforms designed to make the market supreme have cautiously, and by the back door, allowed clinical need to assume something of a pre-eminence over competition.

Education

The Labour years saw significant investment in schools, in terms of both staff and, via PFIs, a long-delayed refurbishment and replacement of school buildings. Its Building Schools for the Future programme was a £55 billion package aimed at updating and replacing the existing aged and, in several cases, crumbling estate. Again, while impressive in scale and celebrated as one of Labour's enduring legacies, it did not break qualitatively with the Major government's approach to and governance of schooling. Like the Tories, New Labour believed that excellence in education was best served through metrics, competition and league tables. Local democratic input via local authorities was a hindrance.

Indeed, Labour moved to effectively privatise several local education authorities by inviting in the private sector to take them over if schools in their charge were deemed failing by Ofsted. Local accountability was further eroded via Labour's flagship academies scheme. Announced in March 2000, this effectively offered thousands of schools up to privatisation. In a speech to the Keynesian think tank the Social Market Foundation, Education Secretary David Blunkett said,

These academies, to replace seriously failing schools, will be built and managed by partnerships involving the government, voluntary, church and business sponsors. They will offer a real challenge and improvements in pupil performance, for example through innovative approaches to management, governance, teaching and the curriculum, including a specialist focus in at least one curriculum area.[35]

These 'partnerships' handed a school over to anyone who could provide £2 million towards the cost of building a new school, and this gave them the power to name the school and to determine who sat on its governors' board, some direction over the curriculum and an element of selection of the academy's intake. This was despite most funding being provided from public funds. Academies also sat outside LEA control and were built in places where existing provision was determined to be inadequate and failing. Alongside moves to academisation, Labour also put stress on testing pupils throughout their school journey, ostensibly for targeted interventions for children who were falling behind, but this too worked as another disciplinary rod.

As far as the Tories were concerned, the 2010 manifesto promised the renewal of school discipline and the recruitment of more and better teachers. Mathematics and science were singled out as requiring attention, and a new national curriculum emphasising core subjects was promised along with reforms to testing. These were accompanied by reformulating league tables to measure attainment alongside assessment outcomes. The Tories also committed to taking over schools put in special measures by academy chains. The Coalition Agreement accepted all these proposals and added a few of its own, which included reforming 'rigid national pay and conditions rules'.[36]

Within a fortnight of his appointment as education secretary, Michael Gove had moved to extend academisation. He wrote to all primary and secondary schools in England suggesting that they become academies and unveiled proposals that removed 'local authorities' power to veto a school becoming an academy, dispensed with parents' and teachers' legal right to oppose such plans, and allowed "outstanding" schools to "fast-track" the process of becoming academies'.[37] All but six Liberal Democrat MPs supported Gove's bill in the Commons, despite the party's formal opposition to academies and position for the revival of local education authorities.

The flagship project associated with Gove's time in office was free schools. A Swedish innovation, this was sold as the right of parent-led consortia to set up their own institutions if they felt that existing state provision was failing. In practice, this leadership was expanded to include faith groups, universities, businesses and existing independent schools. For Gove they offered greater choice in the education system, and, while subject to Ofsted inspections, they could choose their own curriculum, determine the length of the school year and control the terms and conditions of their staff. Controversially, they could employ teachers without teaching qualifications. Like academies, they sat outside local authority control.

The free schools' initiative met with opposition. The funding of a new free school would come from within existing schools' budgets, which effectively meant less money for existing schools wherever a free school was set up. Second, there was concern it might re-create new grammar schools by the back door. There was nothing stopping middle-class parents from setting up schools leveraging their children's existing advantages in education, drawing in pupils from other nearby schools and driving down their league table rankings.

As per academies, the removal of local authority input meant that Gove was the ultimate regulator of this sector of schooling. Such an unwieldy approach to accountability meant that several instances of malpractice and financial mismanagement came to light after the fact, whereas robust scrutiny by local authority education departments might have prevented them.

Alongside this increased marketisation of schooling, Gove immediately cancelled the Building Schools for the Future programme, a decision that meant suspending some 715 projects, and the 600 allowed to continue now faced significant cost cutting. While this was challenged in the courts by six local authorities, the government pressed ahead with cuts to subsidies available for school meals, trainee teacher schemes and Connexions career advice centres, and forced schools running deficits in excess of £1 million to sack staff instead of receiving extra help.

From 2011, a tranche of Labour-era agencies designed to support the marketised ecosystem of schools were wound up.

The Teach First programme, also set up under Labour, was expanded by Gove as part of the government's battering ram against teachers and teaching unions. It offered extra money to graduates taking up 'shortage subjects', particularly mathematics, while replacing teachers' final-salary pension schemes with career averages and looking at ways of removing 'underperforming' teachers from the classroom. This provoked strike action, which included the National Association of Head Teachers voting for stoppages for the first time in its history.

Despite the breadth of the action of the teaching unions, the government pressed ahead with scrapping national pay deals and introducing performance-related pay from September 2013. Responding to protest and criticism, including his plans to centre the reformulated National Curriculum around the rote learning of facts instead of reasoning and problem solving, at the Tory Party conference Gove argued that teachers were 'enemies of progress' and, ironically, said, 'I have a simple message for the militant teaching unions: please, please, please don't put your ideology before our children's interests.'[38]

The replacement of Gove by Nicky Morgan did not change the direction of policy, though Morgan did not resort to the public baiting of teachers. Nevertheless, the pressures on the system were too much and, according to Department for Education figures, 40 per cent of new teachers were resigning within their first year, while the number of unqualified teachers had mushroomed to over 17,000 by the start of 2015.

At the general election, the Tories promised to turn every failing school into an academy and speed up the delivery of free schools. However, there was no serious legislation forthcoming during the final year of Cameron's government. The facts spoke for themselves; by 2017, 77 per cent of primary schools were run by the local authority, with 22 per cent either an academy or part of an academy chain. The position was practically reversed for secondary schools. Here 62 per cent of schools (6,087) were an academy while only 31 per cent retained local authority input.[39]

There was a key difference between Labour and Tory approaches to the marketisation of schooling. For their part, Tony Blair and his education secretaries created a system geared towards securing healthy metrics and driving standards up while ensuring that teachers were disciplined by the targets and inspectorate system. In other words, there was a regulated neoliberalisation of education. The Tories' approach to schools was a step back to the Thatcher–Major approach: disempower teachers and their unions by undermining professional culture, eliminating intermediary bodies that might present a block on the government's ambitions, erode democratic input by local councils, increase competition between schools while opening the door for private providers and reserving strategic decision making on policy and the curriculum to the government.

Gove and his infamous special adviser, Dominic Cummings, liked to refer to teachers, educational professionals and policy specialists as 'the blob', but in so doing they were merely reheating the anti-expertise strategies and discourse pursued by every government since Thatcher. Free schools and academies have not substantially boosted achievement, have not tackled persistent attainment gaps and certainly have not set free the talents of teachers. Gove brought the ill-informed touch of the opinion columnist to education and reshaped it according to his prejudices and the demands of right-wing lobbyists and business. The creation of a challenging curriculum appropriate to the twenty-first century supported by enthusiastic teachers and facilities equal to the task came, and continues to come, a distant second.

State-Order Politics

Despite governing in coalition with the Liberal Democrats, who, prior to 2010, cast themselves as a centre-left alternative to Labour, the Conservatives pursued a programme entirely consistent with previous Tory governments, albeit occasionally borrowing Blair-sounding rhetoric around inclusion and social justice. On economic policy, workers' rights, social security, the NHS and education in schools, there was little to nothing separating the coalition partners.

Where division did emerge, it was episodic and never likely to split the government. For example, the famed decision of the Liberal Democrats to drop the scrapping of university tuition fees in favour of tripling them to £9,000 a year, albeit payable after the fact and only when a graduate's income crossed a certain threshold, saw twenty-one of the party's MPs rebel against the legislation (along with two junior ministers who resigned, and six Tories), while a further eight abstained.[40] This meant that since Nick Clegg had appeared in the Rose Garden with David Cameron, Lib Dem polling wobbled between 8 and 12 per cent and did not recover until a brief interlude in 2019.[41]

These changes sparked a militant opposition movement among students, with several violent demonstrations characterised by heavy-handed and deliberately provocative policing, and the attempted occupation of Tory Party HQ in Millbank Tower. Contiguous with militant opposition under Labour and Major and Thatcher, the Tories were strong on condemnation and quick to emphasise troublemakers and criminal elements. This pattern was repeated the following summer when, as per 1981 and 1991, large cities, especially London, experienced fierce inner-city rioting.

The first real at-odds confrontation between coalition partners was over the Alternative Vote Plus referendum, which was written into the government's programme. Proportional representation (PR), which by 2010 had become routine for Scottish, Welsh, Northern Ireland, European Union and London Assembly elections, was still controversial for Westminster elections. The 'principled' arguments for retaining the 'first-past-the-post' system were that it enabled strong governments and raised the bar of parliamentary entry for extremist parties. In practice, the strongest advocates for keeping the system were partisans of the two parties who benefited from it. Naturally, this disadvantaged the Liberal Democrats and, as we saw in 2015, UKIP particularly.

The Tories would not countenance PR for Westminster elections and to get the electoral reform ball rolling, both parties settled on the compromise of the alternative vote (AV). This system retained the tie between MP and geographic constituency, while allowing voters to rank candidates, and then eliminate runner-up candidates until over 50 per cent of votes are allocated to the eventual winner.

The referendum fell 68 per cent No and 32 per cent Yes on a 42 per cent turnout, with some indication that Cameron was involved in behind-the-scenes campaigning against AV.[42] Referendum day was also the coalition's first electoral test, with local contests taking place across the UK along with the devolved governments in Scotland, Wales and Northern Ireland.

The results for Labour were very encouraging, seeing it increase vote share by 10 per cent, winning 857 councillors and gaining control of twenty-six authorities. The Tories had a satisfactory night with their vote share remaining static on 35 per cent, gaining eighty-six seats and the control of a further four councils. Not for the last time, the Liberal Democrats proved themselves the Tories' dented shield. They lost 748 councillors and nine councils. As mostly urban seats were in the mix, this played to Labour's strength and benefited them most at the Liberal Democrats' expense.

In Scotland the story was slightly different. All three of the Westminster parties lost ground to the SNP, which increased its representation by twenty-three MSPs. Labour and the Tories lost seven and two seats respectively, but the Liberal Democrat vote more than halved in the constituency and list sections and saw their MSPs plunge from seventeen to five. Labour consolidated its hold on Wales, gaining four seats with 42.3 per cent of the vote, while the Tories recorded a modest rise of 2.6 per cent and two seats. The Liberal Democrats, however, did not suffer as egregiously as elsewhere. Their vote fell by a third, but they only lost a single seat. It was clear that the Liberal Democrats were getting punished for the coalition, which might explain the margin of the No victory in the AV referendum – it was Clegg who was the best-recognised face of the Yes campaign.

Come the 2012 cycle of elections, the Tories felt some of the pain as well. For the local councils, Labour increased its popular support to 38 per cent and gained a further 823 councillors and thirty-two councils. Conservative support fell back four points and they shed 405 councillors and twelve councils. Unexpectedly, the Liberal Democrat vote stabilised with a percentage point increase to 16 per cent, but with the loss of one council and 336 councillors. The Tories comfortably held the London mayoralty, but the Liberal Democrats saw their vote halve again, which was the case with their assembly vote too, returning two AMs. There was no Boris bounce for the Tories, and they significantly underperformed in the mayoral vote, going from eleven to nine seats with 32.7 per cent and 32 per cent for the constituency and list sections respectively. Labour polled 42.3 per cent and 41.1 per cent for the same and returned twelve AMs.

With the special exception of the mayoralty, the Tories were beginning to reap the backlash against their policies, and it was reasonable to assume that this could only continue with more cuts to come. This appeared to be borne out by the result of the Corby by-election that November. Called after celebrity and novelist MP Louise Mensch resigned to move to New York, Labour easily took the seat from the Tories on a 12.6 per cent swing. Unfortunately for Labour, this by-election marked the end of politics-as-usual. UKIP went from virtually nothing to over 5,000 votes and secured 14 per cent. Given the distance between Labour and the Tories it could not be argued that UKIP cost Cameron the seat, but it demonstrated how the party was becoming a force outside EU elections. This was previously shown at the Barnsley Central by-election in March 2011. Labour retained the seat with ease, but again UKIP went from an also-ran to second with 12.2 per cent of the vote, apparently at the expense of the Tories.

The rise of UKIP was a long time coming. The party had tapped into what Rob Ford and Matthew Goodwin referred to as the 'left behind', who were 'older, less-skilled, less well-educated working-class voters' who supported UKIP because it appealed to them along a values axis, and who had lost out or become 'uncompetitive' as Britain was integrated into the global economy.[43] Therefore '"Europe" often functions as a symbol of other problems in society and perceived threats to the nation: unresponsive and out-of-touch elites in Brussels and Westminster; a breakdown in respect for authority and British traditions; and most importantly the onset of mass immigration.'[44]

There was a clear age dimension to UKIP's support, with 90 per cent of its voters aged over thirty-five and 57 per cent over fifty-four. Ford and Goodwin argued that these are not Tory Party supporters in exile because UKIP is more working-class than any other party, claiming that 42 per cent of its voters are drawn from this background. However, because they fuzzily define the working class as 'all those in society who do manual work', we have no sense what 'manual work' means, and where independent traders and the retired sit in the scheme.[45] Furthermore, their own figures to support this contention paint a different picture. Looking at how UKIP supporters voted in previous elections, for those able to provide an answer, in elections that took place in 2004–5, they were 21 per cent Tory and 32 per cent Labour. It was 18 per cent and 14 per cent respectively in 2005–7, 20 per cent and 24 per cent in 2007–10, 29 per cent and 5 per cent in 2010–11 and lastly 45 per cent and 7 per cent in 2012–13. It was obvious that UKIP was overwhelmingly attractive to former Tory voters once Cameron entered Number 10 and had acquired them quite rapidly, a simple fact disregarded to support the view that UKIP represented a unique threat to Labour.

Cameron knew he had to shore up the Tories' right flank. Sponsored by backbench MP David Nuttall, in October 2011 his bill for a referendum on EU membership saw the largest rebellion any Tory prime minister had suffered on Europe. Though it was seen off with apparent ease, eighty-one Conservative MPs voted for it.[46] Given Cameron's propensity for short-termism, at December's EU summit called amid the turbulence and economic collapse afflicting several member states, Cameron vetoed the mooted Stability Pact for not being in the UK's interests. Finance market regulation was apparently too much for him, despite previous rhetoric about regulating the City and banks.[47]

The right was emboldened by Cameron's decision to cleave towards it. Following the local-elections setback and while the prime minister was locked in another round of talks about the future of the eurozone, 100 Tory MPs signed a letter calling on the government to introduce legislation for an EU referendum.[48] They demanded a bill preparing the way for a vote on membership following the next general election. While one parliament cannot bind another in perpetuity, the reasoning was that Labour would suffer if they set their face against what, they believed, was a popular demand.

For his part, Cameron decided to pander some more. On 23 January at his speech on the future of the EU at Bloomberg HQ, he committed himself to a renegotiation of the UK's membership along the lines of more flexibility (i.e., opt-outs) to EU legislation and regulation following the 2015 general election, and fatefully said, 'And when we have negotiated that new settlement, we will give the British people a referendum with a very simple in or out choice. To stay in the EU on these new terms; or come out altogether. It will be an in–out referendum.'[49]

What truly opened the floodgates and strengthened UKIP immeasurably was Cameron's decision to see through legislation allowing full marriage between same-sex couples. This was not covered in the 2010 manifesto but, during the campaign, the party committed itself to a position of 'considering it' when it released its Contract for Equalities.[50] Such a move was consistent with Cameron's attempts to move the Tories towards the socially liberal centre on morality and equalities issues, but it also risked conceding ground to UKIP who, sensing an opportunity, discarded the lip service paid previously to libertarian values and rallied for the 'sanctity' of traditional marriage.

In December, the government announced that it would bring forward its plans with a quadruple lock in place to assuage religious-minded opposition. These included opt-ins for religious organisations happy to host same-sex marriages, exempting others and ordained figures who refused to undertake them from equalities legislation and making no compulsion for these bodies to allow such unions. It was not enough as far as oppositionists were concerned. In February 2013, the *Daily Telegraph* reported that 180 MPs, including four members of the Cabinet and half of the twelve-strong Whip's Office, were prepared to oppose the legislation.[51] Subsequent polling data of party members found that 59 per cent opposed with only 24 per cent for.[52] In the event, the legislation easily passed through the Commons, albeit with 136 Tories rebelling against the government and a further thirty-five abstaining.

Backbench and membership predictions of electoral Armageddon were seemingly borne out by the Eastleigh by-election. Called after the resignation of Chris Huhne, the former climate change secretary arrested and later convicted on traffic and deception charges, the Liberal Democrats retained the seat but only after UKIP came within 1,800 votes of winning while the Tory vote slumped by fourteen percentage points. Cameron blandly commented, 'This is a by-election. It's mid-term. It's a protest. That's what happens in by-elections. It's disappointing for the Conservative Party but we must remain true to our principles, true to our course, and that way we can win people back.'[53]

Winning people back did not extend to the local elections that May. Considering that in 2013 the county councils that were up were disproportionately rural and weighted towards the Tories, hints of how UKIP might eat into the Conservative vote were suggested by the results. Labour topped the poll with a projected 29 per cent of the vote, falling nine points on the previous year, but the Tories lost a further six points and managed a quarter of the vote, losing 335 councillors and ten councils in the process – more or less in line with the figures Major commanded after Black Wednesday. Considering that this was favourable territory in true-blue Tory country, it was concerning. Meanwhile UKIP surged to 22 per cent, bypassing the Liberal Democrats on 14 per cent, and winning a further 139 councillors.

The by-election in the safe Labour seat of South Shields held simultaneously also saw UKIP come from nowhere to capture second place, posting results that were more than double the Tory vote. The split on the right was gathering momentum, and Cameron moved to bridge it by caving in to the demand for draft referendum legislation. The Queen's Speech in May included preparatory laws for a ballot in 2017. Likewise, Tory MPs like Nadine Dorries and Jacob Rees-Mogg made their worries about UKIP plain and suggested some sort of pact in time for the 2015 election, a move UKIP leader Nigel Farage was happy to endorse.[54]

Cameron increasingly found himself stuck. Despite a summer of internal Labour Party rowing, Ed Miliband had begun unveiling a programme aimed at mitigating the worst effects of the austerity programme. Cultivating the idea of the 'squeezed middle', Miliband offered a policy mix of not-too-radical but popular positions, which included frozen energy bills, more house building, tax cuts for small businesses and tax increases for the very rich.[55] Trying to find a middle way, the Tories initially dubbed the energy price freeze as 'Marxist' and a portent of Bolshevist expropriations to come should Labour win in 2015.[56] Inevitably such foolish rhetoric came back at them in December after they announced a 'price rise subsidy'.[57] However, mindful of the threat from UKIP, at Tory conference Cameron outlined a £200 tax break for married couples, hoping this would send the right kind of signal to the UKIP-curious. Unfortunately for Cameron, it continued to consolidate its position.

Ahead of the 2014 EU elections, UKIP splashed with a poster campaign claiming that EU migrant labour undercut wages, that 75 per cent of laws are made in Brussels and provocatively that '26 million people in Europe are looking for work. And whose jobs are they after?'[58] Fanned by a favourable right-wing press, UKIP topped the poll with 26.6 per cent of the vote and eleven extra MEPs, to Labour's 24.4 per cent and seven new MEPs. For the first time in the party's history, the Tories came third in a national election with 23.1 per cent and the loss of seven seats. The punishment of the Liberal Democrats continued with the loss of ten out of eleven MEPs and they were beaten in popular-vote terms by the Greens.

In the local elections held on the same day the Tories came second and partially recovered to post a projected 29 per cent share (versus Labour's 31 per cent), while UKIP's support declined by five points. While the Tories lost eleven councils and 236 councillors, UKIP enjoyed a net gain of 163. Again, in response Cameron resorted to tough talk over the EU. As candidates for the president of the European Commission were paraded before ministers, Cameron made it clear that the leading candidate, Jean-Claude Juncker, was unacceptably Europhile and threatened to bring forward the UK's referendum in EU membership if he was appointed. Leaders of EU member states were not moved, and neither were the electorate Cameron was coveting.

Such threats had little effect on the Newark by-election, which was held a fortnight later. The result reaffirmed UKIP's role as the go-to party of protest. The Tories were able to retain the seat but, again, UKIP went from nowhere to second with a quarter of ballots cast.

With a general election less than a year away, the next blow came from within the parliamentary party. In August maverick backbench MP Douglas Carswell defected to UKIP and announced he was resigning his Clacton seat to seek a mandate as a representative of his new party. Held in October, he retained the seat with ease with 60 per cent of the vote. The Tories managed a humiliating 25 per cent. Held on the same day was another by-election in Heywood and Middleton, following the death of Labour MP Jim Dobbin. Here, the Tory vote evaporated, and they finished a poor third while UKIP came very close, with just 600 votes separating it from Labour. Lastly, at UKIP's party conference, Mark Reckless, the Conservative member for Rochester and Strood, announced his defection and intention to resign and hold a confirmatory by-election. Again, the gamble paid off and UKIP saw its second elected parliamentarian returned in November. The spectre of UKIP doing well at the Tories' expense and the Liberal Democrats losing substantial ground to Labour made it appear, at times, as if 2015 was a foregone conclusion.

There was also another difficulty of the Tories' own making. In October 2012, Cameron signed the Edinburgh Agreement with Scottish first minister Alex Salmond to hold an independence referendum within two years. Having settled the question of electoral reform to his satisfaction, Cameron believed that a referendum in Scotland might becalm Scottish politics by strengthening the union and stymying the rise of the SNP, which was elected as a majority government in 2011 under a system specifically designed to engineer cross-party coalitions.

With Cameron distracted by his party's travails, the campaign for No – organised under the Better Together umbrella – was outsourced to Scottish Labour. Reasoning that he might negatively impact the No campaign's chances given Scottish anti-Tory sentiment, the campaign was led by former Labour chancellor Alistair Darling, who debated Salmond head to head in a series of live televised contests. At this point Cameron appeared sanguine – polling in the two years since the agreement gave the No vote big leads and as late as August the projected vote was 43 per cent Yes and 57 per cent No.[59]

Then, in early September, YouGov published a poll giving independence a small lead with 51 per cent saying Yes. This spurred a round of panicked headlines and a belated realisation that the referendum could be lost.[60] There followed a flurry of ministerial visits to Scotland, including Cameron himself. The queen was pressed into action in a national broadcast urging voters to 'think very carefully' about their decision, and on 15 September Cameron, Clegg and Miliband signed a joint document – brokered by Gordon Brown – committing all three parties to conferring more powers on Holyrood and promising to preserve the Barnett formula, the mechanism by which Scotland receives more public money per head than the rest of the UK.

Caution won out over enthusiasm and independence fell 45 per cent to 55 per cent. The morning after the referendum Cameron immediately struck an English nationalist note, declaring, 'We have heard the voice of Scotland and now the millions of voices of England must be heard', and resolving to introduce legislation that would limit the right of MPs for Scottish seats to vote on laws for England and Wales.[61]

Another immediate (and welcome) consequence for Cameron was a collapse in Labour's polling position in Scotland. Better Together may have won the war, but it was the SNP who owned the peace; its membership surged to around 100,000 as progressive-minded voters abandoned a Labour Party which joined with Tory attacks on Scottish nationalism, especially in the rows over whether an independent Scotland could carry on using the pound and how both parties would play hardball in post-independence negotiations. Labour's calamity was such that even seven years after the event the party has still to reckon with how its voter base almost entirely disintegrated.

Weathering the UKIP storms, the lead-up to the general election put polling numbers for both parties around the mid-thirties. Cameron raised the idea of stripping the obese, drug addicts and alcoholics of their benefits if they refused treatment as another measure for securing the right flank.[62] Formerly an enthusiastic advocate of pre-election television debates in 2009, Cameron was more reticent this time around, eventually condescending to appear on one show with as many other party leaders as possible, thereby avoiding a one-on-one live debate with Ed Miliband over his record. Then, in March, Cameron announced that his second term, if he were elected, would be his last term as prime minister – thereby letting disgruntled Tory voters know he was not there forever.[63]

Where the Tories excelled was on message discipline, and throughout the campaign Cameron effectively reran his pitch from 2010, minus the distraction of the Big Society. The official launch of their campaign in April saw Cameron nod towards traditional territory, emphasising the number of hate preachers and terrorists who were locked up or had been deported, and promised a new toughness when it came to crime; more decisions to prosecute would be taken from the Crown Prosecution Service and handed to the police themselves.

The long-term economic plan received its umpteenth outing, there were more promises to remove low-paid people from tax (also handing higher earners a tax cut into the bargain) and there was an offer of a new wave of the right to buy for tenants in housing association properties. Alas, no such guarantee for private tenants was considered. Despite the overdone fiscal hawkishness and their record in government, the Tory campaign made £25 billion of unfunded pledges while Labour made sure its promises were all fully costed.

When the election came, the Tories romped home with a majority of twelve seats and 37 per cent of votes cast, while Labour unexpectedly underperformed its poll showing, managing just 30.4 per cent with a net loss of twenty-six seats. The Scottish collapse disproportionately affected Labour, with the SNP winning all the seats save one apiece for each of the main parties. As expected, the Liberal Democrats folded, losing fifteen percentage points and forty-nine seats, leaving them with eight. And lastly, the Tories' UKIP nightmare refused to manifest. Despite winning 3.9 million votes, almost 1.5 million more than the Liberal Democrats, it returned Douglas Carswell as its sole MP.

UKIP took two-and-a-half times more votes from the Tories than from Labour, but the distribution mattered, and they disproportionately impacted the latter in marginal seats, blocking serious advances in England. How did Cameron's strategy work? His pledge to hold an EU referendum stymied an even greater bleed of voters from the Tories to UKIP, but what also proved crucial was the English nationalist turn signalled on the day after the Scottish referendum. During the campaign, the Tories talked up the 'danger' of an SNP/Labour coalition, what this would mean for ending Britain's nuclear deterrent and how the UK would be torn asunder by a second independence referendum. As Cameron's memorable and, subsequently, much-shared tweet put it, 'Britain faces a simple and inescapable choice – stability and strong Government with me, or chaos with Ed Miliband.[64] As the Tories ran a campaign that tugged at nationalist fears, Labour left the ground almost entirely uncontested.

It was not long before Cameron was reminded of the conditional and slender majority he now enjoyed. Just a month into his second term, a group of Tory MPs announced the formation of Conservatives for Britain to campaign for Leave in the upcoming referendum.[65] Cameron himself was caught up in a row after saying that ministers would be expected to toe the party line in the referendum, but within the space of a day was forced to clarify that ministers would in fact have a free vote and be able to campaign for whichever side they wished.[66]

And so, apart from difficulties with Osborne's summer statement, it was preparation for talks with the EU over Britain's 'renegotiated' membership that dominated attention. Cameron's first major objective was introducing a four-year bar on EU-origin workers accessing social security in the UK, exempting the UK from moves designed to integrate the bloc further and, somewhat at odds with the opt-out, securing guarantees for moving blockages on the single market and letting it operate more freely.[67]

With this 'renegotiation' done, the question was a matter of timing. He had previously promised a contest by the end of 2017, but in the end decided for a short campaign. Weary of the time Yes had in Scotland to build up its momentum, it seemed reasonable to assume that a short timetable would disadvantage Leave, which would be campaigning from scratch, whereas he could leverage the power of government to push a Remain message. This overlooked the fact that, to all intents and purposes, the Leave infrastructure had long been in place given decades of Tory, press and, in more recent years, UKIP agitation and organisation around the EU.

Political developments did not augur well for Cameron's campaign. On 21 February his long-time rival Boris Johnson declared himself for Leave. Widely interpreted by political commentators as an opportunist move to win the Tory leadership contest in the event of Remain losing and a vacancy arising in Downing

Street, it is difficult to interpret this otherwise when Johnson himself wrote two articles supporting Leave and Remain with a view to publishing one of them depending which side he came down on. A cynical view of Johnson's motives is reinforced by his writing a pro-EU article just two weeks before converting to the Brexit cause.[68]

This was a blow to Cameron, as was the decision of Michael Gove to campaign for Leave. However, domestic political developments prevented the prime minister from focusing his full attention on the referendum and, as it turned out, saving his career. The decision of Iain Duncan Smith to resign over more cuts to disability benefits was followed by a major crisis in the British steel industry and the government's studied refusal to step in. Having already allowed Redcar works to go to the wall the previous autumn, Port Talbot announced it was in severe difficulties.

This, another example of the government not standing with 'the strivers', was followed by allegations of Tory involvement in tax dodging. On 3 April the financial affairs of wealthy clients were leaked from the 'tax efficiency' specialists of Mossack Fonseca of Panama City, among whom was Cameron's late father, which meant he was dogged by questions about whether he had personally benefited from these arrangements. Initially refusing to answer press queries, by the end of the week he relented and said he had dispensed with all holdings in his father's company prior to entering Number 10.

At the end of the month, British Home Stores collapsed, partly thanks to the changing retail environment, but the precipitating factors were the company's pension liabilities and the fact that it had been asset-stripped for twenty years by its previous owner, Sir Phillip Green. This left 11,000 out of work and, again, a government that did nothing. For the Leave campaign, which was mining the anti-elite/anti-politics sentiments versus an uncaring and out-of-touch establishment, it could not have asked for better timing.

The local elections did not give advance notice of the referendum's outcome. After a year of serious infighting, Labour under

Jeremy Corbyn increased its support by two percentage points to 31 per cent but lost eighteen councillors, while the Tories were down five points to 30 per cent and forty-eight councillors. UKIP for its part gained a further twenty-five councillors. The Liberal Democrats recovered slightly and put on four points, beating UKIP into third place with 15 per cent and gaining forty-five councillors. Incredibly, the Tories advanced in Scotland. A campaign centred around their personable new leader, Ruth Davidson, and a message emphasising their credibility as a decent opposition to the SNP, appeared to work – they enjoyed an eight-point swing in the constituency and a 10.2 per cent swing in the list section to gain sixteen seats, taking them to thirty-one. Labour continued to decline, losing fourteen seats whereas the incumbent SNP government lost only one. In the Welsh Assembly the Tories lost ground, losing four points and three seats, while UKIP polled 12.5 per cent in the constituency and 13 per cent in the list sections, conferring on it seven AMs.

When the referendum result came through in the early hours of 24 June a shock wave ripped through British politics. By 51.9 to 48.1 per cent on a turnout of 33,577,342 voters (72.2 per cent), the UK voted to leave the European Union and the scene was set for the crisis politics of the next four years. Outside Number 10 Cameron announced his intention to resign as prime minister pending a new leadership contest, and with that he wandered away from the podium, whistling.

The referendum result itself demographically foregrounded the shape of the next two elections. British Social Attitudes survey data suggested that 64 per cent of eighteen- to thirty-four-year-olds, 80 per cent of twenty-five- to sixty-four-year-olds and 89 per cent of those over sixty-five turned out to vote, and the patterning of their choices have a clear age dimension. Only the fifty-five to sixty-four and over sixty-five age groups voted by a majority to leave the EU. Undoubtedly, had younger cohorts turned out in numbers equal to older voters Cameron's gamble would have paid off. On party identity and voting, two-thirds of Labour voters supported Remain. This was deemed an unacceptable margin by the parliamentary party, which voted no confidence in Jeremy Corbyn and spent the summer unsuccessfully attempting to oust him.

Cameron himself did not attract similar levels of blame either from Remain-minded Tories or from those elements of the establishment who were pro-EU, despite Tory identifiers voting 54 to 46 per cent Leave.[69] The survey also showed that 73 per cent of voters who said they were worried about immigration voted Leave. In other words, the growing age divide demonstrated at the 2015 general election was consolidated in starker fashion at the referendum.

On the Remain side, the more cosmopolitan but, crucially, more excluded voters who had experienced the economic crisis and the unemployment shock voted for stability and continuity while those who were older, mostly retired, had their own property and were relatively sheltered from austerity by the decision to shield pensioners from direct cuts voted to make the lives of their children and grandchildren less certain. This was the logical destination of the Thatcher-voting cohorts of voters – insulation as a reward for past prudence, property acquisition and, in the main, voting the right way. Bootstraps conservatism, self-reliance and entrepreneurialism were for the rest.

As the curtain fell on Cameron's premiership, his time in office was characterised by short-termism and headline chasing. While his predecessors were concerned with media management, Tony Blair famously above all, no previous prime minister subordinated government and policy quite so crassly to the perceived electoral and immediate reputational interests of the ruling party. The austerity programme, economic policy, punitive social security policies and particularly the three referenda were big gambles. Like the worst sort of addict, the more meagre the reward the more willing Cameron was to bet the house.

For someone who spent his time in the spotlight talking about broken Britain, no occupant of Number 10 had been as reckless with and departed from the traditions of Tory statecraft, nor left the country in as polarised a state, as when he entered office. He was the preface for what was to come.

7

The One Nation Affectation: Theresa May

Following the referendum result, both main parties were plunged into crisis. Jeremy Corbyn was blamed by the Parliamentary Labour Party for the Yes campaign's loss, though he had stayed away from official Remain events by mutual consent, and it attempted to oust him in a hastily and badly organised coup. And the Tories suddenly had to deal with a vacuum at the top.

With Cameron's pending resignation, they were consumed by a leadership contest. Very quickly, the contours of the competition were starkly visible. Boris Johnson and Theresa May were the obvious front runners, but all leadership elections offer an opportunity for junior figures to chance their arm and raise their profiles in the party and the country. Stephen Crabb, the recent substitute for Iain Duncan Smith at the DWP, launched a joint campaign with Sajid Javid on an explicitly blue-collar Tory ticket. They were joined in the contest by Andrea Leadsom and serial leadership contender Liam Fox.

The contest was not without moments of high drama or, if you prefer, high farce. On 30 June, Johnson's key ally during the Leave campaign and highest-profile backer of his bid withdrew his support and announced he would stand instead. Michael Gove said,

> I came in the last few days, reluctantly and firmly, to the conclusion that while Boris has great attributes he was not capable of uniting that team and leading the party and the country in the way that I would have hoped. So I tried as hard as I could but last night,

reflecting on this, I came to the conclusion that ultimately Boris could not build that team, could not provide that leadership and that unity.[1]

Hours later at his putative campaign launch, Johnson stunned the assembled MPs and journalists by withdrawing from the contest.[2] Undoubtedly, Gove's move was enough for him to err on the side of caution, but in truth Johnson had been by no means been guaranteed to win. In Theresa May, the Tories would have been hard pressed to find a more contrasting rival. Cautious, unshowy, strategic and with a reputation for seriousness, May had sailed through the referendum with one careful speech making a reluctant case for staying in the EU before disappearing from sight again, an approach that had earlier earned her nickname of 'the submarine' by the press pack.

Less of a surprise was Osborne's decision to sit the contest out. On 28 June he said he could not provide the Tories the requisite 'unity' (interestingly, a theme Gove visited a couple of days later) but wanted to stay on as chancellor to provide stability. He said the economy was strong enough to put Britain in a good place to weather Brexit.[3]

The contest's wild card was Andrea Leadsom, the energy minister who had previously enjoyed twelve months at the Treasury. Largely unknown to the public, she was considered to have had a good referendum campaign, representing Leave alongside Johnson and the Labour MP Gisela Stuart on one of the televised debates. As a Leaver and seemingly without baggage, she was well placed to attract support from the party's right.

With five names on the paper, the first ballot of 5 July awarded May an absolute majority of 165 MPs, or 50.2 per cent. Second place went to Leadsom with sixty-six MPs (20.1 per cent), Gove forty-eight (14.6 per cent), Crabb thirty-four (10.3 per cent) and Fox sixteen (4.9 per cent). Fox then withdrew and endorsed May, whose support increased to 199 (60.5 per cent) on the second ballot, versus Leadsom's eighty-four (25.5 per cent) and Gove's forty-six (14 per cent). With the last eliminated, May and Leadsom were poised for referral to the members' ballot.

Leadsom's bid, however, was scuppered by injudicious remarks made during a *Times* interview.[4] She said,

> I am sure Theresa will be really sad she doesn't have children so I don't want this to be 'Andrea has children, Theresa hasn't' because I think that would be really horrible but genuinely I feel that being a mum means you have a very real stake in the future of our country, a tangible stake.

This was considered especially cruel as May had previously spoken about her and her husband's inability to have children, and the Tory Party agreed. On 11 July following 'quiet words', Leadsom withdrew from the race. May was left unopposed, and she entered Downing Street as prime minister two days later.

May's three-year tenure can be divided into two clear periods: before and after the 2017 general election. Yet there are important continuities running between the two. May's pitch to members and then to the country was one of a different kind of Tory prime minister, of someone interested in social justice and inequalities but without the fulsome parading of one's socially liberal credentials. In something of a remarkable rhetorical departure, she talked about class and poverty, words that were anathema under her predecessor. This was a theme returned to time and again during her three years at the top, and so was the other. From the outset May's conception of a post-Brexit relationship with the European Union was determined by her efforts to keep the Tory Party together as a going concern, which she identified with cutting free from EU influence as much as was practicable and, above all, defining her hard Brexit in terms of 'returning' the UK's ability to control its own borders. Having acquired an authoritarian anti-immigration reputation as Cameron's home secretary, it was inevitable that this would become a key theme of her premiership.

There was also another interesting departure from Tory orthodoxy. While her predecessors, including Blair and Brown, used office to reshape government and bed down the neoliberal settlement, May did not do so. This was less a case of turning the Tories towards Keynesian economics and more one of exigency; Brexit utterly dominated May's government. Even in the pomp and circumstance of her triumphant year before the calamitous election, little to nothing was done in this regard. This was also a pattern repeated by Boris Johnson's immediate period in office, in which Brexit and COVID-19 crowded out all else. The problematic political economy was, at best, addressed rhetorically, but in practice was left to carry on its polarising work.

Strong and Stable

May's introductory address to the nation from the steps of Downing Street struck a tone that could not be more different from that of her predecessor.[5] Moving from the Cameron–Osborne emphasis on cutting, free markets and distinguishing between in-groups of strivers and out-groups of skivers, May's speech appeared to owe more to Ed Miliband than to Tory thinking . She offered a picture of a capitalism in which the state was active on the industrial front and compassionate on matters of disadvantage. It was arguably the first one-nation speech a Tory leader had made since the early days of John Major. She invoked the precious nature of the union, and the injustices of racial, sexual and class inequality, saying,

> We will do everything we can to give you more control over your lives. When we take the big calls, we'll think not of the powerful, but you. When we pass new laws, we'll listen not to the mighty but to you. When it comes to taxes, we'll prioritise not the wealthy, but you. When it comes to opportunity, we won't entrench the advantages of the fortunate few. We will do everything we can to help anybody, whatever your background, to go as far as your talents will take you.

Having come through a divisive referendum, it captured something of the popular mood. In contrast to a Labour Party plunged into infighting, the quick resolution of the leadership vacuum and a very different-sounding Tory leader saw the Tories take a commanding poll lead. From the end of June all the way through to the late stages of the general election campaign, double-digit leads were the rule rather than the exception.[6]

For a time, it appeared that a new Tory hegemonic project was under construction. This was rhetorically one nation but combined the governance regimes inherited by May's predecessors with authoritarianism and a more Keynesian approach to economics, albeit with Conservative characteristics. As with previous Tory leaders, May's relatively novel approach to statecraft was concerned with the preservation of class relationships first and foremost. This contrasted with the 'essay-crisis' approach of Cameron and Osborne, whose policies on economic matters were as short-termist as they were vindictive. As such, the damage they inflicted on the social fabric had called forth significant opposition by the time they left office. The growth and utter dominance of Scottish politics by the Scottish National Party, followed by the unexpected election of Jeremy Corbyn as Labour leader in summer 2015, saw a mass revival of socialist politics. Likewise, though the Leave campaign during the EU membership referendum was characterised by atavistic, nationalist and occasionally racist politics, another key driver was the opportunity to protest against (perceived) out-of-touch elites. May, perhaps mindful of the monsters Cameron had assembled, was keen to talk up inclusivity and a willingness to tackle outstanding injustices.

May promised stability and a steady hand, affecting an unshowy but serious persona prepared to govern for the whole nation. However, this did not and would not have universal appeal. Those most likely to respond positively were disproportionately the middle-aged to elderly. These cohorts were most predisposed to turn out to vote, and so the political system was structurally tilted towards them. In other words, the age effect seen at the 2015 election and for Leave in the referendum became increasingly more polarised as May and later Boris Johnson cultivated the politics of Brexit.

As May settled in to her first summer, the immediate issue was what to do about Brexit. To leave the EU the UK needed to trigger the Article 50 process, which provided for a two-year period to negotiate the manner of the UK's departure; come to some agreement about continuity; and scope out the shape of the subsequent trade deal once the UK was outside the union. At the Conservative Party conference in October, May said she would write to the EU Commission in March to begin the process, meaning that the UK would formally leave the bloc in March 2019. What exactly Brexit would look like was left ambiguous.

In the brief leadership campaign, May had explicitly ruled out backsliding or attempting to remain in the EU by stealth and, in coining the slogan 'Brexit means Brexit', fused a jarring if nonsensical juxtaposition of certainty with radical uncertainty.[7] In a further sign of intent she announced that the prerogative of activating Article 50 rested with her and not with a Commons vote.[8] As for the character of her objectives, she took aim at commentary made in the lead-up to her conference speech. In front of the party faithful, she spoke of her intention to introduce a 'Great Repeal bill' to negate the primacy of EU law as affected by the 1972 European Communities Act, and said,

> There is no such thing as a choice between 'soft Brexit' and 'hard Brexit'. This line of argument – in which 'soft Brexit' amounts to some form of continued EU membership and 'hard Brexit' is a conscious decision to reject trade with Europe – is simply a false dichotomy. And it is one that is too often propagated by people who, I am afraid to say, have still not accepted the result of the referendum.

To this May counterposed an independent UK that could not be reduced to model relationships enjoyed by other states, such as Norway and Switzerland. In other words, despite rejecting the parlance her Brexit was very much a hard Brexit. This was not to be a negotiation 'to establish a relationship anything like the one we have had for the last 40 years or more', but to raise barriers.

This meant abandoning arrangements that had strengthened the British economy and allowed for the interpenetration of workers, of flows of capital and trade and the circulation of goods, and so could only be disruptive and damaging. Despite this, May wanted a relationship 'to involve free trade, in goods and services. I want it to give British companies the maximum freedom to trade with and operate in the single market – and let European businesses do the same here'.[9]

This was a recipe for incoherence. It held out the fantasy of retaining the rights of EU membership without the responsibilities. Enjoying such poll leads as well as the support of much of the press, even after Jeremy Corbyn was reconfirmed in his position by the party membership following the attempted putsch against him, May was in a position to do as she pleased.

The first test of her new government came in October in two by-elections. The Batley and Spen by-election was called following the murder of Labour MP Jo Cox during the referendum by a self-confessed fascist. The second was in Witney following David Cameron's decision to leave the Commons. Because of the circumstances surrounding Jo Cox, the Tories, Liberal Democrats, Greens and UKIP did not stand and left the field to Labour and a motley collection of far-right parties and also-rans.[10] Witney was held by the Conservatives with ease, though the Tory vote tumbled to 45 per cent from 60 per cent and the Liberal Democrats charged from fourth to second with 30 per cent, a rise of more than twenty-three points, perhaps suggesting that May's dominance was not quite absolute.

If anything could be taken from this first electoral outing, it was that the UKIP threat was apparently neutered. In Witney it fell from third to fifth behind the Greens and lost six points, but this development opened another front: Remain-minded Tory voters supporting the Liberal Democrats in protest against a hard Brexit. This seemed to confirm itself at the Richmond Park by-election in early December. Zac Goldsmith, reputedly the wealthiest MP in the Commons and son of late billionaire and founder of the Referendum Party James Goldsmith, resigned his seat over government plans to progress the development of a third runway at Heathrow Airport. In a peculiar deal with the party he would re-contest the seat as an independent while the party proper would stand aside. It was a risk as the constituency had voted Remain in the referendum and was represented by the Liberal Democrats' Susan Kramer up until 2010. The result confirmed the pattern from Witney; Goldsmith's vote fell thirteen points to 45 per cent while the Liberal Democrats' Sarah Olney enjoyed a thirty-point surge and took the seat with almost 50 per cent of the poll. For its part UKIP, which had run at the previous general election, stood aside and endorsed Goldsmith.[11]

Away from Brexit, there was the small matter of the economy to attend to. Following her Downing Street speech, there was interest in whether a new Tory government meant a shift in policy as well as rhetoric, and in Philip Hammond's first autumn statement as chancellor there was some movement, but only of degree rather than of kind. He scrapped the arbitrary public spending surplus figures. Hammond also announced the abolition of letting fees for tenants, which was perceived as the Tories' attempt to grab working-class support.[12] There were announcements about 40,000 new homes, a 30p-per-hour increase in the minimum wage, and, following the round of cuts to welfare Osborne had made in the previous Budget, a pledge that there were to be no more.

May felt compelled to return to this theme, and did so on 8 January, setting out her vision, which she characterised as the 'Shared Society', and trying to claim the mantle of a reforming prime minister. Moving beyond a 'narrow focus on social justice', May pitched the idea of supportive government. As she put it, 'people who are just managing – just getting by – don't need a government that will get out of the way. They need an active government that will step up and champion the things that matter to them.'[13] This was defined in terms of fixing broken markets, tackling injustice and inculcating new senses of solidarity and community. Again, the rhetoric indicated a decisive break with her predecessor but had not yet leant itself to any substance beyond Hammond's statement.

As the Tories had quickly managed their leadership transition following the referendum, with a Leave vote successfully delivered UKIP appeared to face an existential crisis. On 4 July Nigel Farage announced his resignation as leader, sparking an unseemly and frequently farcical scramble. On 3 August the front runner, Steven Woolfe, an MEP for the North West of England, was excluded from the leadership race for failing to submit his paperwork on time and allowing his membership to lapse for a year. To rub salt into the wound, his rival Diane James moved swiftly to appropriate his campaign slogan and logo.[14] On 16 September she was announced as the new leader with 46.2 per cent of the votes cast, but on 4 October she resigned, citing her lack of authority in the party, and left altogether in mid-November. This resignation was followed a couple of days later by a brawl between Woolfe and fellow UKIP MEP Mike Hookem, which put the former in hospital. Unfortunately, the rumour that the latter was involved in a high-speed car chase as French police tried to apprehend him proved to be false.[15]

It was not long before Woolfe resigned from the party, leaving the field open for three contenders – fellow North West MEP Paul Nuttall, former party chair Suzanne Evans and *Breitbart*'s Raheem Kassem. Of the three, Nuttall was the only candidate offering a coherent strategy, albeit one based on the assumption that northern working-class people were ripe for an anti-immigration and xenophobic party and had 'been abandoned' by Labour. He easily won with 62.2 per cent of the vote and vowed to 'replace the Labour Party in the next five years and become the patriotic party of the working people'.[16] Nuttall was about to have this strategy tested to destruction.

On 21 December Jamie Reed, the Labour MP for Copeland, resigned from the Commons to take up a job in the nuclear industry. This was followed in January by the resignation of Tristram Hunt from Stoke-on-Trent Central to assume the directorship at the Victoria and Albert Museum.[17] Both seats were considered bellwethers in several ways. Copeland, with its strong relation to the nuclear plant at Sellafield, was perceived to be precarious thanks to Jeremy Corbyn's long-standing views on nuclear power and Stoke-on-Trent Central was the archetypal left-behind working-class seat ripe for UKIP's strategy. The stakes, therefore, could not have been higher – defeat for Labour meant it was facing an existential crisis in so-called heartland seats, and failure for UKIP would mean rethinking its Labour-seats-first strategy.

The Stoke-on-Trent by-election, held on 23 February, attracted most media attention due to UKIP standing Nuttall as its candidate, and in part thanks to ease of access from London. In what was frequently a bad-tempered campaign framed by the media as UKIP's to lose, Nuttall found himself embroiled in gaffe after gaffe. Claims about having a PhD, having played professionally for Tranmere Rovers and, most damning of all, that he was in the crowd at Hillsborough during the 1989 disaster were debunked and publicly derided.[18] In the event, Labour's Gareth Snell held on to the seat with a reduced majority of 2,620 (37 per cent). UKIP polled 5,233 votes (24.7 per cent), managing only a 2 per cent increase, despite Nuttall's higher profile. The Tories, running a relatively low-key campaign, managed a creditable third with 5,154 votes (24.3 per cent). Unusually for a by-election where the Tories were not expected to win, May herself visited the constituency. The Tories then took Copeland with a majority of 2,100 and held onto it at the subsequent two elections. This also marked the first by-election gain by a serving government for thirty-five years and was the first time Labour had not held the seat since 1935.

These two by-elections proved crucial for what happened next. In the month following, May encountered the difficulties destined to torpedo her administration. Having earlier committed the Tories to a hard Brexit put strain on the relationship with the Scottish government, which raised the prospect of another independence referendum in 2018 owing to the changed circumstances brought about by the Leave vote (retaining EU membership was a chief plank of the Better Together campaign[19]). There were problems with the Northern Irish border and how it might function after leaving the EU given the advanced integration between Northern Ireland and the Irish Republic – backbenchers feared that this could compromise the 'independence' of the UK by acting as a drag on its ambitions and/or split Northern Ireland from the rest of the UK and lay the ground for a united Ireland. Lastly, there were May's ambitions to clamp down on immigration.

An overhang from the victorious 2015 campaign came back to haunt the Tories as allegations surfaced concerning false expense accounts centred on their battle bus, which led to a £70,000 fine.[20] Later, Tory MP Craig Mackinlay was charged with making a false electoral expenses claim, for which he was acquitted, while Marion Little, the 'campaign specialist' who worked in Thanet for the 2015 election, where Nigel Farage was also standing, was found guilty and received a suspended sentence in January 2019.[21]

With mounting difficulties, a slim Commons majority suscep-tible to disappearing after a wave of by-elections, impressive poll leads and a Labour Party beset by internal strife, despite earlier promises to see out the mandate 2015 had given the Tories, on 18 April May announced that she would be seeking a general elec-tion – which, thanks to the Fixed-Term Parliaments Act, required a majority in the Commons to vote for it. Reaching this conclusion on a walking holiday with her husband in Wales, she set a date for 8 June. She complained about division in Westminster and the desire of some to frustrate the will of the British people. She there-fore required a firm vote to bring stability to politics and see Brexit through.[22]

There was a strong push from the Tory benches and the press to finish the Labour Party off, and recent by-election outings provided further encouragement. Copeland, for the Tories, showed Labour's susceptibility for punishment thanks to Jeremy Corbyn's views but, more crucially, the combined UKIP and Tory vote in Stoke-on-Trent Central suggested that if May could unify a Brexit vote behind her party she stood a chance of taking swathes of seats that commentators had spent years earmarking as UKIP targets.

Immediate polling appeared to vindicate her decision. Over the following week, the Tories were reported to be leading Labour by 48 per cent to 24 per cent (YouGov), 45 per cent to 26 per cent (Opinium) and 50 per cent to 25 per cent (ComRes). May, however, wanted to leave nothing to chance. The Tories engaged the Australian strategist Lynton Crosby, now 'Sir' thanks to the services rendered the party in 2015 and the London mayoral campaigns of 2008 and 2012. This indicated that the Tories were planning on running a right-wing campaign with a splash of populist posturing over immigrants/scapegoats and liberal elites.

In the space of a week, however, issues that were to produce a drag on the campaign began manifesting: chiefly, the person of Theresa May herself. At Prime Minister's Questions she was often noted as appearing less than comfortable and was frequently left looking robotic and unable to think on her feet; this boded ill for any form of leaders' television debates, hence she quickly ruled out participating in them. This had the consequence of her appearing aloof and uninterested in scrutiny, which contrasted unfavourably with the campaign style of Corbyn, who was rarely seen not addressing a crowd or getting swamped by supporters.

The two differences could not be better summated than by their campaigns' press launches. Labour held a rally, while May spoke at a village hall where she refused to take questions from the press. She gave a speech that was her template for the rest of the campaign:

> Only you can give us the mandate, so vote for a strong and stable leadership in this country. Vote for strong and stable leadership this country needs. Give me the mandate to lead Britain. Give me the mandate to speak for Britain. Give me the mandate to fight for Britain. And give me the mandate to deliver for Britain.

She also contrasted her 'strong and stable' qualities to a 'coalition of chaos led by Jeremy Corbyn' – a line highly reminiscent of the 2015 campaign.[23]

Her personal appearances rapidly assumed the trappings of absurdity, with activists bussed in, the press banned and members of the public kept at arm's length. One particularly galling episode on 29 April saw her helicopter into a village hall in Aberdeenshire which had no reception and therefore could not be broadcast live, and all press questions were screened to avoid embarrassing gaffes.

For a finishing touch, it was listed in the halls programme of forth-coming events as a children's birthday party, prompting further accusations that she was hiding from voters.[24] She might also have been accused of hiding the Conservative Party as well. As her personal polling was in advance of the party's, the campaign was consciously modelled on Ruth Davidson's Holyrood effort of the previous year. Tory branding was conspicuous by its absence at events and underwent a partial rebadging as 'Theresa May's Team'.

Such minutiae largely passed by without notice in the early part of the campaign. Indeed, the Tories received an even greater boost after the details of an over-dinner conversation between May and Jean-Claude Juncker, the president of the European Commission, were made public.[25] The leaks revealed how ill-prepared the Tories were for Brexit negotiations, but May successfully spun the revel-ations as attempts by the European Union to interfere in the general election and undermine the only party prepared for a tough negotiation. By being seen to stand up in the national inter-est and adapting herself to a struggle of a (foreign) them versus a (British) us, the Tory poll lead extended to between fifteen and twenty-two points.

On 18 May, the party launched its manifesto, *Forward, Together: Our Plan for a Stronger Britain and a Prosperous Future.*[26] Authored by long-term aide and self-styled blue-collar Conservative Nick Timothy, it consciously fancied itself a one nation document. It promised increases in school spending and the NHS, a formal-ised abandonment of George Osborne's deficit elimination target and increases to the minimum wage to bring it in line with 60 per cent of median earnings. There was traditional Tory fare on limit-ing immigration and driving down corporation tax rates, but perhaps indicative of how invincible the Tories felt, a few policies amounting to direct attacks on the pensioners – the bedrock of Tory support - went into the manifesto. Winter fuel allowances were to be means-tested, the so-called pensions triple lock – whereby payments would rise in line with whatever was the highest out of average earnings growth, inflation or 2.5 per cent – would be abolished, with the guaranteed percentage taken away. It was changes to funding social care that proved most controversial. The policy would defer care costs until after the recipient died, but with the costs falling onto the estate. Surviving family members and/or would-be inheritors could expect only the first £100,000 to be exempt from care costs.

This effectively marked the turning point in the campaign. Amid storms of protests from Tories and hostile press stories, May was forced to publicly dump the policy – immediately dubbed the 'dementia tax' – while pretending that 'nothing had changed' about the party's platform, and blaming Jeremy Corbyn for making 'fake claims'.[27] Slowly at first, and then perceptibly, the polls began shifting, with Labour making up lost ground. May's reticence to engage with the public and the media put the question of her suitability under the spotlight. The three so-called televised debates saw party leaders take turns in front of live audiences – the one which saw leaders go head-to-head was avoided by May, and Home Secretary Amber Rudd took her place instead.

Most confounding of all, Labour refused to behave as Tory strategy predicted. This strategy was premised on making favourable comparisons to Corbyn, establishing May as a leader of national stature and the Labour leader as weak and tied to Britain's enemies. The Tories cast themselves as the custodians of Brexit while Labour was portrayed as the party of saboteurs and advocates of a second referendum. Wisely, Labour's manifesto accepted the referendum result and said,

> We will scrap the Conservatives' Brexit White Paper and replace it with fresh negotiating priorities that have a strong emphasis on retaining the benefits of the Single Market and the Customs Union – which are essential for maintaining industries, jobs and businesses in Britain. Labour will always put jobs and the economy first.[28]

Therefore not only were the Tories unable to fully exploit a Brexit vote, but May's rhetoric – such as no deal being better than a bad deal – and preference for self-imposed distance from the EU undoubtedly contributed to a firming of Labour's support from voters unimpressed with this nationalistic posturing.

The poll convergence carried on right up to election day. With most pollsters still forecasting a strong majority for May, the Tories were able to significantly increase their vote by 5.5 per cent to 42.4 per cent, or 13.6 million votes. Labour, however, increased its support by almost 10 points, topping out at 40 per cent, or just shy of 12.9 million votes. While May's pitch worked to a degree and was able to produce a coalition the size of those enjoyed by Margaret Thatcher at her height, Labour was able to partially overcome the split character of the opposition and ran them much more closely than anyone had forecast.

As such, May lost thirteen seats and Parliament was hung again. May was able to immediately survive the fallout and forge a deal with the Democratic Unionist Party to allow her to govern with a slender majority, but from this point her leadership slipped into permanent crisis.

The loss of the 2015 majority meant that May's real accomplishment, a firm recomposition of the Tory vote, was overlooked. This comprised the usual base of anti-Labour workers, the petit bourgeoisie, the business and professional salariat and the rich. This was topped up by a layer of Scottish unionist voters turning out against Nicola Sturgeon raising the prospect of another independence referendum. Also coming back to the Tory fold were erstwhile UKIP supporters attracted to May thanks to her tough talking on Brexit, and lastly a not insignificant number of former Labour supporters likewise attracted by the same issue, and turned off their usual party by the cultivated antipathy towards Jeremy Corbyn. These new voters were disproportionately older than the general voting population. Younger people found Theresa May's Tories less than congenial bearing in mind they had borne the brunt of austerity on top of stagnating wages, little security at work, not enough jobs allowing for career progression, low levels of house building and therefore higher housing prices and higher rents.

As older people are more likely to turn out to vote, this ordinarily would give the Tories an advantage – and would continue to do so in subsequent local elections – but the problem with hanging on to older voters is whether they are replaced in sufficient numbers as they pass away. For example, YouGov found Labour leads among every age group under fifty, with at least forty-point leads over the Conservatives among eighteen- to twenty-nine-year-olds.[29] A very similar pattern was found by Ipsos MORI, with Labour leading in age groups under forty-four and the Tories enjoying an advantage in the age group immediately above, accelerating to huge leads in older age groups.[30]

Likewise, the 2018 *British Social Attitudes* survey found widening gaps between the two parties at either end of the age range – a forty-point lead for Labour among eighteen- to thirty-four-year-olds, and a twenty-five-point lead among the over-sixty-fives.[31] This demographic distribution was deliberately cultivated by emphasising Leave as the chief accent of the Tory campaign, but by refusing to accept their framing Labour was given political space to talk about other issues hitherto neglected by mainstream politics, such as the experience of the housing crisis and policies to tackle climate change. May united the right-wing vote – UKIP only stood in 378 seats and polled 594,000 votes, or 1.8 per cent – and the slightly elevated turnout, up 2.4 per cent at 68.8 per cent, saw more Labour-disposed layers of voters cast their ballots, and the anti-Tory vote, with the exception of Scotland, largely uniting behind its challenge and depriving May of her expected majority.

The immediate consequence was May's forced sacking of key aides Nick Timothy and Fiona Hill, who had previously irked and antagonised backbenchers and Tory ministers alike, and subsequent polling of party members found that 60 per cent wanted her immediate resignation.[32] Talk was rife of a leadership challenge, which only accelerated following the disastrous Grenfell Tower fire on 14 June, which killed seventy-two people and left hundreds homeless. The suspicion, later confirmed, that inadequate fireproof cladding acted as an accelerant was to blame combined with May's own disastrous response. She pointedly refused to meet with affected residents, unlike Jeremy Corbyn and May's former leadership opponent, Andrea Leadsom.

Despite speculation about her future, a cursory analysis of the party's parliamentary dynamics and Brexit position made an enforced departure seem unlikely. The circumstances besetting May – a Brexit strategy trying to reconcile national assertiveness while weakening the UK's influence in Europe, a reduction in the salience of immigration and the economy (traditional Tory-owned issues), a seemingly insurgent and reinvigorated left-wing opposition and no parliamentary majority were not attractive propositions for any ambitious Tory. Second, at this stage no one had the support to impose their will on the wider party and would face rebellions and internal division, even though most MPs were for Brexit. Thanks to the unique situation and her enemies cancelling one another out, May was simultaneously at the mercy of Tory factions but occupied a position none of them wanted. This conferred a strange, time-limited invulnerability.

May shored up the Tory position by the end of June by agreeing to a confidence-and-supply arrangement with the Democratic Unionists, a deal sealed with the awarding of a further £1 billion to Northern Ireland. This presented some wider issues, such as accusations that the Tories were willing to overlook the DUP's sexist and homophobic positions on social issues. More concerning was the undermining of the government's own position as stipulated by 1998's Good Friday Agreement. Under the accords, if disputes arise between rival parties at Stormont, as was the case at the time with the suspension of power sharing, Number 10 is supposed to neutrally arbitrate – a constitutional fiction exposed as such when the same government was dependent on the DUP for ten parliamentary votes. It also added a further dimension of difficulty to Brexit. While the DUP campaigned to Leave, it was also tied to the status quo of unimpeded border traffic with the Republic of Ireland, which would be jeopardised if the UK was outside the European Union.

After taking a break from the spotlight, the submarine resurfaced at the start of the new parliament with the task of having to make Brexit mean something. The first order of business was getting her Repeal bill through the Commons. Its chief provision was the part-removal of parliamentary scrutiny. The bill proposed conferring on ministers powers to change the law without bringing matters to the Commons.[33] The debate was suggestive of the splits in MPs set to dominate politics for the following couple of years. Some Remain-minded Tory MPs spoke out against the bill while some Leave-supporting Labour MPs called on their party to support it, despite the authoritarian provisions it contained. Still, more than six months following the start of the Article 50 process, no one was the wiser about the specificities of Brexit.

May addressed this uncertainty with a speech to EU leaders in Florence on 22 September. She set out a plan whereby the UK would continue trading with EU countries on the same terms for up to two years following departure, and that the government would meet its financial obligations. May also said that the status of in-country EU residents would be protected under the law, but without saying anything about what these protections might be.[34] Unfortunately for the prime minister, while this was cautiously welcomed across the political spectrum it was immediately trumped by her disastrous Conservative Party conference speech.

She coughed and spluttered her way through an address that spoke of the 'British Dream' and extra funding for new housing (private and public), as well as an energy price freeze that her colleagues had denounced previously as 'Marxist'. She apologised to the party faithful for a 'scripted' and 'presidential' campaign that fell short, in a speech that also fell short of addressing the problems facing the government. Brexit was barely touched on and policy announcements were thin.[35] Proceedings descended into the comedic as the prankster Simon Brodkin invaded the stage and handed her a mock P45, and then the farcical as the backdrop, which read 'Building a country that works for everyone', dropped to the floor one letter after another. A speech less auspicious for reversing one's faded political fortunes is seldom delivered.

May's weakness was reiterated by Boris Johnson, who took to the papers to outline his vision of Brexit, which, coincidentally, was at odds with her own. This promised a bonfire of regulations allegedly holding the British economy back and would enable the country to put the infamous £350 million a week allegedly spent on EU membership – a claim that played very well during the referendum campaign – into public services.[36]

It also served notice that May's stay of execution was temporary, and her premiership on borrowed time. After her speech, former party chair Grant Shapps made claims that he had a list of thirty names, including 'one or two Cabinet ministers', who would be prepared to challenge May.[37] Press speculation named Johnson, Brexit Secretary David Davis and Commons leader Andrea Leadsom. A studiously leaked WhatsApp conversation among leading Tories defending May, including a fulsome intervention by Johnson, failed to convince that May's leadership was not beset by another periodic bout of crisis.[38]

This instability made for shifts in personnel. On 2 November, key May ally and Defence Secretary Michael Fallon resigned following lewd comments he had made to Leadsom, but such was the dysfunctionality and evaporation of May's authority that Chief Whip Gavin Williamson stepped in and appointed himself Fallon's replacement.[39] On 9 November the International Development Secretary Priti Patel was forced to resign after striking secret deals with Israeli politicians and business leaders behind the prime minister's back. She sought to provide UK development funds for disposal by the country's military.[40]

Calamity and diminished authority meant that when Hammond got up to deliver his Budget on 22 November, there was precious little of May's 'British Promise' in evidence and plenty of his own priorities instead. The abolition of stamp duty on houses valued under £300,000 was announced, along with a reduction of the waiting time for support under the Universal Credit system from six weeks to five, but it did not reverse any of the cuts already programmed in. This accelerated period of crisis was all set to come to a head in early December as the outline of a withdrawal agreement was expected, including a solution for the Irish border issue post-Brexit.

In negotiations, it emerged that a position had been engineered that would see the North remain in the EU's customs union while the rest of the UK would be outside it following withdrawal. This would entail a de facto border moving from Ireland and into the Irish Sea – a position unpalatable to the Democratic Unionists, whom, it seemed, May had forgot about, given that their reason for existence is the maintenance of the Union and the six-county statelet within it. And then, four days later, a seeming break-through.

In a joint May–Juncker press conference, they reannounced agreement on the UK's financial obligations and protections for EU residents, and, crucially, if a solution could not be found to resolve the Irish border the UK would default to 'full alignment with those rules of the Internal Market and the Customs Union which, now or in the future, support North–South cooperation, the all-island economy and the protection of the 1998 Agreement'.[41] Surprisingly, this agreement, which was an admission of failure and incompatibility of the Tory Brexit with the provisions of the Good Friday Agreement, was received rapturously by the Tory press desperate for a good-news story. Despite losing her deputy and long-time ally Damian Green to claims that he lied about pornographic material on ministerial computers, as well as a forced apology to journalist Kate Maltby for unwanted sexual touching, May started to look more secure.[42]

The year 2018 was to prove even more excruciating. Trying to salvage some authority, she called in ministers on 8 January for a Cabinet reshuffle, and what was supposed to be an assertion of leadership proved a disaster. She tried removing Jeremy Hunt from the NHS brief to Business, Innovation and Skills (BIS), but he refused and came away with the responsibility for social care added to his portfolio. This was just as well because Greg Clark, the existing BIS minister, refused to be sacked. If this was not bad enough, May attempted to move Justine Greening from education to the Department for Work and Pensions. She refused and resigned, adding to the small but politically experienced phalanx of Remain-inclined backbench Tory MPs.

This occasioned another round of leadership rumours and coup plots, this time from the right, which had discovered that May's Christmas deal was not to its liking after all. In a provocative speech from the chancellor, Hammond spelled out the details of what had been previously agreed: Britain would continue to have a close post-Brexit alignment with the EU. This sparked off a particularly bilious round of open warfare on the Tory benches and saw the right of the party speculate openly about May's future.[43] A week later, Michel Barnier, the head of the EU's Brexit negotiation team, reminded the government – in front of the press – that negotiations were far from over and there were several outstanding issues. He also reminded May that if the UK left the customs union, border checks in Ireland were inevitable.[44]

Rather than tackle these issues head-on, not for the first time May subordinated her negotiating position to managing parliamentary discipline. In an intervention on 2 March designed to offer clarity over Brexit, she instead unveiled a fudge. With that in mind, it was perhaps surprising that she had little to say on the border issue, using cloaked language to refer to the December agreement. In red meat for the right, she did say that her ideal position was to maintain existing trading relationships with the EU while having the right to strike bilateral arrangements outside it, especially with the emerging economies – again, a position impossible within the customs union she was already signed up to in everything but name. Lastly, she noted that the best way forward was if the UK and EU signed a bespoke deal for which there was no previous model, a position that was sensible in the abstract but impossible given her expectations for it.[45]

An inch forward, May must nevertheless have been glad of a relatively Brexit-free couple of months in which she could play up her imagined strengths. On 4 March Sergei Skripal, a former Russian intelligence officer (and double agent in British pay between 1995 and 2004) and his daughter Yulia Skripal were poisoned in a nerve agent attack in Shrewsbury. A police officer attending the scene was exposed and fell ill, and two others were later poisoned after inadvertently finding and exposing themselves to the agent, leading to one fatality.

Novichok was suspected and May pointed the finger at Russia, which denied it, and a tit-for-tat expulsion of diplomats in London and Moscow was undertaken. For his part, Jeremy Corbyn refused to abide by the traditional bipartisan consensus on national security issues and asked for evidence of May's assertions, drawing attention to the Tory Party's close financial relationship with domiciled Russian oligarchs. With the press on her side and the Tories united on this issue, she was able to make hay by appearing tough on the world stage as well as suggesting that Labour, and Corbyn above all, could not be trusted with national security – a charge some Labour backbenchers repeated with alacrity.[46]

Following an apparent chemical weapons attack on Douma in Syria on 7 April, Boris Johnson issued a press release condemning the event and attacking Moscow for frustrating past UN chemical weapons investigations, and within the week US air and missile strikes had taken place against Syrian government targets at British and French urging.[47]

This respite evaporated as suddenly as it descended. As military action loomed the so-called Windrush scandal erupted, which saw several dozen children of the *Empire Windrush* generation wrongly deported back to the Caribbean, partially as a consequence of the Home Office's policy of a 'hostile environment', which had been in place since May took up as home secretary in 2010. May did make an apology to Commonwealth heads at a leaders' summit, but refused to take any blame for the scandal – instead Amber Rudd carried the can and resigned as home secretary on 30 April, despite polling suggesting that the public held May responsible.[48]

As both parties suffered negative press, there were no real shifts in the polls. They remained level at around 40 per cent of the vote each for the remainder of the year and into 2019. The 2018 local elections provided no resolution either. Labour and the Conservatives polled a projected 35 per cent vote share of ballots cast, with Labour gaining just seventy-nine councillors and no councils while the Tories lost three councils and thirty-five councillors. Underlying the logjam of what might loosely be described as a polarised politics were very modest gains by the Liberal Democrats (seventy-six councillors and four councils), but a collapse of UKIP to just over 100,000 votes and the loss of 123 seats.

In truth, the Tories were able to maintain their position simply because they were the only party 'owning' Brexit, but it was increasingly difficult for May to balance the factions in her party. When the withdrawal bill returned to the Commons, she was forced to make an undertaking to her Remain-inclined backbenchers, led by former attorney general Dominic Grieve, that MPs should be given a greater say over Brexit when the legislation returned to the Commons for final approval.

What exercised Grieve and his colleagues was the prospect of a no-deal scenario if an arrangement with the EU had not been reached by the withdrawal date. He wanted MPs to vote on what happened next, whereas May wanted powers limited to a simple noting of the government's position – in other words, wasting parliamentary time with a meaningless boondoggle. May having agreed to the former position to secure the bill's continued safe passage, the amendment was changed following further negotiations back to the government's original position, ensuring that all but two – 'big beast' Ken Clarke and former minister Anna Soubry – Remain-aligned Tory MPs voted against. As Shadow Brexit Secretary Keir Starmer observed, 'Theresa May has gone back on her word and offered an amendment that takes the meaning out of the meaningful vote. Parliament cannot – and should not – accept it.'[49]

While May was under fire from one side, the other reasserted itself in a semi-concerted show of strength. Airbus and BMW issued dark warnings about the consequences of a no-deal scenario. Meanwhile International Trade Secretary Liam Fox and David Davis openly briefed the media that UK threats to leave without a deal were a negotiating tactic, seemingly ignorant of EU negotiators' newspaper-reading skills. Boris Johnson meanwhile took to the pages of the *Sun* to call for a 'full British Brexit' as opposed to a 'bog-roll Brexit', which was 'soft, yielding and seemingly infinitely long'.[50]

Finally, over the weekend of 7–8 July, May and her Cabinet retreated to the prime minister's country residence at Chequers to finalise the withdrawal agreement to be put to the EU negotiators – incredible considering the passage of time elapsed since triggering Article 50. The proposals were based on a 'facilitated customs arrangement', which was not the same as staying in the Customs Union nor, to placate the Brexiteers, a customs alignment. It suggested a common EU–UK rule book governing standards for trade between it and the UK area, and where UK authorities would collect tariffs on the EU's behalf on goods coming through UK ports from outside the EU. Given the respective weight between the two and the fact of leaving, the UK would likely end up being a rule taker as per the EU's arrangements with other neighbouring, non-member states.

Given May's preoccupation with immigration, it sketched an outline of a 'mobility framework' to allow faster post-Brexit movement between the UK and the EU, with current rights of domiciled EU citizens protected but access to social security restricted among new arrivals, a position most member states had already adopted within the EU's framework. To ensure that May's Cabinet united around these proposals, it was suggested that any quitting minister would have to walk down the Chequers driveway alone and order a taxi back to London. In other words, while favouring a Brexit with more ties to the EU than Brexit's self-appointed custodians wanted, it also represented a belated realisation by May of how her weak position was strangely strong. If no one else was prepared to step into her shoes or could impose their will on the party, then her hand was freer than factional alignments suggested. To underline this, May released the following statement:

> During the EU referendum campaign collective responsibility on EU policy was temporarily suspended. As we developed our policy on Brexit I have allowed cabinet colleagues to express their

individual views. Agreement on this proposal marks the point where that is no longer the case and collective responsibility is now fully restored.[51]

Boris Johnson immediately demonstrated his loyalty by leaking his assessment of the process to the press and resigning as foreign secretary two days later.[52] The unity rhetoric was not followed by its assumption in fact. As the date of the Commons vote on her deal approached on 18 July, May was forced to pivot more towards the Brexit wing of the party. She accepted four amendments from backbencher and noted Eurosceptic Jacob Rees-Mogg, ensuring that her customs bill passed the Commons by a margin of just three votes. These three came from the Labour benches, while, interestingly, the Liberal Democrats' leader Vince Cable and former leader Tim Farron were absent for the vote.

This demonstrated the fundamental weakness of the Remain-minded Tory rebels, who could only muster eleven votes between them in opposition to May's bill. While the amendments effectively wrecked what had been agreed at Chequers – no collection of EU tariff fees, no to an Irish Sea border, the removal of the UK from the EU's value added tax regime and the need for primary legislation if the government wants to enter the Customs Union – May had reasoned that this was a price worth paying to get this phase of Brexit through Parliament, and then negotiate away the contradictory provisions she had accepted. Naturally, Rees-Mogg and his allies organised in the European Research Group (ERG) knew this too. It was a case of them flexing their muscles in advance of the votes to come.[53]

The investment and expenditure of political capital did not lead to a profitable outcome; the EU said no to her new position. Sensing that another round of intense crisis was inevitable, at party conference in October ministers 'forgot' that collective responsibility was 'now fully restored' and took turns at the podium as leaders-to-be. Offering a potted biography of herself, DWP minister Esther McVey argued that criticisms of Tory welfare policy were 'fake news' and, in a peculiar attack on Jeremy Corbyn's supporters in the Labour Party, surmised that the 'three M's in Momentum' amounted to 'Militant, Militant, Militant'. Jeremy Hunt, warming to the foreign secretary role, said he was a reformed Remainer and went on to compare the EU to the USSR. And Boris Johnson's star turn talked up the opportunities Brexit afforded, such as exporting bus stops to Peru.[54]

The gathering's absurdity was crowned by May's final leader's speech. The content was thin and duly saw the ritual invocations of one-nationism (councils were to have borrowing caps raised to build social housing), but the manner of delivery was jarring. Having inadvertently gone viral on social media for dancing with South African children in the summer, she made her big entrance by grooving her way to the podium. One aspect of her speech, in trying to separate out the left from the rest of the Labour Party, was expanded on in an *Observer* article the following Sunday.[55] Here, May made the case for what she wished the Conservatives to be – a moderate, patriotic and reforming government determined to tackle social evils. The position, she argued, was closer to the Labour Party as opposed to the 'Jeremy Corbyn Party'.

The real intended audience of this intervention were the Labour MPs needed to help get her Brexit deal over the line, making her less dependent on her own troublesome Brexiteers and rebellions from Clarke, Grieve et al. Indeed, it proved she was susceptible to political damage from this quarter too. On 9 November, Jo Johnson resigned as transport minister in protest against a hard or a no-deal Brexit. He said, 'To present the nation with a choice between two deeply unattractive outcomes, vassalage and chaos, is a failure of British statecraft on a scale unseen since the Suez crisis.'[56]

Finally, on 14 November a draft agreement was reached with the EU over the withdrawal agreement. The main measures, extensively leaked beforehand, were the restatement of a lump sum to settle outstanding EU financial obligations, reciprocal recognition of citizen's rights and finally a solution (of sorts) to the Irish border issue. Despite May having previously said an internal border would be an affront to UK sovereignty, this is effectively what her deal signed up to. There would be a common UK–EU customs territory; Northern Ireland would be more aligned with the EU than with the rest of the UK to allow something like the status quo on the border to be maintained. Other provisions included new rules on state aid limiting the UK's scope for action (clearly designed to thwart the ambitions of a future Corbyn government), but this concession to the right was balanced by a snub; the deal also ruled out the freewheeling bilateral trade treaties that were one of the ERG's holy grails.[57]

With right-wing efforts thwarted, two Cabinet members and four junior ministers resigned, but the subsequent meeting of the EU27 heads of government signed off the draft and helpfully added that there was little appetite for a renegotiation should the agreement fail to pass the Commons. May's position kept deteriorating. Tories suggesting they would vote against the deal increased as the week went by, and there was little sign of succour coming from the Labour benches. On 10 December, right-wing opposition to May boiled over and forty-eight letters were sent in to the 1922 Committee. This met the minimum requirement of 15 per cent of MPs required to trigger a vote of no confidence.

Two days later the parliamentary party voted, and she won, albeit by 200 votes to 117. She did so by conceding in the afternoon's meeting of MPs that she would not lead the Tories into the next general election. It also signalled the partial and temporary surrender of the ERG's machinations. With a second no-confidence vote ruled out for another year, Rees-Mogg spoke unconvincingly in the Commons about how he now supported the prime minister.[58] This did not signal the ERG's capitulation but more a biding of time: vote down any deal May brings to the Commons, but support her when the inevitable no-confidence motion came from the Opposition bench. With May as leader, the last thing the ERG and any Brexiteer wanted at this stage was a general election.

Indeed, 15 January saw one of the darkest days ever experienced by a governing party. Putting her deal to the Commons, May was defeated by 432 votes to 202 and chalked up the worst government defeat ever among her list of achievements. Following the humbling, May's reply struck a conciliatory note and said that the government was now 'listening'. Considering that most of the Commons was opposed to a no-deal Brexit, might suggest a softer approach. Over the following week delegations from parties and factions of parties met May to press their claims, but negotiations did not go well.

With the clock ticking to the expiration of Article 50 and the possible ejection of the UK without a bridging deal, talks were less a listening exercise and more a matter of wasting time. Green MP Caroline Lucas criticised May for agreeing to discussions, but then refusing to budge on her red lines – above all, the end of freedom of movement for EU citizens, but also an assurance that she would not contemplate a no-deal scenario. Meanwhile, an ERG delegation headed up by David Davis and Steve Baker pressed their desire for a Britain outside any customs arrangement and their opposition to what became known as the Northern Irish backstop. They said afterwards they were pleased with progress made.

On 21 January, May returned to the Commons with a statement in which very little had changed. Settlement fees for EU residents were jettisoned, but she was to return to Brussels for more changes to the Irish backstop. Again, this was an obvious waste of time as the EU27 were not about to revisit the issue. From the Labour benches Yvette Cooper put forward an amendment that would see Parliament take over the Brexit process if May was unable to get approval by the end of the month and suspend Article 50 for the rest of the year. In other words, the more May played for time the more it would be an inconvenience to her plans. Fortunately for her, on 29 January the Commons voted down the Cooper amendment. Interestingly, MPs marching and shuffling through the no lobby were joined by Remain-inclined Tory critics like Grieve, Oliver Letwin and Amber Rudd, and fourteen Labour MPs. May responded by whipping the Tories into supporting an amendment put by 1922 chair Graham Brady committing to a renegotiation of the backstop, and so off to Brussels the prime minister went to run the clock down further,

basically committed to undoing what had been previously negotiated and agreed.

While talks were ongoing, on 18 February seven Labour MPs
left the party and announced the formation of the Independent
Group. The following day they were joined by an additional
Labour MP, Joan Ryan, and on 20 February three defectors from
the Tories – Anna Soubry, Heidi Allen and Sarah Wollaston.
While its formation commanded a great deal of media attention,
more significant was the formation of the Brexit Party by Nigel
Farage on 8 February. Formed to fight the EU elections if Article
50 was extended, it was designed to 'defend democracy' by ensuring that the referendum result was honoured.[59] It put the Tories on
notice that even if UKIP was a busted flush, another nemesis was
poised to harry them from the right. It was a headache Theresa
May could do without.

On 12 February, May announced to the Commons that she
would seek a second meaningful vote on her agreement following
recent talks with the EU, and would make another statement if the
vote was not forthcoming by the end of the month. On 27 February
a further statement was voted on noting progress and set the date
for May's 'renegotiated' deal to return on 12 March. This time the
deal fell 391 votes to 242, with seventy-five Tories voting against,
making it the fourth-worst government defeat in parliamentary
history.

This meant that a debate over a no-deal Brexit was scheduled for
the following day, with an amendment around the so-called
Malthouse compromise. Named after the housing minister Kit
Malthouse, this reopened the backstop issue by proposing replacing
customs checks at the border with electronic tagging and registration. This managed to attract some Tory MPs from both sides of
the Brexit divide, but flew in the face of the Irish border being
settled as far as the EU was concerned and as already agreed with
the government. As an effort aimed at patching up Tory differences,
it was doomed, and the amendment fell miserably by 164 to 374.
Unexpectedly the vote against no-deal itself, tabled by former Tory
minister Caroline Spelman, passed by four votes.

On 14 March a vote was held on extending the Article 50 process. The main motion easily passed, but two amendments only fell narrowly. The removal of a new 30 June deadline tabled by the Labour leadership fell by sixteen votes. An amendment moved by Hilary Benn that affirmed the extension and called for back-bench MPs to set the legislative agenda on 20 March fell by just two votes.

After another weekend of plots and rumours of plots, May caught a glimmer of hope despite the Article 50 extension; speaking on the *Ridge on Sunday* show, former housing minister Esther McVey – a serial meaningful-vote rebel – signalled she might be prepared to back the deal if it meant saving Brexit, a sign that perhaps other rebels could be brought around for a third and final vote. May's plans were, however, immediately frustrated by the intervention of Commons Speaker John Bercow. Under parliamentary rules dating from 1604, a government cannot simply bring back the same legislation repeatedly in the hope of eventual acceptance. If May wanted her third vote, it would need to be substantially altered.

To get the Tories out of this hole, on 30 March she made a televised address to appeal to the electorate to pressure their MPs to back her deal and accused 'Parliament' of prevaricating and blocking the referendum decision. Here, the EU threw May a lifeline. Following a request to the European Council to extend Article 50 if a deal was not agreed by 29 March, the EU issued a two-line extension; withdrawal day would be 22 May if the deal passed the Commons, and if it failed May would have until 12 April to formulate an alternative.

The blood price exacted for these movements was the disintegration of her position in the party.[60] On 27 March, May bowed to political realities and informed the 1922 Committee that if MPs voted for her deal she promised to resign in short order. This last gamble appeared to be strengthened by the drama playing out in the Commons over indicative votes called to determine what sort of Brexit would be comfortable for MPs. Out of the options arrayed none of them found a majority, with the two closest – a customs union Brexit and a second referendum – falling 52 per cent to 48 per cent. Notably, the SNP and Liberal Democrats, who had previously called for a softer Brexit, now lined up against it. Enjoying their moment of relevance, they were joined by the Independent Group in voting them down. With no other option available, May's deal returned on the afternoon of 29 March, what was supposed to be Brexit day, and was defeated for a third time by 344 to 286. Previous irreconcilables like Rees-Mogg and Johnson, along with approximately half of the ERG, rode to May's rescue, but it was not enough.

With everything closed and into extension time, the indicative-vote process returned for another try on 1 April. Four options were selected by the Speaker: a Brexit deal based on a customs union brought by Ken Clarke; a customs union, single market access and freedom of movement position championed by Nick Boles, who resigned the Tory whip on the spot during the debate; a confirm-atory referendum sponsored by Labour's Peter Kyle; and revoking Article 50 in the event of no deal pushed by the SNP's Joanna Cherry. Again, all four fell, with Clarke's proposal faltering by just three votes.

The logjam occasioned more talks between the government and Labour leadership about a way through, while on 5 April May wrote to council president Donald Tusk asking for an extension until 30 June. Following the failure to reach a compromise with Labour, May travelled to the emergency EU summit on 10 April with the prospect of striking a humiliating interim bargain. Article 50 was to be extended to the end of October with a meeting of the EC in late June to assess progress made and consider the next steps. If a deal had not been reached by 22 May then the UK would be legally obliged to participate in EU elections, an eventuality the Tories wanted to avoid at all costs considering the threat posed by the Brexit Party to their voter coalition.

Polling in mid-April confirmed this dread prospectus with support from both parties bleeding away to the Brexit Party (BXP) or the Liberal Democrats, who set themselves up respectively as the repository for Leave and Remain voters ahead of the EU elections. By 12 May, for example, ComRes reported BXP on 27 per cent, Labour 25 per cent, the Liberal Democrats 14 per cent and the Conservatives 13 per cent. This was the first time the Tories had been positioned in anything other than first or second since the immediate period following the foundation of the SDP. An Opinium poll published on 8 May was even worse; the Tories were placed fourth with just 11 per cent.

The local elections taking place a week beforehand provided little cheer either. While Labour lost eighty-four councillors and six councils with 28 per cent of the vote, for the same vote share the Tory position imploded with the loss of forty-four councils and 1,330 councillors. UKIP, which by now was a much-reduced force, lost 145 councillors while the self-conscious Remain parties did very well. The Liberal Democrats gained 704 seats and ten councils, and the Greens enjoyed a net increase of 198 seats. The other big success story was for independent candidates, who enjoyed a surge of 606 extra seats. While UKIP was virtually ignored, had BXP decided to stand candidates it undoubtedly would have done well and the result for the Tories would have been much worse. In its absence, discontent with May only found a partial outlet, with large numbers staying at home.[61]

On 16 May the prime minister met with senior Tories to set the timetable for the election of her successor, and made it known to them she intended to resign. On 24 May, the day after the EU elections, she announced her departure following the Tory leadership contest due to begin on 7 June. Certainly, had she not done so the results of that election would have provoked even more public calls for her to step down. The Brexit Party topped the poll with 30.5 per cent of the vote, Labour came third with 13.7 per cent and the Tories suffered their worst ever defeat in a national election with just 8.8 per cent, coming in behind the Greens.

One of the unofficial Labour election campaign slogans from 2017 was 'Make June the end of May'. Two years on, this aspiration was met. Following the Conservative leadership contest, May stood down on 23 July and was replaced by Boris Johnson.

Assessments of May's premiership will forever be associated with Brexit and the difficulties of handling a seemingly impossible situation. Yet one should not cast as her a victim of circumstance. The two years of negotiation with her own party plus episodic interventions from the Opposition and the EU were largely of May's making. From the summer of 2016 May determined that Brexit should be 'hard' to satisfy the appetites of the domineering Leave-voting blocs within the Tories.

Central to this was the Tory fetishisation of sovereignty, of British 'independence' vis-à-vis the EU. This aspiration was entirely consistent with the party's statecraft of the previous forty years, in which successive prime ministers asserted the centrality of the executive within the state's constellation of institutions. For Brexit to be meaningful it had to mean evacuating EU influence from British politics. There was no place for EU institutions and, above all, the European Court of Justice. Common agreements had to be redefined, so the supremacy of the executive was not compromised by any element of pooled sovereignty, which ultimately was why (initially) the customs border in the Irish Sea was a stumbling block for many Brexiteers. Clinging to sovereignty for the Tories was always much more than a nice idea handed down from Oxford PPE lectures and dusty, seldom-opened tomes of conservative philosophy. It is the conceptual expression of state power, the avenue by which their party asserts its interests and can 'legitimately' reshape and carve up society.

By extension, the prospect of ministers touring the world and signing up countries to better bilateral trade deals was the condensed symbolism of sovereignty restored. May's other, central objective and one she nursed while heading up the Home Office was clamping down on immigration. Whether this was motivated by racism, by a belief that Britain was too full or by the political value the Tories could extract from scapegoating overseas workers or refugees is unclear, but it cannot be separated from how Nigel Farage successively and successfully outflanked the Tories to their right by owning immigration and fusing it with Brexit.

Wrestling back this key driver of the Leave vote was fundamental if the Tories were to secure their voter coalition. Therefore, while May was in her imperial phase and the polls flattered the Tories into thinking they could do no wrong, the outlines of what a Brexit deal would look like were already at this stage subordinate to party interests. And following the catastrophe of the general election, this remained the consistent theme. Except that this was now a government of crisis, a reactive administration buffeted by events and rebellion.

The question, then, is why. The patterning of the indicative votes demonstrated that a Brexit of some description was possible. Had May proven more flexible, a majority between Labour and government loyalists for a Clarke–Boles or a customs union Brexit would have been possible had May whipped for it. Again, for her, there was wider politics at play; the continued existence of the Conservative Party as a going concern. When she repeated her irritating slogan 'No deal is better than a bad deal', few ever asked 'for whom?'

May's apparent recklessness on this question, from the standpoint of the continued viability of British capitalism, can only be understood in the context of class relationships – the priority of class over economic-order politics – and the role her party plays in them. May knew that reaching an accord with Jeremy Corbyn to see through a Brexit on anything but her terms would invite ruin for the Tory Party. Having demonised Labour under his leadership as a Bolshevist manifestation, a split between the Tory mainstream and its enfeebled centre right on the one hand, and its hard right on the other, could not have been discounted. A parliamentary and membership revolt would have been likely, especially with the viable menace of Farage's Brexit Party and the previous strength of UKIP exercising their imaginations. Her class instinct then pushed her towards preserving the Tories at all costs because not only had her party proved itself the vehicle and articulator of British capitalism's dominant class factions, but also there was no other viable alternative for straight-down-the-line bourgeois politics. Labour has always been somewhat less preferable because it is compromised by its institutional links with the labour movement, and at that point in time it was not a 'viable' vehicle for capital thanks to Corbyn and the dominance of the left. Nor were the Liberal Democrats (too small), or the clutch of pro-EU centrist parties, of which the Independent Group/Change UK was the most prominent. For someone like May, preserving the coherence and continuity of the Tories came before all because, instinctively, she knew that she was preserving the pre-eminence of the politics of her people, her class and their interests. Sacrificing the profit margins of British capital is a price worth paying if the Tory Party, the chosen organ of bourgeois rule, is to survive. It was and is the only institution that can be relied on to defend their class system.

From this perspective, despite the ignominy she suffered during two-thirds of her premiership, she was the right woman in the right place at the right time. She put the party first above all else, as indeed all her predecessors had one way or the other. And she also pointed her successor to the way out of the hung parliament that hamstrung her. The 42 per cent of the vote achieved in 2017 was near the peak of what the Tories might achieve at a general election.

This coalition was made up primarily of older voters, who have a habitual propensity to turn out and vote and promising them Brexit cohered a solid bloc who even spearheaded an advance in Scotland. The 2019 EU elections demonstrated what could happen to this coalition if Brexit was thwarted and cancelled: the near total disintegration of the party base. May was unlucky and tactically inept, but she provided the dry run for the triumph to come.

8

Creature of Havoc: Boris Johnson

Prior to the 2019 Tory leadership contest, Boris Johnson was an entirely known quantity. When he made his pivot from London's City Hall in 2015 back into the Commons, it was widely accepted that this was not in order to serve an undistinguished dozen years as a diligent backbencher but was about positioning himself for a future Tory leadership contest. As we saw, the EU referendum consumed David Cameron's career and it seemed obvious that Johnson would enter the race, having spent the campaign as the ostensible leader of the Brexit cause – hence the shock among Tory MPs and Westminster watchers when Michael Gove turned on him and he withdrew in July 2016. This was not going to happen again.

While May was clinging to office, Johnson announced he would be running for the leadership. Taking note of the electoral coalition the Tories were able to assemble in 2017 and, latterly, the splash Farage's Brexit Party had made in tearing the Conservative position apart in May's EU elections, Johnson knew that the path to future electoral victory meant owning Brexit as an issue. More immediately, offering a clean, clear Brexit and not getting bogged down in wrangling and messy details was certainly the mood in the wider party. Whoever emerged in the leadership contest as the most credible pro-Brexit politician would win. There was no room for vacillators, let alone someone who leaned more towards Remain. Lastly, Johnson was very aware of his own persona and campaigning record. Despite a well-earned reputation for laziness, he enjoyed a certain celebrity and had won two personality-based elections against left-wing former London mayor Ken Livingstone. The party required someone who could whip it into shape and take the fight to a left-led Labour Party.

Repeating May's strategy by squeezing the Brexit Party was not without risk. In the event of calling an early election, the possibility of firming up Labour's vote by reaffirming Tory commitment to a hard Brexit could not be discounted. While a viable strategy for bringing together a strong coalition around Johnson's leadership was likely, whether this would be enough for a majority government left a great deal to the actions of his opponents. In this instance, Johnson's gamble was to pay off.

Prior to opening the contest, the 1922 Committee announced a new rule change to prevent a crowded field. At one point thirteen prospective candidates had declared their intention to stand. The new process required a proposer and seconder as per the old rules, but for inclusion on the first ballot each candidate required the support of a further eight MPs. The new rules also introduced a floor for support, therefore speeding up the balloting process. Now each nominee must command at least 5 per cent to proceed to the second round, and then a minimum of 10 per cent to proceed to the third (seventeen and thirty-three MPs in raw-number terms). At each stage the lowest placed candidate would be eliminated. Before voting took place, three candidates – Sam Gyimah (later to defect to the Liberal Democrats), Kit Malthouse and James Cleverly dropped out.

While Johnson's campaign got off to an uninspiring start, he was the bookies' favourite from the beginning. Writing in the *Telegraph*, he argued for a tax cut for high earners by raising the threshold from £50,000 to £80,000 at a projected cost of £10 billion. This was to be funded by increasing National Insurance contributions, thereby effecting a transfer of wealth from those on modest incomes to those earning much more, and raiding the funds set aside by Philip Hammond for no-deal preparations.[1]

At the Tory Party hustings hosted by the One Nation grouping of MPs, Johnson went on the record of setting 31 October as the absolute end date for Brexit, and under his leadership the UK would leave whether it had a deal or not.[2] These were points Johnson re-emphasised on an eve-of-ballot address on 12 June. Following the first vote, Mark Harper, Andrea Leadsom and Esther McVey were eliminated for failing to rise above the 5 per cent floor, and the next day Matt Hancock withdrew. Johnson had a commanding lead of 114 MPs (36.4 per cent) versus the closest runner-up, Jeremy Hunt, on forty-three MPs (13.7 per cent).

Media interest temporarily alighted on Rory Stewart. He was second to last in the first ballot but caught attention thanks to Johnson avoiding as many public debates he could get away with, including a televised candidates' hustings on Channel 4.[3] Casting himself as heir to Ken Clarke, Stewart understood that the chances of success were nil and yet there was a career and a profile to be carved out by presenting himself as the voice of moderate Toryism with a pragmatic, EU-friendly edge.

As for Johnson, his debate avoidance might have had something to do with not revealing details of his putative negotiating strategy, but equally his leadership campaign did not want to run the risk of getting upstaged by either Stewart or another rival who might prove themselves a Brexit ultra and trump Johnson. Dominic Raab, for example, said he was prepared to close the Commons to get the deal through. Any worries or jitters were for naught. Between 18 and 20 June Tory MPs were balloted four times and, on each occasion, Johnson increased his vote share, topping out with 160 votes (51.1 per cent). Jeremy Hunt remained runner-up, ending with seventy-seven votes (24.6 per cent), just edging out Michael Gove by two votes in the final round. With the final two set for submission to the membership, there were suggestions that this outcome had been engineered so that Johnson faced someone who was not a hard Brexiteer and came with significant political baggage of his own (as the former health secretary, Hunt was not universally admired on the Tory benches).

Facing the opponent he desired, the Johnson campaign affected minimum effort. Yet news media abhors a vacuum and it fell to outside events to make political weather. On 20 June, Hunt supporter Mark Field was filmed manhandling a Greenpeace protester from the chancellor's Mansion House speech by grabbing her by the neck, for which he was suspended.[4] This was almost immediately overshadowed by an alleged domestic incident at the home of Carrie Symonds, Johnson's partner, to which the police were called. With the emergence of a recording of the argument, Johnson – for the sake of his campaign – refused to answer any further questions about it, saying police intervention was entirely unnecessary.[5]

If these were not embarrassing enough, the Conservative Party faced a by-election defence in Brecon and Radnorshire after a recall petition unseated the incumbent Chris Davies following his conviction for making a false expense claim. It did provide some ammunition to the Hunt campaign after Johnson cancelled an appearance to debate him on 25 June. Given his previous record of avoiding media scrutiny and accountability, there was a faint hope in the Hunt camp that this might damage Johnson's standing from the point of view of suitability for office.[6] Such whimsies were forlorn. A face-to-face debate on 9 July settled nothing, and an excruciatingly painful interview with the BBC's Andrew Neil was unable to blow Johnson off course.

On 22 July, the ballot closed and, as was widely predicted, Johnson won easily with 92,153 votes (66.4 per cent) versus Hunt's 46,656 (33.6 per cent). A turnout of 87.4 per cent – much higher than previous contests – suggested a membership of 159,403, a tally fractionally higher than figures posted by the SNP and the Liberal Democrats, but lower than Labour's by a factor of more than three. Nevertheless, it was much healthier than doom-laden reports from the year previous suggesting that membership had collapsed to around 70,000, and higher than previously published figures from 2013 that placed it at 139,000.[7]

As Johnson entered Downing Street on 24 July, unlike May's address of three years earlier his first speech from a refurbished lectern was much vaguer. He discussed 'British values' and fulminated against 'the doubters, the doomsters, the gloomsters' determined to throttle the country's potential by keeping the UK tied to the EU.[8] The tax cuts for the rich disappeared, having done their work convincing the Tory selectorate that this was their man. He wanted to convey an impression of a bouncing, ebullient prime minister relentlessly optimistic about the future and determined to sell Brexit as an unalloyed positive.

Yet for all the cheerfulness Johnson knew that his premiership would be made or broken by Brexit. The tame character of the leadership contest was a dull prelude to some of the most confrontational tactics ever pursued by a government to get its way. What was at stake was Johnson's career and the future viability of the Tories as a party of government.

Into the Fire

Barely a week into Johnson's premiership and the unwelcome interlude of the Brecon by-election saw the Tory–DUP majority reduced by one. Having formed a 'Remain alliance' under their new leader, Jo Swinson, the Liberal Democrats successfully persuaded the Greens and Plaid Cymru to stand aside for a (clearer) run at the seat. Buoyed by tactical switchers from Labour, and the intervention of the Brexit Party, the Tories lost the seat, yielding the Liberal Democrats a 1,425 majority. Clearly, for the Tories this underlined the necessity of contesting the field as the owners of Brexit, but they undertook a weak campaign characterised by the decision to run Davies with all his expenses baggage.

With the first shot in the latest round of Brexit wars, Johnson announced that he would be seeking the prorogation – closing – of Parliament for five weeks following the Queen's Speech showcasing the government's legislative programme in October. As the Speaker observed, 'it is blindingly obvious that the purpose of [suspending Parliament] now would be to stop [it] debating Brexit and performing its duty in shaping a course for the country.'[9]

Following the prorogation move, Johnson turned on recalcitrant elements in his own party. In the weekend prior to the Commons reopening on 3 September, Johnson warned putative rebels that they would be deselected ahead of the next general election if they collaborated with other parties to seize control of the legislative agenda. This, Johnson correctly divined, was an effort to introduce a new bill forcing an extension to Article 50 under certain circumstances – something he had pointedly refused to countenance throughout the summer.

Former Cameron lieutenant Oliver Letwin put down a motion asking the Commons to spend the following day debating Hillary Benn's motion for extending Article 50, which passed by 328 votes to 301. In response, Johnson said he would table a motion for a general election with the putative date of 14 October. He also made good on his word and the whip was removed from the twenty-one Tories who had voted against the government, which included senior figures like Ken Clarke, Nicholas Soames, Justine Greening and Dominic Grieve. Adding to Johnson's woes, shortly before the vote Tory MP Philip Lee defected to the Liberal Democrats.

Amid more heated scenes in the Commons the following day, the Benn bill passed by 329 to 300, with Caroline Spelman joining the ranks of the expellees. Johnson's motion for a general election, brought under the provisions of the Fixed-Term Parliaments Act, fell far short of the two-thirds Commons majority needed after Labour abstained. Johnson's drastic measures and the biggest open split in the parliamentary party in its modern history caused unease among the ranks, with the One Nation grouping writing a letter, signed by over 100 MPs, asking for the restoration of the whip to all expelled MPs.[10]

Johnson was keen not to appear cowed after this string of defeats. At a speech in front of police cadets on 5 September, Johnson said he would 'rather be dead in a ditch' than ask for an Article 50 extension, despite his obligation to do so following the Benn bill vote.[11] The speech, widely characterised as rambling and incoherent, followed the news of his brother Jo Johnson's resignation as universities minister and intention to stand down at the next election to protest the wrecking ball strategy the prime minister was pursuing.

The crisis appeared to worsen when Tory attempts to filibuster the Benn bill in the House of Lords collapsed, and on 7 September

Amber Rudd resigned as DWP secretary in time for the Sunday political chat shows. She too could not stomach the no-deal posturing.[12] The Benn bill became law on 9 September, and was accompanied by another government defeat, this time a requirement for it to publish details of no-deal planning (passed by 311 to 302). Johnson mounted a second attempt to call an election, but this also fell.

At a bizarre joint press conference with the Irish taoiseach, Leo Varadkar, Johnson appeared to backpedal slightly by saying that a no-deal Brexit would represent a failure of statecraft. He hinted that his new Brexit deal also looked like the one he had voted against as a recent backbencher, except with a return to a position Theresa May (rhetorically) would not countenance: a de facto customs border in the Irish Sea.[13]

The first day of prorogation brought more high political drama. Following a challenge led by the SNP's Joanna Cherry to the suspension of Parliament at the Scottish Court of Sessions, the judges agreed with the litigants that Boris Johnson's closure of Parliament was unlawful. The justification that the government put forward, resting on Johnson's claim that the chamber needed clearing of business so he could have his Queen's Speech to unveil his legislative programme, was rejected. Instead, closing all of Parliament's business, which included select committees, was a measure 'to stymie parliamentary scrutiny' and served as an example of 'failing public authority standards'. In other words, the judgment suggests that Johnson lied to the queen when he asked for prorogation. The only crumb of comfort for the government was the fact their decision was non-binding.

Following this, Cherry joined with campaigning Brexit litigant Gina Miller, who had had an earlier case against prorogation rejected by the High Court on 6 September and brought the matter to the Supreme Court. On 24 September, it judged itself competent to hear the case and upheld the Court of Sessions decision, and said that the government had not provided a good enough reason for prorogation and therefore Johnson's 'advice' to the queen was unlawful. Downing Street 'leaked' its displeasure to the BBC's chief politics correspondent, Laura Kuenssberg, saying, 'We think the Supreme Court is wrong and has made a serious mistake in extending its reach to these political matters.'[14] The fact that the Supreme Court did no such thing and was responding to a political issue brought before it as a matter of law did not trouble the prime minister. The suspension then was immediately lifted and sitting began the next day.

On 2 October, Johnson published the outlines of a new Brexit plan. As previously trailed in the Varadkar press conference, the UK in its entirety would leave the customs union, but to allow unimpeded cross-border traffic between Northern Ireland and the Republic customs checks would take place away from it in special facilities or on the premises of the firms concerned. There was to be no return to the physical infrastructure of the past. Traders would require special licences based on existing trusted-trader schemes, and there would be exemptions for smaller businesses.

Northern Ireland would remain in the EU's single market for goods and continued to be tied to its food safety, food production and manufacturing regulations – while the rest of the UK would not be. Unlike May's deal, Stormont would have a veto over the deal – every four years it would be asked whether it wishes to stay within the EU's orbit, or move back towards the UK's regulatory regime. Johnson hailed this a compromise a 'genuine attempt to bridge the chasm', while the Commission said that 'further work was needed'.[15] Interestingly, neither the DUP nor the ERG demurred, despite having found similar provisions in May's proposals a deal breaker. It also meant that each four-yearly election to Stormont was set on being a mini-EU referendum and had the potential to introduce another political dynamic that could strengthen the possibility of Irish reunification.

This shifting tack from bombastic opposition to Brexit delay to a more constructive engagement continued on 4 October when, following additional litigation at the Court of Sessions, the government admitted that it would indeed apply for an Article 50 extension if a deal could not be struck at the upcoming round of talks. Even more damning, the papers submitted said that it would tell the British public one thing – no delay, deal or no deal – while admitting in talks with the EU that it was quite prepared to extend if required.[16]

On 14 October, Parliament reopened with a thin Queen's Speech. In addition to references to Brexit, the second main item was a new right-wing populist pivot on crime. The ritual Tory promises of tougher sentences and more protections for the police were joined by new penalties facing deportees who return to the UK. Other items included changes to railway franchising, a belated tightening of regulations governing high-rise dwellings, laws on patient safety and plans to change voter identification laws, which, entirely coincidentally, would favour the Conservatives in elections. Far from being ambitious, this was clearly an opportunity for a party-political broadcast aimed at cohering the Tory base. Get Brexit done, be seen to tinker with health and social care, and appear unsparing to designated scapegoats and out-groups.

Three days later, it appeared that Johnson was a step closer to meeting his Brexit promise. Intensive negotiations saw the EU accept, in large part, what Johnson had previously outlined, aided by its (unsaid) fundamental similarity to the May deal. The only real modifications were UK authorities acting as customs agents on behalf of the EU for anything coming into Northern Ireland and duty paid on goods at risk of ending up in the Republic of Ireland (i.e., EU territory). The North would also align with the EU on VAT, and the continuation or cessation of this situation would be affirmed or repudiated by a majority vote in the assembly.

The previously hardcore Brexiteers on the Tory benches again telegraphed their acceptance, with backbencher Andrew Bridgen saying, 'It looks like Brexit and smells like Brexit – that's Brexit for me' – a clear signal, then, that the right flank of the parliamentary party was secure.[17] However, one unimpressed group were the government's erstwhile backers in the DUP. The deputy leader, Nigel Dodds, argued that the new Ireland arrangements were because Johnson was seeking a deal at any price and had not paid attention to his party's concerns about protecting the integrity of the UK. They would therefore oppose it in the Commons.[18]

Thanks to the approaching Brexit deadline, the Commons sat on Saturday 19 October to discuss Johnson's revamped plan and passed the second Letwin amendment. Going through by 322 to 306 votes, it meant that the deal could only be approved if the legislation for enacting it was passed. While portrayed as a means of delaying Brexit further and forcing Johnson to apply for an extension, for its advocates it was a protection against a no-deal Brexit by foisting on the government the order by which Brexit should be enacted. The backdrop to this was rumours or fears that the ERG were prepared to swallow the meaningful vote and then rebel so that its implementation fell, forcing the no-deal outcome they deemed desirable. This meant that Johnson was now forced to write to Donald Tusk for an extension but made great theatre about his refusal to sign the letter and that this was Parliament's request, not his. The Tory press on the Sunday were happy to amplify this line.[19]

On Monday the government was able to win a vote for a second reading of its withdrawal agreement, but the rapid three-day debate Johnson wanted fell 308 to 322 votes. Even Brexit-backing Labour MPs wanted time to try and amend the deal. Speaking in the debate for the latter, Johnson once again said he would seek a general election if the move failed. Indeed, following the debate Jeremy Corbyn ruled out Labour's backing for as long as a no-deal Brexit remained a possibility – he was content to wait to see if the EU would agree to an extension, which it did on 28 October. The new date of departure was 31 January.

Fatefully, the Liberal Democrats and SNP joined forces to try and push for an election sooner rather than later, with the date of 9 December in mind. They thought the presence of students at university might, somehow, swing the vote in ways those parties might find congenial. Adding to the farce, while the government wanted an election the Tories were opposed to their bringing a bill setting aside the Fixed-Term Act.

It seemed that Johnson wanted the theatre of repeatedly bringing motions for dissolution and losing them, as well as the standing accruing for dissolving this most troublesome of parliaments. In truth, the Tories had long reacquired a significant polling lead and wanted to go to the country while Labour was polling between the high twenties and low thirties and the Liberal Democrats were reporting numbers between 15 and 20 per cent. The SNP and Liberal Democrats were in rushes of their own. The SNP wanted an election as quickly as possible to consolidate its rise in support since 2017, and also to defer any political consequences from the trial of former leader Alex Salmond on sexual assault charges which was due to begin early in 2020. For the Liberal Democrats it was a question of keeping hold of their momentum since the EU elections and, following a by-election victory and defections from the Tories and the Independent Group/Change UK, they had almost doubled their parliamentary contingent from twelve to twenty-one.

On 29 October, with the Article 50 extension secured and the risk of a no-deal Brexit off the table, the Commons voted to hold a general election on 12 December. Labour also supported the move because, despite the polling leads enjoyed by the Tories, there was a belief that 2019 would be a repeat of 2017 – a Brexit-centred firming up of the Tory vote would also firm up the Labour vote. Here, the party had a huge advantage in the number of activists it could turn out, thereby delivering its campaigning messages direct to voters and bypassing the almost uniform media hostility Labour faced. In hindsight, these assumptions were misconceived.

As early as 30 October, Nigel Farage was indicating that the Brexit Party would not stand in every seat but field candidates and focus efforts that would disproportionately hurt the Labour vote – i.e., Labour-held seats where the majority voted to leave the EU in 2016.[20] The lead-up to the election also suggested that Johnson's strategy was about going hard on Brexit and leaving the rest of the policy fare somewhat meagre. The Tories had learned the lesson from 2017 when May's attempt to fix things led to her coming unstuck over adult social care and waylaid her from what should have been the central focus of the campaign.

It was a lesson from the 2019 Australian election, which took place in May. There the National–Liberal Coalition defeated

Labor by opposing its limited programme to an extensive and expensive offering from its opponents. The Tories knew that keeping it simple meant that all they had to talk about was either Brexit or how undeliverable (or dangerous) Labour's smorgasbord offering was.

Yet the discipline this strategy asked of its adherents came under pressure almost immediately. Leader of the Commons Jacob Rees-Mogg said, in a live interview, that the victims of the Grenfell Tower fire did not have 'common sense' because they followed Fire Brigade advice to stay in their flats in the event of a fire, comments later defended by Andrew Bridgen, and subsequently disowned by both men.[21] After this brush with controversy, Rees-Mogg retired from public view for the remainder of the campaign.

The next day Welsh Secretary Alun Cairns announced his resignation after it emerged that he lied about knowing that his aide had 'sabotaged' a rape trial.[22] The Tories were also accused of doctoring footage of Labour's Keir Starmer, making him look hesitant and unable to answer a question on *Good Morning Britain* about the party's Brexit position.[23] Accompanying these gaffes was a Johnson-penned front page for the *Telegraph* with a line comparing Jeremy Corbyn to Stalin.[24]

While the Cairns case was an unhelpful accident, the others all played a part in cohering and mobilising the core vote. Heartless comments on Grenfell were a repetition of arguments that appeared under the line in comment boxes and Facebook groups. The fact of peddling untruths about Starmer and Brexit had, from the standpoint of thwarting those who would thwart Brexit, sufficient 'truthiness', and Johnson's nonsense about kulaks and collectivisation preyed upon the anxieties stirred up by four years of anti-Corbyn press. What looked unprofessional and slapdash conferred messages of the sort the Tories wanted to transmit and did so more effectively than a slick delivery.

This set the scene for the coordinated Tory attack on Labour on 10 November. Across all the Tory-supporting press, the front pages led with the claim that Corbyn's manifesto would cost £1.2

trillion, or an extra £650 million every day. The thirty-six-page booklet published by the Conservative Research Department was, unsurprisingly, a deeply flawed document.[25] For example, it totted up every spending commitment from the 2017 manifesto, every commitment made by shadow ministers since, adding to it every policy passed by the Labour conference and every Labour policy discussion paper. Costings were also dated from the very beginning of the next parliament (13 December) and assumed a five-year term, so Labour's policy on basic income trials, for instance, was treated as if enacted from day one. It fell apart under the most cursory scrutiny, but the truth did not matter. Stoking the anxiety and fears of the Tory base did.

On the Monday Farage finally confirmed that he would only stand Brexit Party candidates in Labour-held seats, arguing that Labour's Brexit position was a betrayal of its voters who supported Leave.[26] With signs of Labour's polling numbers recovering at a rate similar to 2017, at the ritualistic speech every party leader has to give at the Confederation of British Industry annual conference, Johnson pitched slightly to the left and, to audible gasps, said he was scrapping planned Corporation Tax cuts to the tune of £6 billion. To sugar the pill, he promised reviews of business rates and employers' National Insurance contributions.[27]

A much wider and less sympathetic audience awaited in the three televised debates/discussions. The first, on 19 November, put Johnson and Corbyn together for their first head-to-head outside the Commons chamber. With no third-party candidates to hide behind or risk ceding the limelight to, Corbyn's opening statement was oriented towards the kind of country we should be building and drew attention to Tory failures on health, the environment, the economy and Brexit.

In contrast, Brexit was all Johnson talked about. He said that the election had come about because of a deadlocked Parliament, and needed clearing because he wanted Brexit to be done and he had a deal ready to go, approved by all 635 Tory candidates (neglecting to mention that signing up was a condition for stand-ing). Once this was done, he could then get on with other issues people care about. Labour, on the other hand, offered nothing but dither, delay and further referenda.

The danger for Johnson in formats of this sort was on matters of detail, so he avoided them completely and stuck with mono-maniacal lines about Brexit. The *Question Time Leaders' Special* on 22 November saw Johnson and Corbyn joined by Jo Swinson and Nicola Sturgeon in half-hour 'interviews' with a studio audi-ence. Johnson did face tough questioning, and his answers referred to Brexit to such an extent that the moderator, Fiona Bruce, had to intervene persistently to direct him to answer the question. To nullify Tory attacks on Brexit, Corbyn said he would be neutral on any second referendum, which was a gift as far as the Johnson campaign was concerned.

The final leadership debate on 6 December was better tempered than the first Corbyn–Johnson clash, but also saw the repetition of the 'Get Brexit done' slogan. On this occasion Corbyn went on the attack on Brexit, arguing that it would take seven years for Johnson to fulfil the hyped trade deal with the United States, criticising the idea the UK's trading relationship with the EU would be unchanged and therefore Brexit would have no ill-effects. These were correct criticisms of Johnson's position, but they would have had more of a chance of getting wider traction if they had been introduced in the first televised encounter.

The different approaches to the debates reflected the different manifestos both parties put out. As expected, Labour's offered a great deal while the Tory manifesto, *Get Brexit Done: Unleash Britain's Potential*, was a thin document at only sixty-four pages.[28] More police, more nurses, a points-based immigration system, a promise not to raise taxes and funding for schools, apprentice-ships and infrastructure all reflected the Queen's Speech. Measures that did not attract the headlines included a planned attack on Traveller communities (p. 19), bans on public bodies participating in divestment or boycott campaigns of other countries (p. 20) and a minimum-service requirement during public transport strikes (p. 27 – the only explicitly anti-trade union measure in the manifesto).

Unfortunately, like 2017 the contest was marred by a terrorist incident that saw two people murdered on London Bridge. The perpetrator, Usma Khan, had a history of Islamist activity and had been fitted with an electronic tag by the authorities. Affecting a mark of respect, Johnson suspended campaigning in London where the Tories were facing difficulties, and took to the pages of the *Mail on Sunday* to make crude political capital out of the murders, promising an end to automatic early release for terrorist prisoners.[29] This, Johnson argued, was in stark contrast to Labour, which wanted to 'give more powers to human rights lawyers' with the net result that it 'would make us less safe'. Again, the politics of the moment were seized by Johnson to satisfy the appetites of the Tory coalition.

UK polling in the final fortnight showed no evidence of a surge in Labour support beyond the initial recovery at the beginning of the campaign. The final surveys showed a lead for the Tories of between eight and twelve points. This was confirmed by the exit poll on the evening of 12 December, which forecast 368 seats for the Tories and 191 for Labour – an eighty-six-strong majority. The actual result was marginally less bad, with 365 versus 202, but it was nevertheless a triumph for Johnson and a vindication of the recklessly single-minded campaign he had pursued since entering the Conservative leadership contest.

Johnson held together the coalition previously built by May, and added 330,000 extra voters, which awarded the Tories a net gain of forty-eight seats and a majority of eighty. Labour, on the other hand, lost sixty seats, including all its recently regained holdings in Scotland bar Edinburgh Central. While the result was abysmal, this was underlined by the seizure of the so-called heartland, or what were christened during the campaign 'Red Wall' seats – traditional Labour areas stretching west to east across northern England. Likewise, the Liberal Democrat challenge did not materialise. They gained 1.3 million votes but suffered the net loss of one seat – their leader, Jo Swinson. For its part, the SNP gained approximately 300,000 votes and was disproportionately rewarded thirteen extra seats.

Explaining the results, at least on the Labour side, has become bound up with polemic and bad-tempered factional argument. Understanding what happened depends on appreciating the coherence and solidity of the electoral coalitions each party assembled. Up until the first extension of Article 50 and participating in the EU elections, Theresa May largely held on to the coalition she assembled during her triumphant phase right up until the 2017 election. Its evaporation in the summer of 2019 underlined how Brexit was the glue holding it together, and therefore Johnson doggedly pursued it. Coming to office, Johnson's bombast, parliamentary shenanigans, rhetorical defiance of the law and willingness to split the Conservative Party – even if it meant dispensing with grandees and his own brother – demonstrated single-minded purpose in seeing the result of the referendum through. Away from Westminster and the gaze of the lobby hacks, millions of Brexit voters noted this determination and Johnson's willingness to blow up establishment politics to deliver their 2016 vote. This included a large numbers of Leave-voting Labour supporters who felt abandoned by their party's switch away from accepting the referendum result to having another vote. To appeal to this potentially wider coalition, the Tory manifesto could not have room for big policy offers or anything that might drive a wedge between the government and its coalescing support. Everything was subordinate to this aim because, in truth, pulling together a coalition on a Brexit-or-bust prospectus was the only option available for the Tories if they wanted to win.

Why did it work where Theresa May, initially feted as a credible, 'grown-up' and serious figure, failed? Because Johnson was lucky in his opponents. On the issue the election was fought on, the Tories owned the Leave side, but Remain was split between three electorally viable opposition parties. For their part, the Liberal Democrats explicitly positioned themselves as the party of Remain and said they would set aside the referendum result in the (unlikely) event of forming a government. In an election polarising around the EU, they offered a more consistent option than Labour's support for a second referendum, and so were able to eat into the party's support. This, however, had the surprising effect of alienating some Liberal Democrat voters who believed the referendum result should be honoured, who then switched to the Conservatives. In Scotland this space was occupied by the SNP, and this helped it scoop back the seats it had conceded to Labour two years previously.

Then there was the 'opposition' provided by Farage's Brexit Party. In an echo of what happened in 2015, while most of its support was drawn from disgruntled Tory voters in the EU elections the decision to stand in Labour seats had disproportionate consequences. There were Leave-voting Labour voters who would not countenance voting Tory under any circumstance but were prepared to protest their party's abandonment of the 2017 position by supporting Farage. The 644,257 votes won by Farage across 275 seats undoubtedly helped the Tories. Lastly, the Green Party had also tried owning the Brexit issue from the Remain side and, though much less successful than the Liberal Democrats, it improved its showing to 835,579 – albeit down on 2015's high of 1.1 million. Again, Labour bled more votes in an election that was not about contesting the fabled centre ground but about who could turn out the greatest number of supporters.

It is a truism that divided parties do not win elections. For all the Tory fractiousness prior to the general election, Johnson united his party by either expelling or cowing his parliamentary opponents. Tory expellee candidatures, such as David Gauke's in South West Hertfordshire, or Anne Milton's in Guildford, came nowhere (though, arguably, the Liberal Democrats could have taken the latter had Milton decided not to stand). The Tories presented a united front to the electorate. The same could not be said for Labour. The divisions in the party dating from the 2015 leadership contest are well documented and do not require detailed exposition here, but their consequences, such as the constant leaking of documents (including the 2017 election manifesto, which contrary to intentions helped Labour's campaign then), anonymous briefings, factionally convenient amplification of anti-Semitism, open attacks on strategic lines taken by the party and a regular flouting of Shadow Cabinet discipline did not help matters. The most important of these, as subsequently shown in polling for why Labour voters switched to the Tories in 2019, was the adoption of the second referendum policy.

When it was first floated in Labour's second leadership election in summer 2016 by Owen Smith, it was subsequently articulated and pushed by a coalition of Remain-minded MPs in and out of the party following the unexpected result of the 2017 election. By 2018, it was clear that the majority of the membership were won over to a second-referendum position and it was a matter of time before it became official policy. The public wrangling helped muddy the waters and reinforce the perception of Corbyn as ineffectual, something the Tories were happy to flag up by employing John Woodcock, Ian Austin and John Mann, former Labour MPs and well-known critics of Corbyn, to campaign against Labour in the election. In another coincidental happenstance, Johnson-nominated peerages were forthcoming for all three.

Then there was the distribution of the Tory and Labour votes. The former was more evenly distributed across England and Wales, which meant more voters in the right seats at the right time. Labour's support was not.[30] This was particularly the case in the big cities, where Labour MPs chalked up huge super-majorities – i.e., Labour's support was concentrated in fewer constituencies. The geographic skew was a consequence of the age profile of Labour's vote. Many of the so-called Red Wall seats were economically depressed, dominated by low-waged labour markets and above-average unemployment and demographically old. For younger cohorts of voters, it simply made sense to move to where the jobs were, hence a long-term greying of the vote in many 'traditional' Labour areas and a political polarisation relatively contained by the first-past-the-post voting system. The great unanswered question, however, is turnout. Satisfactory explanations for the lower turnout among Labour's new core voters are yet to be fully fleshed out at the time of writing, but the impact of the most scurrilous press and media campaign against a labour leader in living memory cannot be discounted. Even though the sharply polarised politics of this election might have been expected to drive turnout.

Another question remains: Why should Johnson's pitch have proven so successful among older voters, especially when his media persona and many scandals, indiscretions and well-documented propensity for laziness and incompetence are the very antithesis of a stable, prime ministerial authority figure like Thatcher, Blair and Cameron? As we have already seen, it is the confluence of ontologies: of the analogies between retirement and a petit-bourgeois-class location and the political consequences of property ownership among older cohorts (and the importance of the minority rentier strata of small landlords and shareholders), and the relative shielding that retirement and favourable government policy provides.

Brexit and Johnson's politically successful pursuit of it are the affirmation of a higher form of authority and certainty: the durability of a mythologised, nostalgic nation harking back to a better age when there was a sense of a national community, when Great Britain acted freely on the world stage and was respected as a leading player – a vassal of neither the United States nor the European Union. Johnson's Tories, just as May tried before him, fed into these small nationalist identity politics and offered a promise of an ideological anchor in the world while, like all previous Tory governments, making it a more anxious, less certain, more capricious place.

Conclusion

The Future of the Tories

When Britain departed the European Union at the end of January 2020, it did so with the Tories at the peak of their powers. Not only had they won convincingly in 2019, but also this was the culmination of rising support since 2001. To talk about the problems the Tories have and to argue, as this book has done, that the party is facing long-term decline might seem premature, if not downright delusional.

The Thatcher and Major governments were corrosive of their own political dominance. Thatcher's successful assault on the labour movement left the door open to rolling back the social wage. The pre-eminence of the executive with its crude but ruthless attacks on independent points of authority within the state system, and the accelerated closure of swathes of the country's industrial base, alienated natural supporters in the professions and among the petit bourgeois who made a living from the working-class communities the Tories destroyed. Compensating for the liquidation and estrangement of these constituencies was the government's hope that new loyal Tory voters could be generated. These efforts revolved around selling off council homes and opening the housing market, while allowing a limited popular capitalism in the public share issue of newly privatised utilities. This kept two-nation politics viable up to a point and was enough to keep the Tories in power until 1997.

After thirteen years of recovery the Tories returned to office in 2010 and Cameron set about fashioning a programme explicitly aimed at keeping this (now ageing) cohort of property owners wedded to the Tories. The following five years were a period in which a layer of this support was radicalised by the nostalgic certainties proffered by Nigel Farage and UKIP, and the Tories chose to pander to them by doubling down on social security attacks and scapegoating while conceding a referendum on European Union membership. As is well known, the result of the referendum yielded a stark age polarisation. For younger workers, their vote to Remain was a vote for stability and certainty. For older workers and the retired, Brexit offered a promise of escape from an uncertain world, aggravated by the ontological angst of their social location and asset holding, via a projected assertion of national vigour. Subsequently, both Theresa May and Boris Johnson divined that their path to election victory meant fundamentally reorienting the party around these voters. Gone were the homilies to modernisation and reaching out. It was a risky strategy, especially when May's gamble failed. But repeating the trick the second time round, Johnson was faced with a divided field.

Yet the pattern of the Tory vote, the concentration of its support among older voters and its continued cultivation of this base prevents them from convincingly intersecting with the bulk of the working-age population and presents them with an inescapable difficulty. People are not acquiring property at anything like the rates they were in the 1980s and 1990s, and therefore the link between ageing and asset ownership is becoming more attenuated. This means that the electoral basis for their 2019 triumph will, with time, grow increasingly difficult to repeat. Unless the Tories do something by the end of the 2020s the prospects for forming a majority government thereafter gets more fanciful. Demography, however, is not destiny. A trend is not the same as hard determinism.

Thinking through the possible futures the Tories have, the successful resolution of the Brexit crisis – from their point of view – throws up a difficulty. Given the character of their coalition, the nationalism running through the Leave campaign and the ugly conflation of exiting the European Union with anti-immigration and racist politics, post-war nostalgia and attempts to escape a

world that is unfamiliar and unerring, the question at the forefront of Tory strategy is what can replace it. With all the other
Westminster parties bar the SNP accepting Brexit, it might seem
that this well has dried up. For example, since taking over as leader
of the Labour Party Keir Starmer has rapidly buried the part he
played in convincing the party to adopt a second referendum
policy, and in late December 2020 he instructed Labour MPs to
endorse the prime minister's EU trade deal.

It seems there are several substitutes the Tories can use to keep
their people on side. They can simply carry on waving the flag
while trumpeting Brexit's success. Despite stories of the multiplication of red tape and added fees and delays on exporting into the
EU's economic area, unsurprisingly the Tory press have crowed
about the EU's difficulties sourcing COVID-19 vaccine and its
humiliating climbdown following a dispute with drug firm
AstraZeneca. This, trumpeted Johnson's client media, was proof
that Brexit was correct and that leaving the EU has literally saved
lives. The same outlets had comparatively little to say about
128,000 Covid deaths and one of the worst death rates in the
world.

Stoking English/British nationalism might have further electoral
uses too. Thanks to surging polling figures favouring Scottish
independence and the SNP's pledge to hold a further referendum,
there is a rich seam of resentment here that the Tories are well
placed to mine in England. As we saw in 2015, with some skill the
Tory campaign was able to present Labour's Ed Miliband being in
de facto alliance with the SNP, and the price of a minority government supported by Nicola Sturgeon and Alex Salmond would be
the break-up of the UK and scrapping the Trident nuclear weapons
system. That Theresa May tried the same in 2017 and failed to
make as much of an impression does not mean that the Tories will
not try again. Casting Labour as somehow weak on the union and
forgetting how the party blew up its Scottish vote and parliamentary representation in its defence dovetail nicely with Jeremy
Corbyn-era attacks on Labour's lack of patriotism and 'softness'
on terrorism and threats posed by foreign powers. This offers the

possibility of cohering a polarising dynamic ahead of the next election against Scottish nationalism and assorted other anti-England demons.

Then there is the predominance of social liberalism that the Tories can use (and are using) as a wedge issue. Concerns of the sort Ed West has with his prophecies of conservative doom lay the blame at liberal lecturers and lefty teachers brainwashing students and pupils. The so-called 'War on Woke' amounts to preserving as much of the prevailing political culture it can so that scapegoating drives and Little England appeals, which have proven indispensable to the Tories over the years, retain their efficacy. Yet as a long-term investment goes, it is destined to repay diminishing returns. For one thing, getting right-wing journalists excited about exaggerated goings-on on university campuses does not have the same weight or resonance as Brexit did, which cut to the quick of national identity. For another, social liberalism and anti-Toryism do not persist in a rarefied realm of ideas cut off from the everyday. Both are rooted in class or, more precisely, the experience of class cohorts; the brute realities of the experience of work and living at the sharp end of sectional policy making are constituting the outlook of the rising generation. The old Marxist aphorism of an ounce of experience being worth a tonne of theory is beyond the ken of conservative thought – assuming one takes the fairy tales of Tory philosophy in good faith.

Then there is fiddling the electoral system. This was a stated objective of Tory governments since David Cameron's election and remains a key objective of Boris Johnson's. At the time of writing, the Boundary Commission is redrawing the political map of the UK to 'equalise' the population size of constituencies and diluting marginal and Labour-held seats, enhancing further the Tory advantage of its more efficiently spread voter base. Other measures such as compulsory identification checks, ostensibly to cut down on the microscopic instances of voter fraud, are also in play to suppress Labour voters. Gerrymandering the system to the Tories' advantage is their confession that the Tories are ill-equipped to face the politics of their long-term decline, and entirely true to the custom and practice of the party. It is a short-term fix that puts off but does not prevent the inevitable pain.

The difficulty of these strategies, which are co-present and actively pursued, is their time-limited efficacy. This might not matter to Boris Johnson and many leading Tories in 2021 as the consequences of long-term decline are not about to immediately pressure their electoral performance. They can afford to kick the can down the road. It is for future Tory leaders to deal with. The question is how the Tories can escape the situation they have contrived for themselves. With the conservatising effects of age breaking down and Tory support destined not to replace itself like for like, the Tories must find new ways of winning over the rising generation of voters. Not a simple task.

There are three overlapping possibilities. The first is simply doing nothing. As the post-war generation pass away over the next few decades, their property will be inherited by their children in the Generation X and Millennial cohorts. Now with assets at their disposal, there is no reason for not believing a certain conservatisation could set in, albeit at a later stage of their adult lives than was the case with their parents and grandparents. Waiting is risky because this might not translate into support for the Tories given their collective memory of Conservative governments during their formative years, and how opposition parties might respond. The New Labour years showed that the party can intersect with and appeal to propertied layers by pandering to their peccadilloes and shielding them from the chill winds of globalisation. It might do the same again.

Another possibility is jump-starting the acquisition of property and getting many millions more younger workers onto the housing ladder. In the 2010s the Tories oversaw a complex array of part-rent–part-mortgage vehicles, help-to-buy initiatives with government loans and the extension of the right to buy to some housing association properties, none of which have made a dent in the housing market. Resistance abides in government to the building of council housing in sufficient quantities to meet demand, and the Tories have allowed developers to shirk requirements to provide social housing quotas in large developments. All the while planning laws have been watered down as if the problem is recalcitrant local authority opposition to more housing, not developers land banking or limiting construction to benefit from asset price inflation. If the Tories were to reverse course and mandate a national house building effort, then property acquisition could be opened with all the political consequences this entails. They do not because more houses increase supply and would threaten prices and create alternatives to the private rental market. In other words, it goes against the interests of their existing coalition of voters, particularly the caste of petty landlords that their policies have done so much to encourage over the last forty years.

The final strategy entails a thoroughgoing detoxification and reckoning with itself. The Cameron years tried to move with the rising social liberal consensus, but it quickly became apparent that this was but a gloss once his government deepened the neoliberal settlement further. Passing equal marriage legislation while marketising public services and pushing people on social security into destitution does not make for a progressive government of any stripe. Instead, it was just another Tory administration with slick PR. If, however, the Tories were to become more consistently socially liberal and actively dumped their attachments to scapegoating, callousness, authoritarianism and opposition to equalities, and were less capricious and more thoughtful, and abandoned persistent short-termism, in conjunction with significant about-turns on policy, a reinvented Tory Party might become a rejuvenated Tory Party. With one caveat – such a transformation is utterly fanciful and can only exist as a thought experiment. If the Tories were to model themselves on the plodding managerialism of Angela Merkel's Christian Democrats but were consistently socially liberal, it would not be the Conservative Party. Indeed, such a transformation would demand a clear-out of most Tory MPs, its cadre of councillors and most of the membership. As with expecting the Tories to go against the interests of their base, refounding the Tories as a moderate, cautious centre-right party is a pipe dream.

Forecasting their futures can only be an assessment of probabilities. Social relations, after all, are not mechanisms grinding out predetermined outcomes. As we survey the political landscape the Conservatives have shaped to their advantage, it is worth tempering an apprehension of their difficulties with what British political history has taught us for two centuries. No one got rich betting against the Tories.

Postscript

The Conservatives and Coronavirus

We end as this book began. At the start of 2020, Boris Johnson tweeted, 'This is going to be a fantastic year for Britain.'[1] Little over twelve months later and affecting a sombre tone, Johnson offered his apologies for every life lost to COVID-19 and took 'full responsibility' as the official death toll passed 100,000.[2] The story of how the Tories have mismanaged the pandemic and visited a catastrophe on the UK is deserving of several books and, one would think, a stigma it would take the party a generation to wash away. Despite the scale of the disaster, the Tories have proven themselves very adept at managing the political fallout of the crisis. Reflecting their success, as of June 2021 the Tories are posting double-digit leads over labour and have made further unroads into its heartland seats during the was local government elections. According to survey work undertaken in the winter by YouGov the public are more likely to blame the rest of the public (58 per cent) for the surge in infections in December and early January than the government (28 per cent). Unsurprisingly, given the arguments presented in this book, there are clear age profiles to the answers, with only a plurality blaming the Tories found among eighteen- to twenty-four-year-olds.[3] Amid tragedy, an unqualified political success story.

How have the Conservatives managed to escape so much pain? People have rallied around the government as the only means to defeat the viral assailant, and this was particularly true after the initial outbreak. Despite three lockdowns and numerous public health failures, this still accounts for some of the Tory support. In the absence of anything else, analysis of Tory policy must concede the success they have had handling the necropolitics of the virus. This unpleasant-sounding term was explored in depth by Achille Mbembe and, among other things, deals with a state's management of the politics of death: who should die and who should be exposed to the risk of dying.[4] As a concept addressed to matters of war, conflict and the deployment of state violence, the management of death lends itself well to a governments' response to potential of mass-casualty disasters and pandemics. As far as the Tories were concerned, their approach to this inescapable fact of governance was entirely consistent with Thatcherite logics: individualise the problem, overrule or ignore expert advice and depoliticise the government's strategy as much as possible.

The initial strategy document issued when global COVID deaths stood at 3,000 and the UK had just fifty confirmed cases reveals these logics.[5] For example, Section 4.8 states that new health legislation confers powers on 'medical professionals, public health professionals and the police to allow them to detain and direct individuals in quarantined areas at risk or suspected of having the virus' (p. 12). The document goes on to specify the separation of COVID patients from the general hospital population and, particularly, Accident and Emergency departments (p. 14). Taken with other public health rules, these appear neutral and sensible precautions for mitigating infection. Later, it addresses the powers of the authorities. Section 4.39 reads, 'There are also well practised arrangements for Defence to provide support to Civil Authorities if requested' (p. 17) – in other words, to use the military when it is deemed necessary. Section 4.45 raises the possibility of 'population distancing strategies' (p. 18), meaning the closure of schools and other public institutions, encourage homeworking and preventing large gatherings from taking place, as has manifested in the famous social distancing rule.

The Tories proved slow to follow their own advice. Football matches went ahead, Cheltenham races happened and, incredibly, hospitals sent elderly patients back to their care homes, precipitating a huge wave of infection that tore through the system.

Peculiarly, this catastrophic blunder has attracted little attention from the growing army of conspiracy theorists, let alone the cadres of the bourgeois press. From the outset, government messaging firmly stressed individual responsibility for abiding by the rules. 'Stay at home, control the virus, save lives' was simple and easily understood. Therefore when Johnson's mercurial adviser Dominic Cummings drove from one end of the country to the other and later broke lockdown rules in an eye-testing (and credulity-stretching) trip to County Durham's Barnard Castle, far from damaging the government the outcry affirmed individual responsibility for sticking to the rules. Backed, as ever, by the Tories' institutional weight in the media, multiple scandals around personal protective equipment procurement, the provision of laptop computers and tablets to schoolchildren and the visible failure of the outsourced test and trace programme barely troubled Boris Johnson. Instead, the press alighted on illegal parties or people going to the beach. Death in the age of coronavirus has nothing to do with government failures. It's an individual tragedy, a stroke of the most atrocious bad luck. The Tories have accomplished self-erasure, and 126,000 deaths were presented as 128,000 unavoidable tragedies.

A seemingly unlikely ally in the Tory management of COVID necropolitics has proven to be the Leader of the Opposition, Keir Starmer. While carefully worded and supportive criticisms might have been appropriate in the period immediately following his election as leader of the Labour Party, he has done very little to contest Johnson's framing of the pandemic. He has focused his criticisms on competency issues and has occasionally scored 'wins' by calling for lockdowns and tougher action before the spread of the disease forced the government's hand. This is quite deliberate, and he has obviously calculated that a wider political critique is too risky. The result is that Johnson is not held to account for the death toll, nor for the unerring coincidence of contracts getting handed to firms with Tory links. Nowhere is this clearer than when it comes to school reopenings. In the summer of 2020 and in the manner of an annoyed headmaster braced for disappointment, Starmer said he 'expected' schools to open for the new term in

September.[6] When teaching unions were concerned about opening schools after the Christmas break with the more infectious and deadly 'Kent variant' in circulation, Starmer refused to back their campaign despite majority public support for the teachers. One (unnamed) Labour frontbencher summed up their perceived bind as they reflected on their focus groups: 'the more we attack the government, the more people don't like it . . . When we criticise the government, people often respond, "You lot wouldn't have done any better."'[7]

The Tories, then, at the time of writing, are winning the necropolitics. They are setting the agenda and framing the issues and the Opposition refuses to contest their terms. This bodes well for the Conservatives and how they try and determine politics after coronavirus. Any hope that an independent inquiry after the conclusion of the pandemic is going to shift the Tory voter coalition when the deaths of 128,000 of their fellow citizens has not is a forlorn one.

The unavoidable conclusion, despite the prospect of a declining voter coalition and other strategic issues gnawing at the Tories, is, again, that they are proving lucky in their opponents. Save an event that can fundamentally shift the country and quickly dissolve the roots of their support in the country's political economy, a fifth election victory is within the Conservative Party's reach.

Acknowledgements

All books are a collective effort, not least the tough and ruthless work done by the editors. I would like to thank Leo Hollis, Caitlin Doherty, John Gaunt and Mark Martin, whose sharp pens and sound advice helped make this book readable and resemble something approaching a coherent argument.

As for the other culprits for this book, I blame Alex Nunns and Tom Mills for encouraging me to write this in the first place. Also responsible are the train crew Alan Colclough, Steve Lennon, Caily Stephenson, Heather Kuduk, Dave Potts, Dave Arrowsmith, Simon Fernyhough, Heather Withington and Bob for the racing tips, the 'considered criticisms' and boozy noms. Lovely colleagues can't escape their share of the blame, so many thanks for kind words, thoughts and understanding go to Helen Brocklehurst, Andrew Wilson, Sung-Hee Lee, Phil Henry, Phil Hodgson, Charlotte Hargreaves, Martyn Kendrick, Matt Hodkinson, Francesco Belcastro, Baris Cayli, Vee Monro, Liz Doherty, Henriette Bergstrom, Kulsoom Pridmore and, of course, our absent friend Simon Speck, to whom this book is dedicated.

To the cream of the Stoke-on-Trent/North Staffs proletariat, much gratitude goes to Ann Harvey, Olwen Hamer, Lawrence Shaw, Aimee Goddard, Tina Natalello, Shaun Pender, Steve Funnell, Ian McLaughlan, Mark Meredith, Chris Spence, Andy Platt, Glen Watson, Jenny Harvey, Rob Wallace, Neil Singh and Brian Doherty.

And something would be amiss if the rabble of lumpens, troublemakers and sectarians on the fringes of the labour movement

avoided a namecheck. Each of these folks has contributed some-
thing at some time, whether they knew it or not. Thanks go to
Ravi Subramanian, Rhiannon Lockley, Scott Newton, Alex
Doherty, Jyoti Wilkinson, Lewis Bassett, Ruth Woolsey, Juliet
Jacques, Paul Ewart, Adriana Bailey, Jake Rowland, Alex James,
Sarah Brown, Paul Hunt, Emilie Marsh, Simon Hedges, Ian Keillor,
Lisa Keillor, Callan Hansrani, Amy Ilson, Charlotte Drayton,
Kyria Hooper, Devan Frith, Natalie Hughes, Malika Belgasmi,
Dawn Jordan, Karen Bennett, the *Reel Politik* scallies and the
regular commentators and readers of All That Is Solid.

Finally, I'm indebted to my family. Mum, Dad, David and
Helen, Gwynneth and Ron, and Nana and Granddad. Especially
Nana Barbara who is entirely responsible for introducing me to
politics. I do wonder what she'd have made of this book. And last
of all my deepest gratitude is for Cat, whose love, support and
encouragement make everything possible.

Notes

Introduction

1. D. Mercer, 'Eat Out to Help Out: businesses claimed £849 million through scheme for 160 million meals', *Sky News*, 25 November 2020, news.sky.com.
2. Gov.UK, 'Coronavirus (COVID-19) in the UK', 20 March 2021, coronavirus.data.gov.uk.
3. The Academy of Medical Sciences, *Preparing for a Challenging Winter 2020/21*, acmedsci.ac.uk.
4. A. Woodcock, 'Coronavirus: UK winter could see 85,000 deaths in second wave, says leaked Sage report', *Independent*, 29 August 2020, independent.co.uk.
5. T. Fetzer, 'Subsidizing the spread of COVID19: evidence from the UK's Eat-Out-to-Help-Out scheme' (2020), Centre for Competitive Advantage in the Global Economy (CAGE), warwick.ac.uk.
6. William Hague at ISDA Legal Forum, London, 30 January 2020, twitter.com.
7. 'How the voters voted in the 2019 election', Ipsos MORI, December 2019, ipsos.com.

1. Dimensions of Decline

1. The latest and bestselling exponent of this reportage is *The Times* chief political correspondent Tim Shipman. See T. Shipman, *All Out War: The Full Story of Brexit*, London: William Collins, 2016; and T. Shipman, *Fall Out: A Year of Political Mayhem*, London: William Collins, 2017.

2. W. Bonefeld, A. Brown and P. Burnham, *A Major Crisis?*, Aldershot: Dartmouth, 1995; P. Dorey, *The Conservative Party and the Trade Unions*, London: Routledge, 1995.

3. R. Seymour, *The Meaning of David Cameron*, Repley, Hants: Zero Books, 2010.

4. A term subsequently used to describe the populist framing of pro-austerity politics. See Chapters 5 and 6 below, or, for its coining, M. Bolton and F.H. Pitts, *Corbynism: A Critical Approach*, Bingley: Emerald Press, 2018.

5. H. Hill, 'Boris' boys and girls: the Conservative Commons intake of 2019', *Conservative Home*, 21 January 2020, conservativehome. com; 'May's men and women: the Conservative Commons intake of 2017', *Conservative Home*, 25 October 2017, conservativehome. com; and P. Goodman and H. Hill, 'The complete Cameron's Children: an analysis of all 74 new Conservative MPs', *Conservative Home*, 7 September 2015, conservativehome.com.

6. D. Bond, 'Class of 2019: meet the new MPs', *The House*, 16 December 2019, politicshome.com.

7. Subscribe 2020/21, Conservative Councillors' Association, conservativecouncillors.com.

8. Local Government Association (2018), *National Census of Local Authority Councillors 2018*, local.gov.uk.

9. Fawcett Society, 'New Fawcett data reveals that women's representation in local government "at a standstill"', 2 July 2019, fawcettsociety. org.uk.

10. Operation Black Vote (2019), *BAME Local Political Representation Audit 2019*, obv.org.uk.

11. R. Keen and L. Jackson (2018), 'Membership of UK political parties', House of Commons briefing paper SN05125.

12. 'Conservative leadership race: voters "issued two ballots"', BBC News, 6 July 2019, bbc.co.uk.

13. J. Blanchard, 'Cleverly does it', *Politico*, 1 October 2019, politico.eu.

14. 'Donate to the CWO', Conservative Women's Organisation, conservativewomen.uk.

15. *Central Office* v. *James R. S. Burrell (Inspector of Taxes)*, All England Law Reports, 1982, p. 60.

16. P. Stephens, *Politics and the Pound: The Tories, the Economy and Europe*, London: Macmillan, 1996.

17. 'Party structure and organisation', Conservative Party, conservatives.com.

18. Constitution of the Conservative Party, Fourth Amendment, April 2009, 24.5, p. 8, politicalpartydb.org.

19. Ibid., p. 6.

20. For example, see P. Mair, *Ruling the Void*, London: Verso, 2013; and C. Crouch, *Post-democracy*, Cambridge: Polity Press, 2004.

21. P. Burton-Cartledge, 'Case studies in political atavism', *All That Is Solid*, 20 May 2019, averypublicsociologist.blogspot.com.

22. T. Bale, P. Webb and M. Poletti, *Footsoldiers: Political Party Membership in the 21st Century*, London: Routledge, 2020; T. Bale and P. Webb), 'Members only: views of the Conservative Party's rank-and-file', *Political Insight* 4(3), 2013, pp. 4–8, psa.ac.uk.

23. P. Whiteley, P. Seyd and J. Richardson, *True Blues*, Oxford: Oxford University Press, 1994, p. 42.

24. G. Wheatcroft, *The Strange Death of Tory England*, Basingstoke: Macmillan, 2005; E. West, *Small Men on the Wrong Side of History: The Decline, Fall and Unlikely Return of Conservatism*, London: Constable, 2020.

25. John Ross, *Thatcher and Friends*, London: Verso, 1983.

26. E. West, 'Why conservatism is doomed', *UnHerd*, 9 March 2020, unherd.com.

27. R. Inglehart, *The Silent Revolution*, Princeton, NJ: Princeton University Press, 1977.

28. West, *Small Men*, pp. 128–9.

29. S. Childs and P. Webb, *Sex, Gender, and the Conservative Party*, Houndmills: Macmillan, 2012.

30. Wheatcroft, *The Strange Death of Tory England*, p. 1.

31. A. Gallas, *The Thatcherite Offensive: A Neo-Poulantzasian Analysis*, Chicago: Haymarket Books, 2015.

32. Wheatcroft, *The Strange Death of Tory England*, p. 182.

33. Ross, *Thatcher and Friends*, p. 48.

34. J. Ross, 'Election 2010: Conservatives remain in long-term decline', *Guardian*, 5 May 2010, theguardian.com.

35. J. Ross, 'The Tories will get 30.3% at the next general election. Here's why', *Guardian*, 5 March 2013, theguardian.com.

36. For an account on the Western adoption of Keynesian/corporatist policy, see E. Mandel, *Late Capitalism*, London: New Left Books, 1975; and for Britain particularly see Gallas, *The Thatcherite Offensive*.

37. R. Gledhill, 'Why do people stop going to church? Church of England fails to halt decline', *Christian Today*, 28 October 2016, christiantoday.com.

38. K.H. Thompson, 'Upward social mobility and political orientation: a re-evaluation of the evidence', *American Sociological Review*, 36 (2), 1971, pp. 223–35.

39. For an elaboration of this argument, see M. Lazzarato, 'Immaterial labour', in P. Virno and M. Hardt (eds.), *Radical Thought in Italy*,

Minneapolis: University of Minnesota Press, 1996, pp. 132–47; and M. Hardt and A. Negri, *Empire*, Cambridge, MA, and London: Harvard University Press, 2000.

40. A. McDonnell and C. Curtis, 'How Britain voted in the 2019 general election', *YouGov*, 17 December 2019, yougov.co.uk.

41. C. Curtis, 'How Britain voted at the 2017 general election', *YouGov*, 13 June 2017, yougov.co.uk.

42. P. Moore, 'How Britain voted at the EU referendum', *YouGov*, 27 June 2016, yougov.co.uk.

43. P. Kellner, 'General election 2015: how Britain really voted', *YouGov*, 8 June 2015, yougov.co.uk.

44. Unfortunately, UKIP was not included in the age breakdowns. See 'How Britain voted in 2010', Ipsos MORI, 21 May 2010, ipsos. com.

45. K. Marx, *The Eighteenth Brumaire of Louis Bonaparte*, Moscow: Progress Publishers, 1971; L. Trotsky, *Fascism: What It Is and How to Fight It*, New York: Pathfinder, 1969.

46. 'Almost a third of graduates "overeducated" for their job', BBC News, 29 April 2019, bbc.co.uk.

47. R. Miliband, *The State in Capitalist Society*, London: Quartet Books, 1969, pp. 110–11.

48. Ibid., p. 168.

49. B. Jessop, *State Power*, Cambridge: Polity, 2007.

50. J. Goldthorpe, *On Sociology: Numbers, Narratives, and the Integration of Research and Theory*, Oxford: Oxford University Press, 2000.

2. Thatcher

1. 'I would just like to remember some words of St. Francis of Assisi which I think are really just particularly apt at the moment. "Where there is discord, may we bring harmony. Where there is error, may we bring truth. Where there is doubt, may we bring faith. And where there is despair, may we bring hope" . . . and to all the British people – howsoever they voted – may I say this. Now that the Election is over, may we get together and strive to serve and strengthen the country of which we're so proud to be a part.' M. Thatcher, remarks on becoming prime minister (St Francis's prayer), 4 May 1979, margaretthatcher.org.

2. John Ross, *Thatcher and Friends*, London: Verso, 1983.

3. The terms economic order and class politics are elaborated in A. Gallas, *The Thatcherite Offensive: A Neo-Poulantzasian Analysis*, Chicago: Haymarket Books, 2015.

4. M. Richardson (undated), 'Trade unions and industrial conflict', humanities.uwe.ac.uk.
5. J. Freedland, 'Enough of this cover-up: the Wilson plot was our Watergate', *Guardian*, 15 March 2006, theguardian.com.
6. S. Hall, B. Roberts, J. Clarke, T. Jefferson and C. Critcher, *Policing the Crisis: Mugging, the State, and Law and Order*, London: Macmillan, 1978.
7. S. Hall, *The Hard Road to Renewal*, London: Verso, 1988.
8. Peter Dorey, *The Conservative Party and the Trade Unions*, London: Routledge, 1995.
9. J. Critchley, *Westminster Blues: Minor Chords*, London: Elm Tree Books, 1985, p. 50.
10. Gallas, *The Thatcherite Offensive*, 2015.
11. Interestingly, opposing consumers to producers in this way was a keynote of New Labour thinking about industrial relations. For instance, see G. Rosen, *Serving the People: Co-operative Party History from Fred Perry to Gordon Brown*, London: The Co-Operative Party, 2007; and more recently W. Streeting, *Let Us Face the Future Again*, London: Fabian Society, 2020.
12. D. Kavanagh, *Thatcherism and British Politics: The End of Consensus?*, Oxford: Oxford University Press, 1990.
13. However, recent revisionist history suggests that the SDP split from Labour was just as harmful for the Conservatives. See M. Singh, 'Did the SDP really split the left in 1983?', *Prospect*, 20 February 2019, prospectmagazine.co.uk.
14. H. Paterson, *Look Back in Anger*, Nottingham: Mushroom Books, 2014.
15. Employment Act 1988, Dock Work Act 1989, Employment Act 1990.
16. Conservative Party (1979), *1979 Conservative Party General Election Manifesto*, margaretthatcher.org.
17. S. Peplow, *Race and Riots in Thatcher's Britain*, Manchester: Manchester University Press, 2019.
18. 'What happened in the hunger strike?' BBC News, 5 May 2006, news.bbc.co.uk.
19. P. Taylor, *Provos: The IRA & Sinn Féin*, London: Bloomsbury, 1997, pp. 242–3.
20. M. Thatcher, 'Speech to 1922 Committee ("the enemy within")', 19 July 1984, margaretthatcher.org.
21. P. Stephens, *Politics and the Pound: The Tories, the Economy and Europe*, London: Macmillan, 1996.
22. For background on and the legacy of the letter, see P. Booth (ed.), *Were 364 Economists All Wrong?*, London: Institute of Economic Affairs, 2006.

23. P. Jenkin (1980), Foreword, in *The Black Report*, sochealth.co.uk.
24. E.J. Evans, *Thatcher and Thatcherism*, London: Routledge, 1997.
25. I. Cobain, ' "Subversive" civil servants secretly blacklisted under Thatcher', *Guardian*, 24 July 2018, theguardian.com.
26. C. Haddon, *Reforming the Civil Service: The Efficiency Unit in the Early 1980s and the 1987 Next Steps Report*, London: Institute for Government, 2012, instituteforgovernment.org.uk.
27. HC Deb (8 May 1981), Vol. 4, col. 458, available at parliament.uk.
28. See L. Castellani, *The Rise of Managerial Bureaucracy: Reforming the British Civil Service*, London: Palgrave Macmillan, 2018, pp. 89–91.
29. A. Hodder, 'Employment relations in the UK civil service', *Personnel Review*, 44 (6), 2015, pp. 930–48.
30. A.E. Mueller, *Working Patterns: A Study Document by the Cabinet Office*, London: HMSO, 1987.
31. A. Chisholm, 'Next Steps in retrospect', *Civil Service*, 12 September 2017, civilservice.blog.gov.uk.
32. NHS Management Enquiry, 6 October 1983 (Griffiths Report), reproduced in S. Harrison, *National Health Service Management in the 1980s: Policymaking on the Hoof?*, London: Avebury, 1994, p. 175.
33. A. Pollock, *NHS Plc*, London: Verso, 2004.
34. C. Knight, *The Making of Tory Education Policy in Post-war Britain 1950–1986*, London: Falmer Press, 1990, p. 154.
35. C. Benn, 'A new 11-plus for the old divided system', *Forum*, 22 (2), 1980, pp. 36–42.
36. R. Garner, 'Special report: working-class pupils went to private schools under Margaret Thatcher's abolished assisted places scheme – how did they get on?', *Independent*, 4 October 2013, www.independent.co.uk.
37. D. Gillard (2018), 'Education in England: a history', education-england.org.uk.
38. Department of Education and Science, 25 September 1987, educationengland.org.uk.
39. For a first-hand account from Militant's perspective, see P. Taaffe and T. Mulhearn, *Liverpool: A City That Dared to Fight*, London: Fortress Books, 1988.
40. Local Government Act 1988, legislation.gov.uk.
41. Conservative Party (1987), *The Next Moves Forward: 1987 Conservative Party General Election Manifesto*, conservativemanifesto.com.
42. Conservative Party Political Broadcast, 21 April 1988, youtube.com.
43. M. Thatcher, 'Mrs Thatcher: the first two years', *Sunday Times*, 1 May 1981, margaretthatcher.org.

44. The clearest exposition of this view can be found in D. Harvey, *A Brief History of Neoliberalism*, Oxford: Oxford University Press, 2005.
45. R. Fevre, *Individualism and Inequality*, Cheltenham: Edward Elgar, 2016.
46. Ibid., p. 37.
47. For an overview, see R. Ronald, *The Ideology of Home Ownership: Homeowner Societies and the Role of Housing*, London: Palgrave Macmillan, 2008.
48. C. Pattie and R. Johnston, 'The Conservative Party and the electorate', in S. Ludlam and M.J. Smith (eds.), *Contemporary British Conservatism*, Basingstoke: Macmillan, 1996, pp. 37–62.
49. M. Thatcher, 'The owner-occupiers' party', *Daily Telegraph*, 1 July 1974, margaretthatcher.org.
50. M. Thatcher (1983), 'Foreword: the challenge of our times', *Conservative General Election Manifesto 1983*, margaretthatcher.org.
51. Institute for Government (1984), *The Privatisation of British Telecom*, instituteforgovernment.org.uk, p. 54.
52. See 'British Gas – if you see Sid tell him', youtube.com.
53. Polling carried out by Ipsos MORI in 1989 suggested that 18 per cent of people thought privatisation was the worst thing Thatcher had done. See Centre for Public Impact (2016), *Privatising the UK's Nationalised Industries in the 1980s*, centreforpublicimpact.org.
54. J. Moore, 'British privatization: taking capitalism to the people', *Harvard Business Review*, January–February 1992, hbr.org.
55. J.J. Hukka and T.S. Katko, *Water Privatisation Revisited: Panacea or Pancake?*, Delft: IRC International Water and Sanitation Centre, 2003.
56. C. Pierson, 'Social policy under Thatcher and Major', in Ludlam and Smith, *Contemporary British Conservatism*, pp. 202–21.
57. See M. Evans, D. Piachaud and H. Sutherland, 'The effects of the 1986 Social Security Act on family incomes', *Social Policy Research*, 54, August 1994, jrf.org.uk.
58. T. Bale, *The Conservative Party: From Thatcher to Cameron*, Cambridge: Polity, 2016.
59. Wheatcroft, *The Strange Death of Tory England*, p. 179.
60. R. Thomas and S.H. Williamson (2018), 'What was the U.K. GDP then?', measuringworth.com.
61. Completions fell to 29 per cent by 1997 and 51 per cent by 2013–14. See K. Albertson and P. Stepney, '1979 and all that: a 40-year reassessment of Margaret Thatcher's legacy on her own terms', *Cambridge Journal of Economics*, 44(2), 2020, pp. 319–42.

62. R.S. Katz and P. Mair (eds.), *Party Organisations: A Data Handbook*, London: Sage, 1992.
63. P. Whiteley, P. Seyd, and J. Richardson, *True Blues: The Politics of Conservative Party Membership*, Oxford: Clarendon Press, 1994.
64. Wheatcroft, *The Strange Death of Tory England*, p. 171.
65. J. Charmley, *A History of Conservative Politics, 1900–96*, New York: St Martin's Press, 1996, p. 233.

3. The Major Interregnum

1. For example, on his election, see P. Norman, 'Tory leader who rose without a trace', *Financial Times*, 28 November 1990.
2. J. Major, *The Autobiography*, London: HarperCollins, 1999, p. 90.
3. W. Bonefeld, A. Brown and P. Burnham, *A Major Crisis?*, Aldershot: Dartmouth, 1995.
4. P. Stephens, *Politics and the Pound: The Tories, the Economy, and Europe*, London: Macmillan, 1996.
5. D. Dorling and J. Cornford, 'Who has negative equity? How house price falls in Britain have hit different groups of home buyers', *Housing Studies*, 10 (2), 1995, pp. 151–78.
6. For a comprehensive set of historic polling data, see A. Wells, 'Polls from 1987–1992', ukpollingreport.co.uk.
7. For historic Gallup data, see https://web.archive.org/web/2011081 1013721/http://www.hks.harvard.edu/fs/pnorris/datafiles/Gallup. xls.
8. Major, *The Autobiography*, p. 668.
9. Ibid., p. 670.
10. In May 1993, Brenda Procter, Bridget Bell and Gina Earl of North Staffs Miners' Wives occupied a pit shaft at Trentham Colliery and chained themselves to the railings inside. They only emerged after NUM president Arthur Scargill arrived personally to greet them. See *Staffs Live*, 9 March 2018, staffslive.co.uk.
11. Major, *The Autobiography*, p. 671.
12. HC Deb (29 June 1992), vol. 210, col. 688, available at hansard. parliament.uk.
13. F. Mullin, 'How UK ravers raged against the ban', *Vice*, 15 July 2014, vice.com.
14. In the context of a debate about crimes committed on bail, John Major uttered this famous line in an interview with the *Mail on Sunday*. See D. Macintyre, 'Major on crime: condemn more, understand less', *Independent*, 21 February 1993, independent.co.uk.
15. A. Fogg, 'The prophecy of 1994', *Guardian*, 21 July 2009, theguardian.com.

16. R. Robinson, 'The impact of the NHS reforms 1991–1995: a review of research evidence', *Journal of Public Health Medicine*, 18 (3), 1996, pp. 337–42.
17. Major, *The Autobiography*, pp. 682–3.
18. Pollock, *NHS Plc*, p. 3.
19. Major, *The Autobiography*, p. 262.
20. D. Gillard (2018), 'Education in England: a history', education-england.org.uk.
21. Major, *The Autobiography*, p. 398.
22. A. Bevins, 'Major unveils his lean welfare machine', *Independent*, 8 October 1996.
23. Major, *The Autobiography*, p. 217.
24. M.J. Smith, 'Reforming the state', in Ludlam and Smith, *Contemporary British Conservatism*, p. 159.
25. J. Major, 'Mr Major's Commons statement on the Citizen's Charter', *John Major Archive*, 22 July 1991, johnmajorarchive.org.uk.
26. J.M. Lee, G.W. Jones and J. Burnham, *At the Centre of Whitehall: Advising the Prime Minister and Cabinet*, Basingstoke: Macmillan, 1998.
27. L. Castellani, 'The Citizen's Charter: towards consumer service in central government', *History and Policy*, 24 September 2017.
28. Major, *The Autobiography*, p. 259.
29. Ibid., p. 250.
30. I. Hollingshead, 'Whatever happened to the Citizen's Charter?', *Guardian*, 17 September 2005, theguardian.com.
31. B. Wheeler, 'The cones hotline legacy . . .', BBC News, 6 January 2009, news.bbc.co.uk.
32. J. Major, 'Mr Major's speech to 1993 Conservative Party conference', *John Major Archive*, 8 October 1993, johnmajorarchive.org.uk.
33. Major, *The Autobiography*, p. 387.
34. Joseph Rowntree Foundation (2019), *Pensioner Poverty*, jrf.org.uk.
35. D. Macintryre, 'Rebels defeat Major on fuel tax', *Independent*, 7 December 1994, independent.co.uk.
36. J. Rankin and J. Waterson, 'How Boris Johnson's Brussels-bashing stories shaped British politics', *Guardian*, 14 July 2019, theguardian.com.
37. M. Thatcher, 'Speech to the College of Europe ("The Bruges Speech")', Margaret Thatcher Foundation, 19 September 1988, margaretthatcher.org.
38. M. Major, 'Mr Major's Commons statement on qualified majority voting', John Major Archive, 29 March 1994, johnmajorarchive.org.uk.

39. Major, *The Autobiography*, pp. 606–7.
40. Ibid., p. 620.
41. M. Thatcher, 'Keith Joseph Memorial Lecture ("Liberty and limited government")', Margaret Thatcher Foundation, 11 January 1996, margaretthatcher.org.
42. See, for example, the Conservative Party's election broadcast on YouTube, 'Conservative Party Political Broadcast: New Labour, New Danger', 23 November 2016.
43. S. Ludlam and M.J. Smith, 'The character of contemporary conservatism', in Ludlam and Smith, *Contemporary British Conservatism*, p. 267.
44. Major, *The Autobiography*, p. 687.
45. M. Pinto-Duschinsky, 'Tory troops are in a worse state than feared', *The Times*, 6 June 1997.

4. Into the Abyss

1. D. Cameron, leader's speech, Conservative Party conference, 1 October 2006, britishpoliticalspeech.org.
2. Bale, *The Conservative Party*.
3. W. Hague, speech to Conservative Party conference, 1977, youtube. com.
4. 'Ann Widdecombe "tested out" Howard quip', BBC News, 31 December 2009, news.bbc.co.uk.
5. P. Dorey, M. Garnett and A. Denham, *From Crisis to Coalition: The Conservative Party, 1997–2010*, Basingstoke: MacMillan, 2011, p. 137.
6. F. Abrams, 'Hague's reforms jar with the faithful', *Independent*, 17 February 1998, independent.co.uk.
7. 'We care too, claims Hague', *Guardian*, 11 October 1997, theguardian.com.
8. HC Deb (2 July 1997) vol. 297, col. 318, at api.parliament.uk.
9. Institute for Government (1998), *The Introduction of the National Minimum Wage*, p. 69, instituteforgovernment.org.uk.
10. M. Garnett, 'Win or bust: the leadership gamble of William Hague', in M. Garnett and P. Lynch (eds.), *The Conservatives in Crisis*, Manchester: Manchester University Press, 2003, pp. 49–65.
11. W. Hague, speech at INSEAD, Fontainebleau, 19 May 1998.
12. P. Wintour, 'Hague risks Tory split over Europe', *Guardian*, 16 May 1999, theguardian.com.
13. E. MacAskill and L. Ward, 'Happy Hague cashes in on pound', *Guardian*, 15 June 1999, theguardian.com.
14. 'William Hague's battle plan', *Economist*, 7 October 1999, economist.com.

15. W. Hague, 'Full text: William Hague's conference speech', *Guardian*, 7 October 1999, theguardian.com.
16. See P. Dorey, 'Conservative policy under Hague', in Garnett and Lynch, *The Conservatives in Crisis*, pp. 125–45.
17. 'Tories stage petrol protest', BBC News, 29 July 2000, news.bbc.co.uk.
18. See B. Doherty, M. Paterson, A. Plows and D. Wall, 'Explaining the fuel protests', *British Journal of Politics and International Relations*, 5 (1), 2003, pp. 1–23.
19. 'Hague slams Blair, backs ending blockades', BBC News, 13 September 2000, news.bbc.co.uk.
20. J. Murphy and D. Foggo, 'Labour poll lead collapses in wake of petrol crisis', *Daily Telegraph*, 17 September 2000, telegraph.co.uk.
21. D. Hencke, 'Portillo in shadow cabinet row over fuel cut', *Guardian*, 5 October 2000, theguardian.com.
22. For polling between 1997 and 2001, see A. Wells, '1997–2001 polls', ukpollingreport.co.uk.
23. 'Last chance to save the pound', *Daily Mail*, 26 May 2001, dailymail.co.uk.
24. N. Watt, 'Portillo reveals homosexual past', *Guardian*, 9 September1999, theguardian.com.
25. T. Heppell, 'The ideological composition of the parliamentary Conservative Party 1992–97', *British Journal of Politics and International Relations*, 4 (2), 2002, pp. 299–324.
26. C. Blackhurst, 'The contradictory world of Iain Duncan Smith', *Independent*, 9 October 2001, independent.co.uk.
27. A. Chrisafis, 'I'm a normal Conservative with perfectly normal views', *Guardian*, 25 August 2001, theguardian.com.
28. Bale, *The Conservative Party*, p. 148.
29. A. McSmith, 'Duncan Smith supports Iraq action', *Daily Telegraph*, 2 September 2002, telegraph.co.uk.
30. 'Huge turnout for countryside march', BBC News, 22 September 2002, news.bbc.co.uk.
31. M. White and A. Perkins, ' "Nasty party" warning to Tories', *Guardian*, 8 October 2002, theguardian.com.
32. M. Davies, 'Duncan Smith: the Tories are back', BBC News, 11 October 2002, news.bbc.co.uk.
33. G. Jones, 'Tory leader defied over gay adoption', *Daily Telegraph*, 5 November 2002, telegraph.co.uk.
34. A. Grice, 'Tory party chief quits amid claims of a purge', *Independent*, 15 February 2003, independent.co.uk.
35. A. Pierce, 'Duncan Smith in £160,000 wrangle', *The Times*, 9 May 2003, thetimes.co.uk.

36. For polling between 2001 and 2005, see A. Wells, '2001–2005 polls', ukpollingreport.co.uk.
37. 'IDS: quiet man is here to stay', *Daily Mail*, 9 October 2003, daily-mail.co.uk.
38. 'Howard launches leadership bid', BBC News, 31 October 2003, news.bbc.co.uk.
39. Dorey, Garnett and Denham, *From Crisis to Coalition*, p. 149.
40. Bale, *The Conservative Party*, p. 211.
41. 'Blair blackmails top-up rebels', *Daily Express*, 27 January 2004.
42. M. Howard, 'The British Dream: speech to Policy Exchange', *Conservative Party Speeches*, 9 February 2004, conservative-speeches.sayit. mysociety.org.
43. 'Full text of Howard's speech', BBC News, 19 February 2004, news. bbc.co.uk.
44. Bale, *The Conservative Party*, p. 217.
45. C. Brown, F. Govan and C. Hastings, 'Kilroy-Silk: I won't be gagged about the evils of Arab states', *Daily Telegraph*, 11 January 2004, telegraph.co.uk.
46. M. White, 'Collins joins Kilroy in UKIP's battle for Britain', *Guardian*, 25 May 2004, theguardian.com.
47. M. Howard, 'Full text: Michael Howard's speech on Europe', *Guardian*, 12 February 2004, theguardian.com.
48. Bale, *The Conservative Party*, p. 223.
49. T. Hames, 'Mouse that roared was amplified by Tory terror', *The Times*, 14 June 2004, thetimes.co.uk.
50. J. Glancey, 'What does the Tories' new logo mean?', *Guardian*, 4 October 2004, theguardian.com.
51. M. Howard, 'Full text: Michael Howard's speech', *Guardian*, 5 October 2004, theguardian.com.
52. M. Kettle, 'Are you thinking what I'm thinking about the election?', *Guardian*, 8 March 2005, theguardian.com.
53. Conservative Party (2005), *Are You Thinking What We're Thinking? Conservative Election Manifesto 2005*, news.bbc.co.uk.
54. 'Howard will stand down as leader', BBC News, 6 May 2005, news. bbc.co.uk.

5. The Rise of Liberal Toryism

1. P. Wintour, 'Howard defeated on leadership vote change', *Guardian*, 28 September 2005, theguardian.com.
2. See A. Cooper, *The Case for Change*, London: C-Change, 2005.
3. M. Tempest, 'Tories crown Cameron their new leader', *Guardian*, 6 December 2005, theguardian.com.

4. M. Tempest, 'Davis under fire over blonde gaffe', *Guardian*, 9 November 2005, theguardian.com.

5. L. Fox, 'Liam Fox's speech to the Tory conference 2005', *Guardian*, 5 October 2005, theguardian.com.

6. 'How Cameron won . . . and Davis lost', *Conservative Home*, 6 December 2005, conservativehome.blogs.com.

7. J. Robinson and D. Teather, 'Cameron – the PR years', *Guardian*, 20 February 2010, theguardian.com.

8. Bale, *The Conservative Party*, p. 101.

9. 'In full: Cameron victory Speech', BBC News, 6 December 2005, news.bbc.co.uk.

10. D. Cameron, 'I don't believe in isms', *Mail on Sunday*, 1 January 2006.

11. See A. Wells, '2005–2010 polls', ukpollingreport.co.uk.

12. A. Wells, 'Labour and Conservatives neck and neck', 31 March 2006, ukpollingreport.co.uk.

13. 'At a glance: Conservative poll launch', BBC News, 18 April 2006, news.bbc.co.uk.

14. Conservative Party (2006), *Built to Last: The Aims and Values of the Conservative Party*, news.bbc.co.uk.

15. Dorey, Garnett and Denham, *From Crisis to Coalition*, p. 76.

16. P. Dorey, 'A Conservative "Third Way"? British Conservatives and the development of post-Thatcherite Conservatism', in D. Ozsel (ed.), *Reflections on Conservatism*, Newcastle: Cambridge Scholars Publishing, 2011, p. 173.

17. P. Hitchens, 'The Tories are doomed', *Guardian*, 14 December 2005, theguardian.com.

18. M. Hastings, 'Cameron is about to discover his big problem: the Conservative party', *Guardian*, 2 October 2006, theguardian.com.

19. 'Top Tory axed over Army race row', BBC News, 8 March 2007, news.bbc.co.uk.

20. D. Cameron, '2007 speech to Conservative spring forum', ukpol.co.uk, 30 December 2015.

21. 'Quentin Davies MP defects to Labour!', *Conservative Home*, 26 June 2007, conservativehome.blogs.com.

22. 'Five Southall councillors defect', BBC News, 9 July 2007, news.bbc.co.uk.

23. M. Kite, 'Tory by-election candidate is Labour donor', *Sunday Telegraph*, 15 July 2007, telegraph.co.uk.

24. M. Pack, 'Exclusive: Grant Shapps says "realistically we're not going to win" in Ealing', *Liberal Democrat Voice*, 10 July 2007, libdemvoice.org.

25. 'Brown to complete "government of all the talents"', politics.co.uk, 29 June 2007.
26. M. Kite, 'Crunch time as Cameron faces his disillusioned ranks', *Sunday Telegraph*, 22 July 2007, pressreader.com.
27. G. Hinsliff, 'Cameron softens crime image in "hug a hoodie" call', *Guardian*, 9 July 2006, theguardian.com.
28. G. Rayner and A. Porter, 'Northern Rock: Gordon Brown's big gamble', *Daily Telegraph*, 18 September 2007, telegraph.co.uk.
29. D. Summers, '"Go ahead and call that election"', *Guardian*, 3 October 2007, theguardian.com.
30. For an insider's view, see D. McBride, 'Gordon Brown and the 2007 election: why it never happened', *Daily Telegraph*, 9 October 2012, telegraph.co.uk.
31. M. Kite, 'Gordon Brown "breaking military covenant"', *Daily Telegraph*, 11 November 2007, telegraph.co.uk.
32. P. Hennessy, M. Kite and C. Hastings, 'Revealed: Blair's secret role in loans scandal', *Daily Telegraph*, 19 March 2006, telegraph.co.uk.
33. 'Labour boss quits over donations', BBC News, 27 November 2007, news.bbc.co.uk.
34. 'Timelines – Hain resigns after funding row, Reuters, 24 January 2008, uk.reuters.com.
35. P. Inman, L. Elliot and D. Hencke, 'Darling under fire as Northern Rock is nationalised', *Guardian*, 18 February 2008, theguardian.com.
36. A. Gimson, 'Gordon Brown: from Stalin to Mr Bean', *Daily Telegraph*, 29 November 2007, telegraph.co.uk.
37. 'Tory whip withdrawn from Conway', BBC News, 29 January 2008, news.bbc.co.uk.
38. J. Kirkup, 'Gordon Brown backs down over 10p tax', *Daily Telegraph*, 23 April 2008, telegraph.co.uk.
39. For example, J. Freedland, 'Attacks on toffs will ring hollow until Labour proves its meritocratic mettle', *Guardian*, 21 May 2008, theguardian.com.
40. J. Djanogly and A. Duncan, *Labour and the Trade Unions: An Analysis of a Symbiotic Relationship*, London: Centre for Policy Studies, 2007.
41. J. Kirkup and N. Paris, 'Tories attack "something for nothing" culture', *Daily Telegraph*, 8 January 2008, telegraph.co.uk.
42. C. Grayling, 'A new kind of welfare', *Conservative Home*, 8 July, conservativehome.com.
43. D. Cameron, 'David Cameron's speech in full', *Guardian*, 1 October 2008, theguardian.com.
44. 'Expenses: How MP's expenses became a hot topic', *Daily Telegraph*, 8 May 2009, telegraph.co.uk.

45. K. Walker, 'Have they no shame? Duck house and moat MPs fought expenses payback call', *Daily Mail*, 31 January 2010, dailymail.co.uk.
46. '"Appalled" Cameron leads payback', BBC News, 12 May 2009, news.bbc.co.uk.
47. A. Pierce, 'European elections 2009: David Cameron's victory tempered by UKIP surge', *Daily Telegraph*, 8 June 2009, telegraph.co.uk.
48. D. Cameron, 'David Cameron: Conservative Party conference speech in full', *Daily Telegraph*, 8 October 2009, telegraph.co.uk.
49. 'Labour's lost it', *Sun*, 30 September 2009, thesun.co.uk.
50. A. Smith, 'Hoon and Hewitt call for secret ballot over Brown's leadership', *LabourList*, 6 January 2010, labourlist.org.
51. 'Cameron calls for inquiry into No 10 bullying claims', BBC News, 22 February 2010, news.bbc.co.uk.
52. Conservative Party, *Invitation to Join the Government of Britain: The Conservative Party Manifesto 2010*, London: Conservative Party, 2010.
53. K. Grant, 'Gordon Brown's "bigoted woman" quits Labour because of Jeremy Corbyn', *i News*, 13 May 2016, inews.co.uk.
54. Dorey, Garnett and Denham, *From Crisis to Coalition*, p. 160.
55. Conservative Home (2010), *Falling Short: The Key Factors That Contributed to the Conservative Party's Failure to Win a Parliamentary Majority*, conservativehome.blogs.com.
56. M.A. Ashcroft, *Minority Verdict: The Conservative Party, the Voters, and the 2010 Election*, London: Biteback, 2010.
57. Dorey, Garnett and Denham, *From Crisis to Coalition*, p. 177.

6. Liberal Toryism in Office

1. 'Tory/LibDem leaked agreement', *All That Is Solid*, 12 May 2010, averypublicsociologist.blogspot.com.
2. S. Lee, 'Indebted and unbalanced: the political economy of the coalition', in M. Beech and S. Lee (eds.), *The Conservative–Liberal Coalition*, Basingstoke: Palgrave Macmillan, 2015, pp. 16–35.
3. L. Elliott, 'Public finance watchdog installed "to stop chancellors fiddling the figures"', *Guardian*, 18 May 2010, theguardian.com.
4. 'Cameron: "Difficult decisions" on pay and benefits', BBC News, 7 June 2010, bbc.co.uk.
5. T. Onanuga, 'Emergency budget: George Osborne's speech in full', *Guardian*, 22 June 2010, theguardian.com.
6. B. Chu, 'The chart that shows UK workers have had the worst wage performance in the OECD except Greece', *Independent*, 5 June 2017, independent.co.uk.

7. 'Budget 2012: Labour attack package "for millionaires"', BBC News, 21 March 2012, bbc.co.uk.

8. G. Osborne, 'Autumn statement 2012: the full speech', *Daily Telegraph*, 5 December 2012, telegraph.co.uk.

9. J. Williamson, 'Government bribes employees to give up employment rights', *Touchstone*, 20 March 2013, touchstoneblog.org.uk.

10. L. Kuenssberg, 'When is a job not a job? The rise of "zero hours" contracts', *ITV News*, 2 April 2013, itv.com.

11. 'UK unemployment total falls to 2.16m', BBC News, 11 June 2014, bbc.co.uk.

12. J. Doward and T. Helm, 'Fears grow over Conservatives' links to fossil fuel lobbyists', *Guardian*, 21 October 2012, theguardian.com.

13. 'Osborne confirms Budget surplus law', BBC News, 10 June 2015, bbc.co.uk.

14. P. Wintour, 'Nick Clegg to speak up for "alarm clock Britain"', *Guardian*, 11 January 2011, theguardian.com.

15. A. Grice, 'Tories fear return of nasty party in attacks on welfare "scroungers"', *Independent*, 9 January 2013, independent.co.uk.

16. G. Cordon, 'David Cameron defends welfare reforms as "moral mission"', *Independent*, 19 February 2014, independent.co.uk.

17. Conservative Party, *Invitation to Join the Government of Britain*, p. 15.

18. R. Crisp and D. Fletcher, *A Comparative Review of Workfare Programmes in the United States, Canada and Australia*, Department for Work and Pensions research report no 533, London: HMSO, 2008.

19. R.M. Page, 'The coalition, poverty, and social security', in Beech and Lee, *The Conservative–Liberal Coalition*, pp. 68–85.

20. T. Ross, 'Iain Duncan Smith's Work Programme "worse than doing nothing"', *Daily Telegraph*, 27 November 2012, telegraph.co.uk.

21. P. Butler, 'Sanctions: staff pressured to penalise benefit claimants, says union', *Guardian*, 3 February 2015, theguardian.com.

22. M. Oakley, *Independent Review of the Operation of Jobseeker's Allowance Sanctions Validated by the Jobseekers Act 2013*, London: HMSO, 2014.

23. S. Preece, 'Record disability benefit appeal success rates show this "cruel" system is "unfit for purpose"', *Welfare Weekly*, 14 December 2018, welfareweekly.com.

24. J. Chapman, 'End this housing benefits hysteria: figures demolish claims that cities will be "cleansed" of the poor, say ministers', *Daily Mail*, 31 October 2010, dailymail.co.uk.

25. 'DWP benefit cap briefing', *All That Is Solid*, 8 March 2013, averypublicsociologist.blogspot.com.

26. T. Helm, 'Labour will be tougher than Tories on benefits, promises new welfare chief', *Guardian*, 12 October 2013, theguardian.com.

27. Conservative Party, *The Conservative Party Manifesto 2015: Strong Leadership, a Clear Economic Plan, a Brighter, More Secure Future*, London: Conservative Party, 2015, p. 28.

28. I. Duncan Smith, 'In full: Iain Duncan Smith resignation letter', BBC News, 18 March 2016, bbc.co.uk.

29. Conservative Party, *Invitation to Join the Government of Britain*, pp. 45–9.

30. A. Porter, 'Biggest revolution in the NHS for 60 years', *Daily Telegraph*, 9 July 2010, telegraph.co.uk.

31. The Mid Staffordshire NHS Foundation Trust Inquiry, *The Mid Staffordshire NHS Foundation Trust Independent Inquiry into Care Provided by Mid Staffordshire NHS Foundation Trust, January 2005–March 2009*, London: The Stationery Office, 2010.

32. National Audit Office, *Managing the Transition to the Reformed Health System*, London: The Stationery Office, 2013.

33. C. Ham, B. Baird, S. Gregory, J. Jabbal and H. Alderwick, *The NHS under the Coalition Government*, London: The King's Fund, 2015.

34. N. Triggle, 'Are Andrew Lansley's NHS reforms being binned?', BBC News, 11 January 2019, bbc.co.uk.

35. C. Chitty, *Education Policy in Britain*, Basingstoke: Palgrave Macmillan, 2009, p. 103.

36. HM Government, *The Coalition: Our Programme for Government*, London: The Stationery Office, 2010, p. 29.

37. Gillard, *Education in England: A History*, educationengland. org.uk.

38. D. Hayes, 'Conservative conference: Gove urges teaching unions to put children's interests above "ideology"', *Children and Young People Now*, 2 October 2013, cypnow.co.uk.

39. 'Academies and maintained schools: what do we know?', fullfact.org, 26 May 2017.

40. 'Tuition fees vote: plans approved despite rebellion', BBC News, 9 December 2010, bbc.co.uk.

41. For a summary of all polls between May 2010 and May 2020, see A. Wells, 'Voting intention', ukpollingreport.co.uk.

42. J. Murphy, 'Cameron aide "met No campaign leader before AV poll"', *Evening Standard*, 12 May 2011, thisislondon.co.uk.

43. R. Ford and M. Goodwin, *Revolt on the Right*, Abingdon: Routledge, 2014, p. 10.

44. Ibid., p. 146.

45. Ibid., p. 152.

46. 'EU referendum: rebels lose vote in Commons', BBC News, 25 October 2011, bbc.co.uk.

47. I. Traynor, N. Watt, D. Gow and P. Wintour, 'David Cameron blocks EU treaty with veto, casting Britain adrift in Europe', *Guardian*, 9 December 2011, theguardian.com.

48. 'EU referendum: 100 Tory MPs back call for vote', BBC News, 28 June 2012, bbc.co.uk.

49. D. Cameron, 'David Cameron's EU speech in full', *Daily Telegraph*, 23 January 2013, telegraph.co.uk.

50. S. Porion, 'The implementation of same sex marriage in 2013: Cameron's modernising social agenda in the Conservative Party since 2005', *Observatoire de la société brittanique*, 14, 2014, pp. 42–65.

51. R. Watts, 'Conservative Party ripped apart by gay marriage vote', *Daily Telegraph*, 2 February 2013, telegraph.co.uk.

52. P. Webb and T. Bale, 'Why do Tories defect to UKIP? Conservative Party members and the temptations of the populist radical right', *Political Studies*, 62 (4), 2014, pp. 961–70.

53. 'Eastleigh by-election: Cameron vows to "win people back"', BBC News, 1 March 2013, bbc.co.uk.

54. M. Chorley, 'UKIP leader Nigel Farage offers to endorse Eurosceptic Tory MPs with his party's logo as a stamp of approval in the 2015 election', *Daily Mail*, 13 May 2013, dailymail.co.uk.

55. E. Miliband, 'Transcript: Ed Miliband's 2013 conference speech', *LabourList*, 24 September 2013, labourlist.org.

56. A. Bienkov, 'The Tories love Theresa May's energy bill freeze – which is weird because when Labour proposed the same thing they said it was a "Marxist" plot', *Business Insider*, 9 May 2017, businessinsider.com.

57. 'Government outlines plans to cut energy bills by £50', BBC News, 1 December 2013, bbc.co.uk.

58. 'UKIP anti-immigration posters – what do they actually say?', *Channel 4 News*, 21 April 2014, channel4.com.

59. 'Scottish independence: "invaluable second chance" for Alex Salmond', BBC News, 25 August 2014, bbc.co.uk.

60. R. Greenslade, 'Scottish referendum – London national press reflects panic at Yes poll lead', *Guardian*, 8 September 2014, theguardian.com.

61. P. Wintour, 'David Cameron raises West Lothian question after Scotland vote: "English votes for English laws"', *Guardian*, 19 September 2014, theguardian.com.

62. 'Obese could lose benefits if they refuse treatment – PM', BBC News, 14 February 2014, bbc.co.uk.

63. 'David Cameron "won't serve third term" if elected', BBC News, 24 March 2015, bbc.co.uk.
64. D. Cameron, 4 May 2015, at https://twitter.com/David_Cameron/status/595112367358406656?s=20.
65. T. Ross, '50 Tories plot Britain's exit from EU', *Daily Telegraph*, 6 June 2015, telegraph.co.uk.
66. J. Groves and M. Chorley, 'The great EU-turn! Now Dave says: I won't sack ministers who campaign to leave the EU after he claims remarks were "misinterpreted"', *Daily Mail*, 8 June 2015, dailymail.co.uk.
67. 'EU referendum: draft reform deal worth fighting for, says Cameron', BBC News, 2 February 2016, bbc.co.uk.
68. B. Johnson, 'Voters have to ask Donald Tusk some hard questions before they accept his EU "deal"', *Daily Telegraph*, 7 February 2016, telegraph.co.uk.
69. E. Clery, J. Curtice and R. Harding (eds.), *British Social Attitudes 34*, London: NatCen Social Research, 2017.

7. The One Nation Affectation: Theresa May

1. 'Michael Gove: Boris Johnson wasn't up to the job', BBC News, 30 June 2016, bbc.co.uk.
2. H. Stewart and J. Elgot, 'Boris Johnson rules himself out of Tory leadership race', *Guardian*, 30 June 2016, theguardian.com.
3. N. Slawson, 'George Osborne will not contest Tory leadership race', *Guardian*, 28 June 2016, theguardian.com.
4. R. Sylvester, 'I'm sure Theresa will be really sad that she doesn't have children', *The Times*, 9 July 2016, thetimes.co.uk.
5. C. Doherty, 'Theresa May's first speech to the nation as Prime Minister – in full', *Independent*, 13 July 2016, independent.co.uk.
6. A. Wells, 'Voting Intention', ukpollingreport.co.uk.
7. M. Mardell, 'What does "Brexit means Brexit" mean?', BBC News, 14 July 2016, bbc.co.uk.
8. S. Swinford, 'Theresa May will trigger Brexit negotiations without Commons vote', *Daily Telegraph*, 27 August 2016, telegraph.co.uk.
9. T. May, 'Theresa May – her full Brexit speech to Conservative conference', *Independent*, 2 October 2016, independent.co.uk.
10. 'Batley and Spen by-election: Tracy Brabin victory for "hope and unity"', BBC News, 21 October 2016, bbc.co.uk.
11. F. Gillett, 'Goldsmith stunned as Lib Dem Sarah Olney wins seat', *Evening Standard*, 2 December 2016, standard.co.uk.
12. J. Watts, 'Conservatives pitch for the working class with help on letting fees, benefits and housing', *Independent*, 23 November 2016, independent.co.uk.

13. T. May, 'I'm determined to build the shared society for everyone', 8 January 2017, facebook.com.
14. A. Bennett, 3 August 2016, at twitter.com/asabenn/status/760834174316081152.
15. J. Mill, 'Who is Mike Hookem, accused of punching Steven Woolfe in Ukip meeting?', *Metro*, 6 October 2016, metro.co.uk.
16. M. Chorley, 'Oppose migration or lose your seat, Labour MPs told', *The Times*, 28 November 2016, thetimes.co.uk.
17. P. Burton-Cartledge, 'Goodbye to Tristram', *All That Is Solid*, 13 January 2017, averypublicsociologist.blogspot.com.
18. 'Nuttall aide offers to quit over Hillsborough mistakes', BBC News, 15 February 2017, bbc.co.uk.
19. 'Scottish independence: Better Together boss sets out Union case', BBC News, 1 February 2013, bbc.co.uk.
20. J. Elgot and R. Mason, ' Conservatives fined record £70,000 for campaign spending failures', *Guardian*, 16 March 2017, theguardian.com.
21. 'MP Craig Mackinlay cleared of election expenses fraud', BBC News, 9 January 2019, bbc.co.uk.
22. 'Theresa May's general election statement in full', BBC News, 18 April 2017, bbc.co.uk.
23. ' "Give me the mandate to lead Britain" – Prime Minister Theresa May launches election campaign at Walmsley Parish Hall, Bolton', *Bolton News*, 19 April 2017, theboltonnews.co.uk.
24. L. Dearden, 'Theresa May faces fresh accusations of "hiding" after Scotland rally publicly listed as child's birthday party', *Independent*, 30 April 2017, independent.co.uk.
25. S. Swinford and J. Huggler, 'How Theresa May's Downing Street dinner with Jean-Claude Juncker unravelled', *Daily Telegraph*, 1 May 2017, telegraph.co.uk.
26. Conservative Part, *Forward, Together: Our Plan for a Stronger Britain and a Prosperous Future*, London: Conservative Party, 2017, s3.eu-west-2.amazonaws.com.
27. L. Hughes, 'Theresa May announces "dementia tax" U-turn', *Daily Telegraph*, 22 May 2017, telegraph.co.uk.
28. Labour Party, *For the Many Not the Few: The Labour Party Manifesto 2017*, London: Labour Party, 2017, labour.org.uk, p. 24.
29. C. Curtis, 'How Britain voted at the 2017 general election', *YouGov Politics and Current Affairs*, 13 June 2017, yougov.co.uk.
30. Ipsos MORI, 'How Britain voted in the 2017 election', 20 June 2017, ipsos.com.
31. D. Phillips, J. Curtice, M. Phillips and J. Perry (eds.), *British Social Attitudes: The 35th Report*, London: The National Centre for Social Research, 2018, p. 107.

32. Shipman, *Fall Out*. R. Merrick, 'Election result: Theresa May has lost the support of Conservative party members who want her to resign, finds survey', *Independent*, 10 June 2017, independent. co.uk.

33. 'Brexit: Davis and Starmer clash over key legislation', BBC News, 7 September 2017, bbc.co.uk.

34. 'The Guardian view on May in Florence: a small step towards reality', *Guardian*, 22 September 2017, theguardian.com.

35. T. May, 'Theresa May's Conservative conference speech – full text', *Spectator*, 4 October 2017, spectator.co.uk.

36. B. Johnson, 'Boris Johnson: my vision for a bold, thriving Britain enabled by Brexit', *Daily Telegraph*, 15 September 2017, telegraph.co.uk.

37. R. Roberts, 'Grant Shapps: all you need to know about the man with two names plotting to overthrow Theresa May', *Independent*, 6 October 2017, independent.co.uk.

38. S. Williams, 'Senior Tories defend Theresa May in leaked Whatsapp messages', *i News*, 7 October 2017, inews.co.uk.

39. J. Vesey-Byrne, 'Gavin Williamson: 14 of the most brutal things MPs are saying about Theresa May's new Defence Secretary', *indy100*, 2 November 2017, indy100.com.

40. R. Syal and A. Asthana, 'Priti Patel forced to resign over unofficial meetings with Israelis', *Guardian*, 8 November 2017, theguardian.com.

41. 'Joint report from the negotiators of the European Union and the United Kingdom Government on progress during phase 1 of negotiations under Article 50 TEU on the United Kingdom's orderly withdrawal from the European Union', TF50 (2017) 19–Commission to EU 27, 8 December 2017, p. 8, ec.europa.eu.

42. G. Rayner and C. Hope, 'Damian Green sacked over porn cover-up as Theresa May suffers third Cabinet departure in two months', *Daily Telegraph*, 21 December 2017, telegraph.co.uk.

43. O. Bennett, 'Tory civil war over Brexit spills into Parliament as MPs turn on each other', *Huffington Post*, 30 January 2018, huffingtonpost.co.uk.

44. 'Brexit: transition period not "a given", says Barnier', BBC News, 9 February 2018, bbc.co.uk.

45. 'In full: Theresa May's speech on future UK–EU relations', BBC News, 2 March 2018, bbc.co.uk.

46. K. McCann, 'Jeremy Corbyn mocked by his own MPs after claiming Russia should be given the right to test nerve agent itself', *Daily Telegraph*, 20 March 2018, telegraph.co.uk.

47. Foreign and Commonwealth Office, 'Foreign Secretary responds to reports of chemical weapons attack in Douma, Syria', 8 April 2018, gov.uk.

48. H. Carr, 'Poll: Britons blame May more than Rudd for Windrush scandal', Sky News, 30 April 2018, news.sky.com.
49. 'Brexit rebel Dominic Grieve says May's compromise "a slap in face"', BBC News, 15 June 2018, bbc.co.uk.
50. B. Johnson, 'The people want us to deliver a full British Brexit and we MUST bust out of the corsets of EU regulation, says Foreign Secretary Boris Johnson', *Sun*, 22 June, thesun.co.uk.
51. B. Kentish, 'Theresa May faces Brexiteer backlash hours after ordering MPs to stop public dissent', *Independent*, 7 July 2018, independent.co.uk.
52. E. Wills, 'Brexit latest: Boris Johnson in crude outburst on Theresa May's EU deal', *Evening Standard*, 8 July 2018, standard.co.uk.
53. 'Brexiteers' Customs Bill amendments accepted by government', BBC News, 16 July 2018, bbc.co.uk.
54. 'Theresa May on why Boris Johnson speech made her cross', BBC News, 2 October 2018, bbc.co.uk.
55. T. May, 'Labour voters should look afresh at the Conservatives', *Guardian*, 6 October 2018, theguardian.com.
56. H. Stewart, 'Jo Johnson quits as minister over Theresa May's Brexit plan', *Guardian*, 9 November 2018, theguardian.com.
57. 'Brexit: Cabinet backs draft agreement', BBC News, 14 November 2018, bbc.co.uk.
58. 'Jacob Rees-Mogg says Theresa May has his "confidence" after winning vote of Tory MPs', Sky News, 17 December 2018, news.sky.com.
59. N. Farage, 'My new Brexit party stands ready to defend democracy', *Daily Telegraph*, 8 February 2019, telegraph.co.uk.
60. A. Wickham, 'Cabinet ministers are plotting to oust Theresa May as even her fed-up whips say her Brexit deal is doomed', Buzzfeed News, 23 March 2019, buzzfeed.com.
61. A. Briscoe, 'And the local election results show . . .', *Britain in Numbers*, 6 May 2019, simonbriscoeblog.wordpress.com.

8. Creature of Havoc: Boris Johnson

1. 'Tory leadership contest: Boris Johnson pledges income tax cut for high earners', BBC News, 10 June 2019, bbc.co.uk.
2. C. Mason, 'Notes from the first Tory leadership hustings', BBC News, 4 June 2019, bbc.co.uk.
3. B. Glaze, D. Bloom and L. Dunphy, 'Channel 4 leaves EMPTY PODIUM for Boris Johnson as MP snubs TV leadership debate', *Mirror*, 16 June 2019, mirror.co.uk.
4. K. Rawlinson, 'Mark Field urged to quit as minister after grabbing climate protester', *Guardian*, 21 June 2019, theguardian.com.

5. 'Boris Johnson refuses to answer questions about "row with part-ner"', BBC News, 22 June 2019, bbc.co.uk.

6. 'Tory leadership race: Hunt tells Johnson "don't be a coward"', BBC News, 24 June 2019, bbc.co.uk.

7. B. Wheeler, 'Tories must come clean on membership figures – ex-chairman', BBC News, 5 January 2018, bbc.co.uk.

8. B. Johnson, 'Boris Johnson's first speech as Prime Minister', Prime Minister's Office, 24 July 2019, gov.uk.

9. 'Parliament suspension: queen approves PM's plan', BBC News, 28 August 2019, bbc.co.uk.

10. A. Tolhurst, 'More than 100 Tory MPs urge Boris Johnson to rein-state the 21 no-deal rebels', *PoliticsHome*, 4 September 2019, politicshome.com.

11. K. Devlin, F. Karim and R. Ford, 'I'd rather die in a ditch than ask for Brexit delay, says Boris Johnson', *The Times*, 5 September 2019, thetimes.co.uk.

12. A. Rudd, 'Amber Rudd: resignation letter in full', BBC News, 7 September 2019, bbc.co.uk.

13. A. Woodcock, 'Leo Varadkar confronts Boris Johnson with wither-ing assessment of his Brexit strategy in strained joint press conference', *Independent*, 9 September 2019, independent.co.uk.

14. L. Kuenssberg, 24 September 2019, at https://twitter.com/bbclaurak/status/1176508349845823488?s=20.

15. 'Boris Johnson: Brexit plan "genuine attempt to bridge chasm"', BBC News, 3 October 2019, bbc.co.uk.

16. 'Brexit: Boris Johnson will send extension letter – court document', BBC News, 4 October 2019, bbc.co.uk.

17. J. Snow, 'ERG's Andrew Bridgen says: "It looks like Brexit, it smells like Brexit"', *Channel 4 News*, 17 October 2019, channel4.com.

18. 'Brexit: EU and UK reach deal but DUP refuses support', BBC News, 18 October 2019, bbc.co.uk.

19. G. Russell, '"House of fools": how the papers covered Johnson's latest Brexit defeat', *Guardian*, 20 October 2019, theguardian.com.

20. S. Payne and G. Parker, 'Brexit party considers pulling out of hundreds of seats to boost Tories', *Financial Times*, 30 October 2019.

21. 'Grenfell Tower: Jacob Rees-Mogg criticised for "insulting" comments', BBC News, 5 November 2019, bbc.co.uk.

22. 'Alun Cairns resigns in Ross England rape trial "sabotage" row', BBC News, 6 November 2019, bbc.co.uk.

23. J. Waterson and R. Syal, 'Keir Starmer: Tories' doctored TV footage is "act of desperation"', *Guardian*, 6 November 2019, theguardian.com.

24. A. Gregory, 'General election: Boris Johnson compares Corbyn to Stalin over "hatred" of billionaires', *Independent*, 6 November 2019, independent.co.uk.

25. Conservative Research Department, *The Real Cost of a Labour Government*, London: Conservative Party, 2019, assets-global. website-files.com.

26. K. Proctor and G. Wearden, 'Brexit party will not contest 317 Tory-won seats, Farage says', *Guardian*, 11 November 2019, theguardian. com.

27. B. Johnson, 'Prime Minister Boris Johnson's CBI conference speech', 18 November 2019, conservatives.com.

28. Conservative Party, *Get Brexit Done: Unleash Britain's Potential. The Conservative and Unionist Party Manifesto 2019*, London: Conservative Party, 2019, assets-global.website-files.com.

29. B. Johnson, 'BORIS JOHNSON: Send me back to Number 10 and I will end automatic early release of violent offenders and terrorists', *Mail on Sunday*, 30 November 2019, dailymail.co.uk.

30. J. Mitchell and R.C. Jump, 'Labour, the "red wall", and the vicissitudes of Britain's voting system', *openDemocracy*, 20 August 2020, opendemocracy.net.

Postscript: The Conservatives and Coronavirus

1. See B. Johnson, 2 January 2020, twitter.com/BorisJohnson/status/1 212679425629859840?s=20.

2. G. Rayner, L. Fisher and S. Knapton, 'Boris Johnson "deeply sorry for every life that has been lost" to Covid', *Daily Telegraph*, 26 January 2021, telegraph.co.uk.

3. 'Who do you hold most responsible for the rise in coronavirus cases over the last month?', YouGov, 11 January 2021, yougov.co.uk.

4. A. Mbembe, *Necropolitics*, Durham, NC: Duke University Press, 2019.

5. Department of Health and Social Care, *Coronavirus: Action Plan*, London: HM Government, 2020, assets.publishing.service.gov.uk.

6. E. Chappell, 'Starmer: I expect all children back at school in September', *LabourList*, 16 August 2020, labourlist.org.

7. A. Rawnsley, 'The bad taste question about Covid that everyone in Westminster is asking', *Guardian*, 31 January 2020, theguardian. com.

Index

and collective bargaining by workers,
28, 46, 50
and Conservative Party (Tory Party),
3, 50, 52, 55, 57, 98, 189, 271
and David Cameron, 171, 190
and elections, 57, 165
and employment tribunal panels, 185
and John Major, 92
and Labour Party, 55, 165, 167, 171
legislation against, 57, 122
and manufacturing unions, 54
and membership decline, 86, 93
and National Association of Colliery
Overmen, Deputies and Shotfirers,
56
and National Coal Board (NCB), 55,
56
and National Union of Mineworkers
(NUM), 55, 56, 57, 73, 97
and National Union of Railwaymen,
56
and National Union of Teachers, 69
penalties for, 53
power of, 75, 190
and print unions, 57
and protection of living standards, 47
and the Public and Commericial
Services union (PCS), 110
and teachers' unions, 67, 104, 203,
204
and Thatcher, 49, 52–3, 60, 85, 86,
93, 204
and trade union movement, 28–9
and Trade Union Reform Acts, 98,
189
and Union of Democratic Mineworkers, 55

United Kingdom
and Britain's Leave or Remain vote,
32, 252
and British National Party, 148, 149,
159
citizenship in, 59, 148
and closing of coal mines, 97, 121
and Conservative Party (Tory Party),
2–3, 4, 7, 21, 31, 97
economy of, 45–7, 61–3, 70, 85, 92,
94, 96, 99, 112–3, 121–2, 183–7

education in, 66–69, 179
and Europe, 93, 94, 208
and the European Union, 113, 118,
149–50, 151, 182, 208, 209, 216,
218, 226, 237, 240, 241, 244, 265–6
and the Exchange Rate Mechanism,
93, 94, 96–7
and fracking, 187–8
and global crash of 2008, 99, 168
and housing, 183, 193–4
and increase of pension age, 183
and increasing of interest rates, 96–7
independents and minor parties in,
12, 212
and inflation, 45–6, 94, 99
and infrastructure investment bill,
186
and international exchange markets,
199
and Irish border, 240
and labour relations policy, 96
and local government under
Thatcher, 70–3
and manufacturing problems, 62
and Members of Parliament, 206
and mining pit closure, 55
and nationalisation of Bradford and
Bingley, 168
and Northern Ireland, 230–1, 264
and nuclear weapons, 279
and Paul Nuttal, 229, 230
political parties in, 87
and the poll tax, 121
poorest in, 83, 85
and privatisation of British Rail, 99
and proportional representation
(PR), 205–6
and protections for EU residents,
240
and Raheem Kassem, 229
and recession, 45–7, 94, 107
and returning deportees, 265
and social security, 83, 179
and spending, 183
and state, business and trade unions,
43
state system of, 41
and Suzanne Evans, 229
and tariffs, 244